GI )

Gangster

The Rise, Fall, and Redemption of

a Notorious Hustler

By Gregory Marshall

BROWN GIRLS BOOKS

Houston, Texas * Washington, D.C.

Growing up Gangster © 2015 by Gregory Marshall

Brown Girls Publishing,
LLC www.browngirlspublishing.com
ISBN: 9781625176059

Dedication

My best friend Joseph (Jay) Campbell. I think about you every single day, Homie. May God rest your soul. I'll see you when I get there. Delores (Misty) Jackson. My right-hand man Vincent Ridley. Tupac Shakur, thanks for the fun memories. Cousin Barry, Aunt Lena, and Aunt Thelma. You will never be forgotten.

Acknowledgements

First and foremost, I'd like to thank my Lord and Savior, without whom none of this would be possible. Thank you, my Father, for giving me a second chance at life and blessing me with this gift to write.

I want to thank Eb Lottimer for discovering me as a writer. Thank you for believing in me, Eb. To my publishers, ReShonda Tate Billingsley and Victoria Christopher Murray. Thank you for taking a chance on me.

To my wife of nineteen years, thank you Debbie Pilgram for dealing with all that I've put you through and for nursing me back from my death bed. To my good friends Robert Manzanilla and his wife, Betty. Thank you for sharing my vision and breathing life into this project.

To Lottris and Tressie Clayborne, thank you for opening your home to me and treating me like family. But more importantly, I thank you guys for getting me back into church after thirty years. You guys were there for me at a very critical time in my life. Your home was always filled with love; your living room is where my spiritual transition truly began. Tressie, thank you for giving me my first bible ever. I still have it and I shall forever cherish it.

To my childhood friend, Renee Gray, thank you for all that you've done. You came on board and shared my vision. Thank you for helping me manifest my dream into a reality.

To my old Comrade, Sanyika (Monster Kody) Shakur. Thank you for being that living example and inspiration in motivating me to follow your path. To my lawyer, Chokwe Lumumba.

To my publishing consultant, editor, and mentor Lissa Woodson. . . you know I adore you. To my editorial consultant, Janice Pernell, you are a wizard of words.

To Tyruss (Big Syke) Himes, thanks for all your advice and support. To Myra Thomas, Jason Ludwig, Christian Simmons, John Calhoun, my son Greg Jr., and his mother, Tina Robinson. I'd like to thank all the folks from Natchez, Mississippi. You welcomed me back to this beautiful little town and gave me the opportunity to finish writing my book.

To Sheriff Chuck Mayfield, Deputy D.A. Ronnie Harper, Officer Thomas Borum, my favorite cousin, Stacey Woods, Avis Norman, Gregory Gaylor, Geniece Cain, Verlene (Ma'dear) Gaylor, Gwen Morris, Roy Woods, Uncle Ernest Woods, Ernest L. Woods, Tiffany Woods, and Leonard Woods.

I'd like to give special acknowledgements to Julia (Sugar Baby) Henry. Mama, you are one special woman. Thank you for always being there for me no matter what. You are my true inspiration. You raised me with all the morals and principles that I apply to my everyday life. Thank you for never giving up on me.

My Blue-Eyed Angel. Deputy Julius Cotton, thank you for being God's designated helper. You saved my life on that fateful night of the shooting. None of this would be happening had it not been for you.

Pastor Johnny Quinn, thank you for being such a great spiritual leader and advisor. I'm so blessed to have you in my life. You and the rest of my church family at St. Paul A.M.E. are the foundation which my new life revolves around. I love you all dearly.

"If your hand or foot causes you to sin, cut it off and cast it from you. It is better for you to enter into life lame or maimed, rather than having two hands or two feet, to be cast into the everlasting fire." - Matthew 18: 8

Author's Note

For me, this passage from the Bible sums up my whole life. Getting shot was the best thing that could've happened to me. I had to die to live. I was living a life that offered me only two options — certain death or life in prison.

I used to have this nightmare where I had to choose between losing my arm or leg. I always chose my arm. I did lose the use of my right arm, but I won't complain. The words you are reading at this very moment are being tapped out with the use of one index finger on my left hand. I wrote the entire book this way. That's my gift from God. My life was spared so I would share this living testimony with you. God is still working miracles every day. I'm one of them.

I've committed some heavy sins along my journey. No sin is greater than the other. I'm asking anyone who I've hurt to please forgive me. I realized that I was an angry, fatherless child in search of love from a man who would never be there for me. I knew that I would have to forgive him before I could move on.

Recently, I reached out to him after eighteen years of silence. It's still a work in progress. There are many messages in my story. I'd like to focus on one in particular. If any passage affected you emotionally concerning the fact that one, or both, of your parents were not there for you, why would you –in turn – do the same thing to your child? Change has to start somewhere. Why not let it start with you?

Prologue

The End of a Turbulent Beginning

November 5, 1996
1:02 a.m.

*S*o this is what it feels like to die...

No amount of training in the streets could ever prepare me for this moment. Gun smoke swirled, lingering inside the car like a bad dream on a good day. The cool air whipping about the car barely brushed against my heated skin. From the passenger seat, I could make out only parts of the dark scenery, which stretched from the heart of Natchez to the murky waters of the Mississippi River.

I'd chosen a less populated spot on a deserted country road, believing it was the perfect place to conduct our transaction. The likelihood of being spotted by the police or anyone else was slim. Unfortunately, it also meant that there would be no one who could save me.

Everything was happening so fast, as though the moment the bullets hit my head, someone put time on fast forward and left it there. Death was in the air; I could feel it. Just like I could feel the vibrations from the pager settled between my thighs. I tried to move, but nothing from the neck down responded to my mental commands.

I could speak, though, and so I called out, "Jay!"

Nothing.

I called my partner's name once again.

This time I heard a response, though I couldn't understand him. The sound he made was unlike anything I'd heard before – the weary sound of a man slipping from life and embracing death.

Jay was trying to tell me something, but he choked on his own blood before he could utter a coherent word. His eyes grew dim and his chest heaved in an attempt at one last breath. He expired before my eyes, and I actually felt his spirit move past me.

Jay's death was confirmation: they meant to kill us.

One down. One still breathing—barely.

I was surprised that I was still able to think about that or anything, for that matter. Warm blood flowed down my chest and one thing came to mind: I survived the deadly streets of Los Angeles only to get gunned down in the Deep South — a place where relatives sent their children in the summers to escape gang-infested cities. I accepted the fact that an empty lot on the outskirts of hell was where my life would end.

The pager signaled another call coming through. My wife had been so worried about me doing this deal. She was right to be concerned, but I couldn't think about who was right or wrong. My heartbeat was my only focus; it was all I had left.

The consistent thumps against my chest were so loud, it was as though someone turned up the sound. When my heartbeat slowed down, would that be the end? Where was Jay's spirit? Would I go to the same place? Would I see him again?

I had never felt so alone, not even my first time in jail when the door slammed and plunged me into an abyss, separating me from the outside world. Fear gripped me so hard that tears pooled in my eyes, but it was too late to cry. Life was being measured in seconds, and I couldn't help but think about my mother, wishing she were here. She was like Superwoman—she always made everything right. But even her super powers couldn't save me now.

I waited on that moment when my life was supposed to "flash before my eyes." I anticipated a temperature change; I had a feeling it was about to get real hot for me. Five gunshots at close range was a sign that I'd finally gotten what was coming to me; I was just another victim of this street game called hustling.

Closing my eyes, I focused on my heartbeat, ready to meet my Maker.

A light appeared and a voice echoed around me. I opened my eyes — slowly, as though that effort would be the last move I'd make. The temperature was still cool—a good sign.

I could barely see the face, but I could make out the pale skin and deep blue eyes.

This must be my angel, a blue-eyed angel.

My mother told me all about this as a child and a sense of comfort enveloped me. I'd been given a pardon! I was going to heaven, even with all the dirt I'd done.

My angel talked to me, asking questions. But the questions...something didn't feel right. I'd never died before, I knew it wasn't supposed to go like this.

My eyes are too heavy to keep open, but I didn't want my angel to leave me. I could see him more clearly now because of the blue lights from a policeman's cruiser that flashed behind him. A cowboy hat was perched on his head and I heard the crackle of conversation flowing in and out of a two-way radio.

This is an angel?

When did angels start carrying holstered guns? When did they wear gold badges?

I closed my eyes again, searching for answers, but none came. My pager vibrated once more, and another thought caused me to panic. I was a black man, a known criminal, in a place where racial injustice is as common as fresh air.

Pale skin, blue eyes, and a badge? Maybe this wasn't an angel of mercy.

Maybe this was the angel...of death.

Chapter 1
The G True Hollywood Story

Los Angeles, California - 1980

O ne hour's worth of work would make me richer than I ever imagined. Weeks ago, I had plotted the moves, plus pumped a Viking Freight driver for vital information about which truck carried the biggest payload.

This operation could bring in thousands, if not millions, all in one solid sweep. My plan was ingenious and I was only seventeen!

My partner in crime was my cousin Vince, the black sheep of his family, just like I was quickly becoming the black sheep of mine. When I handed Vince a .32 semi-automatic pistol, I scanned his expression for signs of fear. His dark brown face registered a determination that matched my own. I had the perfect accomplice.

A Viking Freight truck filled with cash and high-end jewelry was set to leave a lot in Culver City on Thursday. For two nights before, I found it impossible to sleep, but I was ready today.

Though I wasn't the oldest child, I was considered the "man of the house," and my mother woke me up early to start everyone's day. Despite my activities on the "less than legal" side of life, I took my family responsibilities seriously. My mother gave me a list of things to do and I got my four siblings off to school.

Vince showed up about ten minutes after everyone left. My mother had never liked him, even though we were related, and she had good reasons to distrust his influence. But, I was just as bad an influence on him. I just kept my dark side away from my family.

I was supposed to be going to school, but I had other plans today. Vince and I left on our mission, and within fifteen minutes, we stole a dark green '72 Chevy Nova, then drove to Viking Freight's main yard, arriving right before the driver pulled out.

I trailed him as he made the first stop at a jewelry store in Beverly Hills. When the truck turned Northbound off Wilshire Boulevard, it came to a stop sign at the end of a residential street lined with million dollar homes.

When he stopped, I rammed my car into the back of the truck. The driver put his vehicle in park and jumped out.

We were on him before he could blink — flanking him with guns pointed. Vincent scrambled into the passenger seat and gathered up the most valuable of items — diamonds, emeralds, rubies, and gold. I moved into the shadows, keeping my pistol pointed toward the wide-eyed, trembling man.

"Get in the back of the truck," I ordered. I located the moneybag, then turned to him. "Hand over that wallet."

I jumped into the driver's seat and we took off; my first instinct was to take him with us. Instead, I made a split-second decision and ordered Vincent to throw him out of the passenger side door.

Twenty seconds later, I encountered our first problem. I had never driven a huge truck; the brakes failed and I ran through the stop sign and onto somebody's beautiful lawn. That gate tore apart with a bang. I recovered and drove like a mad man, making up for those lost minutes.

We made it to the onramp of the 405 Freeway. Only a red light and three cars stood between me and freedom. Celebrating came to mind, but it was short-lived. A LAPD cruiser hit the corner, speeding, with lights flashing.

Come on light. Change!

I tried not to make eye contact and looked in the rearview mirror after the cop car passed. The cruiser traveled about twenty feet, made a hard U-Turn, then gunned in our direction.

I turned to Vincent. "Get out!"

We grabbed the guns, jumped out of the truck, and took off. He went one way and I ran in the opposite direction, heading for the chain link fence along the freeway. My gun was still cocked, so I carefully scaled the fence, then disappeared into the heavy brush and took a moment to put the pistol on "safety."

My heart was beating so hard. I wasn't prepared for this part of the game.

What had gone wrong? The plan was simple—take the truck to the buyer I had set up, unload the goods, and make a cool killing. Nowhere in that three-step plan had I allowed for being chased by LAPD's finest.

This was worse than any scenario I could imagine. A young black male – a robbery suspect with a firearm – in white Beverly Hills. This was a recipe for justifiable homicide.

I spotted a huge tree and moved to it, using it as a cover from the slow-moving traffic only feet away. Searching the bumper-to-bumper traffic, I looked for a vehicle to carjack. I was about to jump onto the freeway -- then, trouble.

Two cops with their guns drawn cautiously approached the tree, their gazes sweeping the area. Car horns erupted in a chorus of honks as motorists tried to alert the police to me. I pinned my back against the tree and inched around it as the police passed right by.

The sounds of traffic were distracting, so I made a break. As I scrambled down the embankment, I glanced over my shoulder. The cops hadn't seen or heard me. Escape seemed possible.

I ran as fast as I could, tearing up the pavement, jumping fence after fence. Besides Vincent, I was probably the *only* young black male within twenty miles, which served to make me a target for that fact alone.

Commotion from above made me look up. White people on rooftops of businesses were yelling and pointing out my every move. I felt as trapped as a runaway slave that the bloodhounds had chased up a tree.

Tired and scared, I found cover in a heavily shaded area. I couldn't run another yard. My feet were on fire. Tendrils of pain shot up my thighs. My chest heaved, but I couldn't draw in a good breath.

I bent over, bracing both hands on my knees. Sweat

drenched every solid inch of me, making my trendy two-tone Adidas jogging suit feel like an extra ten pounds. Salty liquid burned my eyes and blurred my vision.

After a few moments, I stood, scanned the area, and was about to give up when I noticed a white building about fifty feet ahead that looked like the perfect hideaway. The open door was all the invitation I needed.

I half ran, half staggered and entered a cool, dark room. My eyes adjusted to the darkness. Only a single window was in the small shack and labels on boxes that were stacked against the wall let me know that this was a supply room for the Veterans Hospital. If I waited until dark, I just might get away.

I stretched out on the floor and the cold cement felt good against my hot, sweaty face.

Had Vincent been caught? Would he snitch if he had?

Then, I thought about my mother. Being captured and arrested would be the ultimate letdown for her. How would she handle this?

The distant sound of a helicopter snapped me back, and with each second, the blades of the chopper sounded closer, until they hovered right above. A flurry of activity outside made panic grip me once again. Car doors slammed and chatter from police radios flooded the air. Then, panic turned into terror the moment the dogs started barking.

I eased over to the window and peeked outside. Police were everywhere! A command post had been set up about fifty yards away.

The pistol was still in my hand, though sweat pooled around the handle. The situation was getting worse by the minute, but I couldn't bring myself to release the weapon.

Would this be where my life ended?

I paced the concrete floor. "Fuck! How did I get myself into this shit?" I muttered.

The helicopter still hovered and the barking became louder and closer.

Then, "This is the Beverly Hills Police Department!" a voice blasted. "You're surrounded; throw out your weapon and come out with your hands up!"

I crouched down on a nearby crate thinking I'd watched this shit on television a thousand times. Now I was in the starring role.

The voice through the bullhorn jarred me again. "You have thirty seconds to throw out your gun or we're sending in the dogs."

My mind said, "Move!" but my body wouldn't.

Suddenly the door exploded off the hinges and a huge black German Shepherd lunged at me, putting a death grip on my right wrist. My gun fell to the ground.

"Okay, okay! Please call your dog off me, please!"

The dog chewed on my wrist, even as I sank to the ground in a submissive position. The police flooded in like a tidal wave -- white, brown, and beige bodies.

"Freeze, motherfucker! Get down on your motherfucking stomach before we kill your Black ass!"

A boot lodged on my neck and pressed me to the concrete.

While it would have taken hours to get this type of police coverage where I lived in Inglewood, a full platoon of officers had arrived within minutes on the "rich" side of town.

They snapped on handcuffs and lifted me off the floor like a rag doll. The chase had the officers all pumped up. Their expressions told the story — anger, anxiousness, and excitement; the wrong combination for a young black male with a master plan, a gun, and the balls to attempt a million dollar heist in the heart of Beverly Hills.

I was definitely in trouble.

Chapter 2
Crime & Punishment

T he dog continued biting my leg as they led me away. The more I screamed, the harder he bit. One of the officers finally asked the magic question, "How old are you, boy?"

I had never been to jail, but my time in the streets had taught me that youngsters were treated differently, so I replied, "Seventeen, Sir."

They called off the dog, though they weren't happy about it.

A crowd of police, and a few reporters with news cameras awaited me at the command post.

One of the officers said, "He's a *juvenile*."

A rumble of disappointment followed, as filming stopped and reporters trudged away. The officer threw me into the back seat of a cruiser, and then, they transported me to jail.

The car pulled into the Beverly Hills Police Headquarters, where the officers questioned me. Based on what they asked, I figured they hadn't caught Vince.

The officers took turns putting on the pressure, trying to find out the name of my accomplice. Snitching was forbidden, so my cousin was safe.

I was given a procedural once-over by a nurse and I was thankful to learn that the dog's teeth hadn't penetrated my skin. The nurse halfheartedly cleaned and bandaged the scrapes, and then I was thrown into a holding cell. They turned the air conditioner up super high; after several minutes, my teeth clattered.

They left me there for several hours before an officer came in. "You're being transported to Eastlake Juvenile Hall."

I stared at him, wondering, *What the hell is juvenile hall?* I thought they would simply call my mother, she would pick me up, take me home, and I would be at school and work the next day.

The officer smiled at my confused expression.

It was about ten o'clock when I was chauffeured into downtown Los Angeles. The squad car stopped in front of a gate fortified with barbed wire. The brick building was lit up like a football stadium and minutes ticked by before the gates to Eastlake Juvenile Hall slowly slid open. Several guards waited as we pulled into a secure entryway.

The tallest of the bunch opened the back door and grinned. "Well, well, well. We've been waiting on you, Mr. Hijacker."

They escorted me through a set of steel double doors. Several holding cells were on my left, with a color television mounted on the wall in front of each one. They slipped my handcuffs off and threw me into the first cell.

As the Beverly Hills cops turned to leave, one said, "He's all yours, guys. He's got some pretty serious shit pending against his ass."

That shattered any illusions I had of going home.

A bologna and cheese sandwich was sent my way while I went through the booking process. When the eleven o'clock news came on, I froze as the top news story was video footage of me being escorted to the police car.

Being black and committing a crime in Beverly Hills turned out to be big news. In Inglewood, it wouldn't have made a blip on anyone's radar.

The guard walked over to my cell, wearing a gap-tooth grin. "Damn, youngster. You decided to go big-time on your first beef, huh?"

At midnight, the guard opened the main door to the housing unit and an explosion of screams and shouts made it sound like a prizefight was in progress. Twenty rooms lined each side, with small windows on each door. Curious and angry glares were aimed my way as I walked by.

Halfway down the hall, the officer stopped, opened a door, handed me a thin blanket, and shoved me inside. When he slammed the door behind me, I collapsed onto the thin mattress on top of the concrete bed.

Though I was exhausted, sleep was the furthest thing from my mind. Seventeen years old and charged with armed robbery with the use of a firearm and hijacking a Viking Freight truck.

My mother had to know of the arrest by now. It had probably traumatized her beyond repair. She depended on me, and I refused to visualize my mother's face once she heard of my arrest.

I would rather die.

And that's just what I thought about during my first night in Eastlake Juvenile Hall – suicide. But even if I wanted to, they had taken my shoelaces and there wasn't a damn thing around I could use.

I was scared as hell. The cold, small area was nothing but concrete, steel, and two panels of glass. One gave me a small view of the outside world, and the other a direct line to the hallway.

My physical surroundings were bleak and foreboding and I'd been left alone with the one thing that I didn't want to face – the truth.

I did not have to be in jail, not after having been raised by a God-fearing, hard-working, loving woman who worked one and sometimes two jobs, so that my siblings and I wouldn't meet this end. Despite my father's abandonment, she *ha*d been there. If I had listened to *her* wisdom, had followed *her* lead, I would not have been left alone to endure this empty stretch of time, with nothing but the cold uncertainty of my future and warm memories of my past.

* * *

Though I was born in 1962, six years later was the real starting point of my story. That year was the beginning of what would become a young life filled with love, pain, pleasure, mistakes, and regrets.

My mother, Julia Marshall, was a beautiful woman with dark brown eyes and a warm smile, employed as a machinist at Northrop Aircraft. My mother was an honest, caring, religious woman with morals and principles shaped by the years she spent growing up in the Deep South – Natchez, Mississippi. She was the youngest of thirteen children, earning her the nickname "Sugar Baby."

My mother had five children of her own. Marvin and Melvin came first, identical twins born in 1961. Melvin died a few days after he was born and the doctor explained that since identical twins shared a unique bond, Marvin would never be normal. I was born a year later, and pushed into the role of big brother since Marvin still grieved for his twin. Jerome, the quiet and reserved brother, was born in 1963.

Sheila, the only girl, was born in 1965 during the height of the Watts riots and Anthony, the baby of the family, came a year later.

Sheila and Anthony's father came from a strong Native American bloodline, giving them light skin and curly, silky hair. The rest of us had proud African features, which mirrored my mother's family.

We lived on 61st and Denker Avenue in the middle of Los Angeles. My mother was a single parent who lived her life for the success of her children, especially since my father had stepped out on us and my stepfather didn't stick around either.

Despite the lack of a father figure, we did have other family. My mother's sister, Lena, stayed on 48th Street and Arlington Avenue, not too far from us. She had two sons, Watani and Barry, and we spent almost every weekend, and every day during the summer at Auntie Lena's house.

While my mother was conservative, Auntie Lena was laid back. A hint of sweet incense filled the air at her place, and Marvin Gaye or some other cool artist always played on the stereo as a backdrop to the flurry of activity at her house.

There was always something going on over there because my cousins Watani and Barry were older and popular, so their friends loved to drop by. The garage was their hangout spot and music and laughter came from behind the closed doors all the time.

I always managed to find my way back there, even though it was off limits to the younger kids. All I could do was stand outside and listen, which only increased my curiosity.

One day I was playing in the backyard, when everyone piled out of the garage in a stampede and jumped into Watani's '56 Chevy. I waited until they pulled out of the driveway, then I tipped into the garage. The place was windowless and reeked of marijuana and incense.

I scanned the room and spotted brass knuckles lying on a weight bench. I slipped them on; the cold, smooth brass felt good on my small fingers and my mind instantly went to my cousin Barry. Part of me idolized Barry; he was the big brother I didn't have. But he had this streak in him that made me call him The Torturer because he was a monster to me and my brothers.

He would make us play these horrible games, one that he called 'The Boogie Man,' which was an evil episode of hide-and-seek. When Barry found us, he bit us, like he was trying to take a plug out of our skin. Every time we vowed to hide better, but there was a price to pay if he *couldn't* find us.

Another game: He put a sheet over our heads, spun us around until we became disoriented, then he turned off the lights and made us run through the house. This game resulted in a bloody nose at a bare minimum.

Sometimes he made us sit on a floor heater with our pants down until the grill burned an imprint on our asses.

Looking down at the brass knuckles, I wondered if this strip of strong steel could make Barry think twice about messing with me.

I wanted to explore some more, so I closed the sliding door and was pitched into endless darkness. I felt my way across the room, and located the light switch. Somebody had replaced the regular bulb with a black light and the posters on the walls illuminated the room.

A poster of Pam Grier snapped me to attention. Large breasts were stuffed into a tight, low-cut blouse tucked into skin-tight bell-bottoms that ended at tall platform heels. She had a big red afro and held a machine gun. The black light made the smoke coming from the barrel look so cool.

The next poster, the one of Malcolm X, appeared to be all eyes. His eyes were intense, as though he watched my every move.

A tattered sofa was pushed against one wall. I took a seat, but jumped right back up. I removed the cushion and my eyes widened — there were three handguns and two rifles. I was too scared to touch them, but I couldn't stop looking.

Then, I heard, "Greg!"

I froze and broke into a cold sweat.

My mother! She sounded like she was only a few yards away. If she found me, I would be in trouble. I slid over to the door, and flicked off the lights. But my mother's voice grew louder as she came closer.

I watched her through a sliver in the door. She looked around outside, then turned to go back into the house.

I was home free!

Until the brass knuckles fell from my sweaty hands and clanked onto the cement floor.

Mama spun around, quickly covering the distance to the garage door. "Greg, I just *know* you're not in there."

If she came in and found the things that I had uncovered, everybody would be in trouble. I couldn't have my cousins mad at me.

I answered with a defeated, "Yeah, mama."

Mama reached the door just as I opened it. Sugar Baby wasn't so sweet when she snatched my little butt, and led me to a peach tree. The perfect switch was in her hands in less than thirty seconds. My mother had perfected the skill of preaching as she wore my butt out.

After the whipping, she said calmly, "We're holding a family meeting."

I was still crying, but aware enough to understand that family meetings were serious business, even more serious than getting a whipping.

Auntie Lena and my siblings were already gathered in the living room and that's when they told us that Los Angeles was becoming too dangerous.

"For your safety, in a couple of weeks, we'll be moving down south…to Natchez, Mississippi."

* * *

So how did Mama's desire for us to escape the dangerous streets of South Central Los Angeles end up with me embracing the things she didn't want? Now that I was in the belly of Eastlake Juvenile Hall, I had all the time in the world to figure that out.

Chapter 3
The Beginning of the End

S itting on that concrete bed, my mind couldn't process everything — the chill in the air, the scratchy blanket, the gray, dingy coloring everywhere I looked. And then outside my cell, what sounded like a thousand voices bellowed simultaneously.

Why can't they just shut the fuck up?

I wasn't prepared for this — dealing with the consequences of my actions. This should've been my father's job to teach me, to tighten me up on the pitfalls and challenges of the world. Maybe hearing him explain that sticking to the master plan —finishing school, getting a job, buying a house, starting a family — did have its rewards.

I was always hungry for survival lessons, but never learned any from my father. I learned my lessons in the streets.

But now, it felt like those lessons weren't enough. I was alone, I was scared, and since nobody could see me, I let my tears flow.

All the prison horror stories I'd heard flooded my mind. What would happen to me in the next hour? The next day? The next week? Would I make it in here with all of these criminals?

I curled up with the blanket, and wept so hard that convulsions racked my body. I cried and pinned all of my troubles on the one parent who was never there.

How could my father do this to me? How could he bring me into this world, then leave me to fend for myself? How could he leave Mama to take care of us? Leave us to make our own way as if we didn't matter? Animals protected their offspring better than he had protected us.

Because of my father, I never had any stability in my life.

* * *

It was 1970 and we were living the ideal life in the country in Mississippi. My mother was working two jobs. One was at a small restaurant, "The White House," where she met Clarence.

Clarence was tall with keen Native American features and a chiseled square chin. His skin was pock-marked, almost leathery and he wore his hair in a short afro.

And there was always a huge smile on his face.

I saw right through that smile. The hair on the back of my neck stood up the moment I shook his hand. It was that smile and his eyes. There was evil in his eyes.

I put my personal feelings aside because Mama seemed happy. Clarence had a good job at the paper mill and he was cool to Mama - until the honeymoon was over. That's when we found out that his alcohol tolerance was very low. He could look at a can of beer and get drunk. And when he was drunk, he became a completely different person.

It all started when Clarence convinced my mother to move to a newly built subdivision called Lagrange. We'd been living in a house my mother built across the road from her brother, my Uncle Ernest. Uncle Ernest was our father figure and we felt safe being near him.

That all changed when Clarence moved us to a home right next door to his mother and siblings. The house *was* beautiful - a three-bedroom brick home, where the four boys shared a room and Sheila had her own. But even though it was nice, we hated being so far from our people.

The whippings started right after we moved in. I was signaled out for being the strong one, and received the majority of the beatings. Jerome became his favorite and Clarence would let him stay up late, watching old war movies and eating popcorn, while the rest of us were in bed.

We dreaded the days when our mother left us alone with Clarence. I couldn't do anything right and the intensity of the whippings increased with each drink he had. My resentment grew with each lash of the extension cord across my body.

Mama had no clue of the torture we endured, even though she and Clarence had their problems. We spent many a night listening to Clarence and our mother argue.

Then, one September night, things exploded. Clarence was drinking, and for no reason, he sent us to bed without dinner. Mama came home from work at about nine o'clock and the fighting began.

His voice was loud and his speech was slurred as he accused her of seeing another man because she was twenty minutes late.

Doors slammed and Clarence cussed, "You lying bitch. Don't you run from me!"

Another door slammed. Then a few moments of silence.

My brothers and I stayed still in our bunk beds. Marvin slept on our top bunk, and below, I felt the vibrations from his shaking. Then, the silence was broken by a loud scream.

"Please, Clarence," my mother cried. "Just let us leave!"

A heavy thump followed with more rumbling. His next words stopped my heart.

"Bitch, you can't leave me. I'll kill you first!"

I jumped out of bed and watched Clarence drag my mother across the floor by her hair, while holding his 12-gauge shotgun. My mother and I locked eyes.

Words couldn't describe the horror in her eyes. That was when I became full of courage and screamed, "Leave her alone, Clarence!"

He released his grip on her, turned back to me, and the world stopped spinning. His blood red eyes looked right through me, but that was all the time my mother needed to make a break for it.

Clarence was quick though, and grabbed her blouse, ripping it just as she made it out the door. The last thing I saw was my mother running, heading to the woods behind our house and into the pitch black night. Clarence was right behind her, carrying the shotgun.

I stood at the door listening for any sound of distress from Mama, but then I heard Clarence muttering angry words as he came back toward the house.

All that courage I had went back to where it came from. That man was going to kill me!

I ran to the kitchen, grabbed a butcher knife, then hid it under the covers on my bed. I was standing at the foot of my bed when he came in.

He grabbed me by my throat, lifted me off the floor, and tossed me onto my bed. Seething with anger, he said, "Y'all better not move. If I catch anyone trying to go out a window, I'll blow your head off."

We were so quiet that you could hear a rat piss on cotton. I snuck my hand under my blanket and gripped the knife. If he came near me, I was going to use it.

When he left the room, my mind filled with all kinds of questions: Where was my mother? Was she all right?

I was only ten, but I felt so bad about not being able to protect my siblings and our mother. Clarence would never have gotten away with this around my Uncle Ernest.

That was when I had my first thoughts ever of killing a man. Uncle Ernest had taught me how to hunt and thoughts of cutting Clarence's throat like a hog flashed through my mind. I laid in my bed and thought of the many ways I would kill him before the night was over.

Just as the sun rose, I finally drifted off to sleep. I thought I was dreaming when I heard the sound of my mother's voice. She was alive!

There was no sign of Clarence as she got us out of bed, dressed, and then swiftly loaded us into the car. A Mayflower moving truck pulled up just as we pulled off. As we rode, Mama explained that we were heading back to California.

Chapter 4
Moving On Up

The two years after we came back from Natchez were rough. We moved around like gypsies since my mother had to leave so much behind when she left Clarence. But despite all that, Julia Marshall always found a way. She was determined to make our lives better and one Friday evening, Mama came in from a long day at work smiling more than usual.

"I've got some good news," she said. "We're moving into a new house in Inglewood. I'll take you to see it tomorrow."

Mama fried up some chicken and all the excited chatter about our new home felt good. We were so happy, we even ate our vegetables with no fuss.

After my bath, I stretched out on my bed, trying to envision our new house. I couldn't wait and was the first one up the next morning.

My mother fixed the Saturday morning special — pancakes, eggs, and bacon; but on that morning it was *really* special. It felt as if the hard times were behind us.

After breakfast, we changed into what poor folks called our "good clothes" and I went into big brother mode, helping get everyone ready and loaded into the car before I slipped into the front seat. When Mama took her place at the wheel, she looked beautiful. She was beaming with confidence and pride.

It was a crisp morning and the sun hovered behind us from the east. We pulled out of the driveway in an avocado green '70 Ford Galaxy station wagon to begin our journey to a better life.

As she drove, I was proud to sit up front next to my mama. With her two-job work schedule, I was her right-hand man. That put some weight on me at the age of eleven, but I didn't mind. I did my part because I didn't want her to think that she *needed* to have a boyfriend or husband. After Clarence, I felt that any man she'd date would mistreat us because we were not his very own. Hell, our flesh and blood fathers had done nothing good for us.

We went south on Denker Avenue and Mama said, "Greg, make sure you pay attention to the streets."

I smiled. She was preparing me for my new responsibilities. When we turned west on Imperial Highway, the area transitioned from all black to a neighborhood where only a sprinkle of blacks colored the landscape. The quality of the houses, apartments, and cars was so much better than what we were used to seeing.

Our family might not fit in, was the first thought that came to mind. I shook that off; if my mother felt that a move from South Central to Inglewood was best, then it was.

We pulled up to a major intersection, Crenshaw Boulevard and Imperial Highway.

Mama said, "Greg look to the left. That's the Bank of America building."

A huge digital clock and temperature display was perched on top of the fourteen-stories-high building.

Mama said, "I'm almost sure we can see it from our house. Use it as landmark to find your way home if you ever get lost." Then she added for the benefit of my siblings, "And use it to tell time to bring your butts in the house before curfew."

Everybody laughed.

The Bank of America building was in a big shopping center, and Thrifty's caught my eye. There weren't many of those kinds of stores on our side of town, but they had best damn ice cream in the world.

We continued west on Imperial, made a left on Cherry Avenue, then a right at the first block. Mama parked in front of the second house from the corner, where Aunt Lena sat in her car waiting. She gave me a big smile. "Well Grego, how do you like our new house?"

My high spirits crumbled. Did that mean Barry, the monster, was moving in with us?

Then she said the magic words: "There are two houses on this lot. The front one is yours."

I looked over her shoulder and fell in absolute love — with a brick building! The grass on the front lawn was manicured and as I glanced down the block, every lawn on the street looked as good as ours.

Mama took a key out of an envelope and held it out to me. She was giving me the gold, passing the torch. I put the key in the door, and my siblings flew past, almost knocking me to the ground. I moved forward, took a deep breath, and to this day I remember that new paint smell.

The kitchen was huge, with a little breakfast nook area that extended into the backyard — just right for our family. A magnolia tree like the ones in Natchez stood in the middle of the backyard between the two houses, thick leaves offering a much-needed shade. My aunt's elevated porch was about ten feet behind that tree. The large glass window in the front of her house gave a perfect view of the whole yard. Another small yard behind Auntie Lena's house was next to the alley, where the two garages connected to her house. A six-foot-high gray brick wall flanked the property, making it feel as if we were in a family fortress.

I was taking it all in when I heard the sound of music: *soul* music. James Brown!

Mama had told me that the neighborhood was predominately white with only three black families living on our street. Chatter and loud laughter floated from the house next door, I strolled to my aunt's porch for a better view.

Right then, their screen door slammed, and a young black girl with an athletic build burst from the house, ran through their yard, and hopped the front fence. I saw just enough of her to know that she might be a tomboy, but she was very pretty.

The screen door slammed again, and this time, a dark-skinned girl of about six came out. We locked gazes, then, she rolled her eyes, stuck out her tongue, and hit me with the middle finger before she went back inside, slamming the door behind her.

I was rooted to the spot. *Damn, there goes the neighborhood.*

* * *

On Sunday after church, my mother and I gathered cleaning supplies from our house on Denker before we went to our new home.

We'd only been there for a little while when Mama said, "I need you to go the store and buy two light bulbs." She reached into her purse, scraping up just under a dollar. "Hurry up."

I took a shortcut through the alley, but that probably wasn't the best move since I would have to cross in the middle of Imperial Highway. I was preparing to navigate the six lanes of traffic when two dudes on dirt bikes started in my direction.

A bad vibe put me on guard. I ran to the center divider, hoping to avoid them, but traffic held me, and the bikers made it on the divider at the same time. Cars whizzed by; I couldn't move.

The bikers said to me, "What's your name, homie? And where you from?"

"Greg. It's my first day in the neighborhood." Then in my nervousness, I made the huge mistake of telling them, "Mama gave me money to buy light bulbs for our new house. . . " I couldn't believe I'd been dumb enough to tell two obvious thugs that I had money. And I was probably looking like I felt — scared as hell.

When they said, "Let me see your money," and pulled out a small switchblade, I knew I couldn't let them take my mother's money. So I jumped into the street just as there was a break in traffic, and I fled toward Gordon's Market.

I hung around the store, making sure the coast was clear before I took the long way home. A full hour had passed on what should have been a fifteen-minute trip. When I finally reached the house, my cousin Barry and another dude were in the front yard.

"Greg, where in the fuck have you been, little nigga?" Barry yelled. "Your mother told me she sent you to the store an hour ago. It don't take that long to get some fucking light bulbs." He gave me a knuckle-thump on the forehead.

I was forced to tell him what happened and as I talked, Barry fumed. He didn't play that robbery shit. Him torturing the hell out of us was fine, but robbery — not so much.

"That's Pookie and Larry," Barry's friend, Duke, said just from my description. "They're known for jacking everybody in the hood."

Barry said, "Don't worry, little cousin, I'll deal with them."

Maybe Barry living close to us was going to be a good thing after all. But not too long after that incident, I didn't need Barry anymore. I found a new "mentor" who taught me more about being down and dirty than Barry ever could.

Mackie, "Mr. 315," was no joke. Keeping up with him had landed me in a place that no young black man ever wanted to be —Eastlake Juvenile Hall.

41

* * *

Another chill in my solitary cell snatched me back to the present. I closed my eyes, hoping to cry myself to sleep. Because in the morning, I would have to walk out of the cell and face the unknown.

Chapter 5
In Through the Out Door

Sleep finally came, but I didn't find much comfort. Seconds after I closed my eyes, the cell was suddenly flooded with bright light. Then at 5:30 a.m., an oldie-but-goodie blared through the PA system.

Clicks from the unlocking doors preceded a booming voice, "All right, rise and shine, you little punks! You've got fifteen minutes 'til breakfast and school."

The hallway filled with chatter and slamming doors. When the guard unlocked my door, he tossed in a small clear plastic bag and I caught it in mid-air.

"That's your care package," he said. "Head to the bathroom and get ready for breakfast. Make sure you make your bed first." He was gone before I could even ask a question.

I poured the contents onto my bed, then threw on my new jailhouse outfit — blue jeans and dark blue shirt. Grabbing my toothpaste and toothbrush, I headed out. Bodies were everywhere, and I felt lost. All eyes seemed to be on "the new guy."

I made my way to a huge bathroom with ten sinks lining both sides and inmates of every race crowded around. Since most of them had their shirts off, all kinds of tattoos were on display. This was supposed to be juvenile hall, but some of those dudes looked like grown ass men — true thugs.

Trying not to look too nervous, I waited my turn for a sink, then rushed back to my room and made my bed.

We were instructed to line up in front of our rooms as they were inspected before breakfast. At that moment, I realized, I was no longer in control of my life.

At breakfast, everyone ate in silence and I avoided eye contact with my fellow thugs. Afterward, the inmates formed a single file, and we walked across the compound to the school. I was told to wait in the unit counselor's office.

School in Eastlake wouldn't be much of a problem. Crime life aside, I had managed to stay in school and receive decent grades. Even with my street cred, I was a borderline nerd.

I got through that day in school and that night back in my cell. And again I worried and cried myself to sleep because the next day, I was to appear in court.

It turned out, I had much to worry about.

The judge informed me, "You are close to being eighteen and combined with the severity of your case, you'll be tried as an adult." He also made it clear that state prison was a good possibility.

My first thought was to cry like a sissy, but I was in the system now. I had to suck it up and focus on survival. That meant crying was not an option. As a first-timer, one sign of weakness and my ass was grass.

Over the next couple of days, I made friends quickly.

The seriousness of my case gave me the edge needed to survive, especially during the early stages. I met a lot of newbies, like me, but it was the seasoned inmates who became our role models. They taught us how to survive by our wits, our might, and any means necessary. We were a bunch of lost souls and they were our only guidance.

After spending just a few days with them, I knew having a future as a normal citizen was practically over. With my time in this detention center, my felony conviction, and being black, my fate was sealed.

We spent our days talking about our crimes. And thanks to my friend, Mackie, Mr. 315, I had plenty of escapades to share.

* * *

The summer of 1976 was the end of my innocence. I was fifteen years old and life was good: I was doing well in school, was into church, had a paper route, and the Boy Scouts were my extended family. My mother was proud that I had stayed on the right track and I was proud that she managed to take care of us without any help from my father, stepfather, or any other man.

I'd learned to block out the many hurtful thoughts I had about them. And it would have worked if they had remained out of sight. But they didn't.

First, my father moved to a house just a few blocks away with his new wife and stepdaughter, and then, Joseph, the father of my two youngest siblings, moved two blocks away with his new wife and family.

On the outside, my mother handled these situations, but I could imagine the anguish she suffered. We had no support coming from either of them, even though they both now lived within five minutes of us.

This only made *our* family bond tighter, though. It was us against the world.

By then, my cousin Barry abandoned his torture tactics and became more of a big brother to me. We built his beautiful electric blue with silver metal flake flames custom Honda 750 motorcycle together. Every single nut and bolt had been dipped in chrome and one of the greatest days of my life was when he let me ride it by myself. I'll never forget the envious stares as I drove around the hood. This was more than a motorcycle between my thighs; it was a work of art.

Barry had started talking on a CB radio. The static crackle of the voices intrigued me. I would sit in his gold '68 Chevy Nova listening for hours. It wasn't long before I was talking on the radio with him.

Barry explained that everyone had a handle — a nickname that CB radio people used. It only took only few seconds to come up with mine: 'The Brainiac.' I was into electronics and had dreams of becoming an inventor.

The people on the CB had names like Double Dealer, Hercules, Paper Boy, Perfect Girl, and California Play Boy. One voice caught my attention; he had to be close to my age, but he seemed to have more confidence than me. He knew all the latest CB jargon and came across as being a little too slick.

Eventually I found out that he was known as Mr. 315. A power struggle ensued between us from the beginning.

He constantly overrode my conversations and insisted that I say "Mister" before the 315. Only then would I get to talk.

Two weeks later, Barry gave me a powerful base station CB radio with a small antenna mounted on side of the house. I couldn't wait for Mr. 315 to come on the air.

I smiled as soon as I heard that cocky voice. When he was completely engaged in conversation, I dropped the hammer on his ass and spoke into the microphone, "Not today 315, it's Brainiac's turn." As usual, I left out the Mister on purpose.

Mr. 315 laughed hard. "That's pretty good, Brainiac, but I got something for that too, buddy."

We shared a laugh and kept chatting, agreeing to meet in person since he only lived about two miles away.

When we met a few days later, Mr. 315 didn't look anything like he sounded. He was two inches shorter than me, with a stocky, muscular build. His complexion was light, his hair silky and curly. He looked Hispanic, but sounded black. Mr. 315 told me that his real name was Maximillian - Mackie for short.

I thought, *What kind of name is that for a nigga?*

Mackie was a savvy street dude who talked and moved with a lot of confidence. I was impressed.

Once we met, I ran home from school every day to finish my homework and chores so that I could get on that CB. During one of our conversations, I found out that Mackie's father was very active in his life and coached the baseball team Mackie played on. I couldn't help but wonder how much fun that must be, but it also made me resent my father that much more.

At first, our friendship proved difficult. He lived in the Watergate Crips neighborhood, and I was from the Imperial Village Crips neighborhood. Our hoods were engaged in a violent gang war — Crips fighting over land they didn't own.

Neither one of us were a gang member, but we could easily lose our lives if we were in the wrong place with the wrong person.

Then one night, Mackie called with good news. "I'm moving to your neighborhood in a couple of weeks."

I celebrated! How great was it going to be to have my friend around all the time.

But having him live only two blocks away was the absolute worst thing that could have happened. I hung out with Mackie every chance I got, and discovered he was into some pretty shady stuff. He'd dropped out of school and had become a master thief.

I was still on the straight and narrow, but was drawn to Mackie like a magnet to metal. I didn't know it, I couldn't see it, but Mackie had a great deal of influence over me and that meant I was headed for trouble.

One night, he was sitting on my front porch, waiting for me when my mother and I returned home from a Boy Scout meeting.

As I approached, the disapproval rolled off of him in waves. He politely addressed my mother, but as soon as she was inside he looked me up and down, and said, "Man, what's up with this Boy Scout shit, homie?"

Two weeks later, I devastated my mother, announcing that I was through with the Boy Scouts. That gave me more time to spend with Mackie.

Mackie showed me the ropes of street hustling, and I was a damn good student. We started off small, breaking into cars and big rigs for the CB radios.

We lived a double life. Our parents were religious and strict, and we were perfect kids in the presence of our elders. But away from them, it was a different story.

During the day, I helped my mother take care of my siblings and I delivered the newspapers on my paper route. But by night, I lived the life of a criminal, learning at the feet of Mackie.

One night, just a little before midnight, Mackie tapped on my window. The fog was so thick I could hardly see him.

"I've got something to show you."

I slipped out of the house and walked up the block with him. "Fog is the best cover for a thief," he taught me. "Rain is second best. Cops hate to get out of their patrol cars when it rains." Mackie pulled out a flathead Craftsman screwdriver from his back pocket. "This is the only tool we'll need for this project."

We walked two blocks into Hawthorne, an all-white neighborhood, before he told me the plan. "I'm about to show you how to steal a car."

I was scared for half a second, then I was excited. Mackie had so much confidence, it was contagious.

We walked about ten more feet before he stopped. His car of choice was a beat up two-door 1962 Chevy Nova. Mackie pulled out the screwdriver and went to work on the vent window. He was inside the car before I could say, "Let me help."

He slid into the passenger seat. "Greg, get behind the wheel."

Mackie worked on the ignition like a heart surgeon. Then, the red light on the dashboard flashed. He passed the screwdriver my way, and I knew I had to get it right on the first try.

I stuck the screwdriver into the ignition, started it up, and pulled off wearing the biggest grin. We took a joyride for a few hours, ditched the car, and were back in bed before the sun rose.

That night, Mackie and I became closer than best friends, closer than homeboys; we were partners in crime. I prayed the fog would return soon.

A few days later, as I was walking through Hawthorne, I spotted an old white couple washing a beautiful 1964 Impala. I asked, politely, if they might be interested in selling.

They yelled, "Get the hell away from our property!"

Then they made the huge mistake of calling me a nigger.

All I could think about was getting to Mackie's house.

As soon as I told him the story, he laughed. "Don't worry, Brainiac, that '64 belongs to you, homie."

It was June, so like a few days before, a thick fog rolled in that night, and with equipment in hand, we headed to Hawthorne.

The car was in an open garage connected to the house. Mackie wrapped a thick lock with duct tape to muffle the sound, worked his magic, and the headlights were on before I had time to play lookout.

Mackie scrambled into the car, and the ignition light flashed a few seconds later. I slipped into the driver's seat and was all set to start that bad boy up, when Mackie gripped my hand.

"Fool, we can't start it here. Everybody knows the sound of his car. We have to push this sucker around the block."

Words can't describe how I felt driving that car home. The satisfaction of making them pay for calling me 'nigger' took a back seat to the beauty of the car. Every piece of the interior was in mint condition, like it had just been wheeled off the showroom floor.

We took it straight to my garage and parked it next to my shell of a car. Mackie showed up early the next day and I ditched school. Three hours of non-stop work, and we had stripped that car and placed everything onto mine. Two weeks later, we snatched a set of custom wheels.

Mackie always stayed ahead of me when it came to cars, but I was the electronics pro, so I always had the best stereo system. Since I was the brains and he was the brawn, our partnership worked out fine.

Running the streets with Mackie earned me a vicious reputation. I was considered one dangerous dude and having a Chevy low-rider and selling drugs bumped me up to gangster level as well. It was a well-known fact: Mackie and I weren't to be fucked with, especially after we taught a local pimp that lesson.

Imperial Highway was a popular whore stroll and the hookers on that stroll were some of my best PCP customers.

A pimp named Pretty Tony jacked me up one day and

demanded that I stop selling to "his bitches." I didn't pay his threats any attention. I just told the hookers to start meeting me around the corner.

A few days later, as three of Pretty Tony's whores huddled around me while I dipped their cigarettes into a bottle of PCP, Tony approached from my backside. I never heard him coming, but I recognized his voice immediately.

"What the fuck is this shit? You're costing me money, little nigga!"

I spun around. Pretty Tony held a small pistol by his side and the whores scattered like roaches.

He looked into my eyes. "The next time I catch you slipping like this, it's gonna cost you, youngster."

He was threatening me, but his threat was about to cost him.

Pretty Tony owned a brand new, dark brown Fleetwood Cadillac—the typical pimpmobile with a huge chrome grill, bumper kit, wire wheels, and all the trimmings.

That night, we stripped that pimpmobile in my garage and while doing that, I found a .44 Magnum Smith & Wesson under the dashboard. It was a blue steel six-inch revolver with a handcrafted wooden handgrip. Love at first sight! I showed it to Mackie, then stashed it inside my garage.

The next morning, we put a set of dummy tires on what was left of the pimpmobile, found a milk crate as a driver's seat, and a pair of vice grips for steering.

We normally dumped those stripped cars in the wee

hours of the morning, but we made an exception that day.

Mackie sat on the passenger side floor and I sat on the crate when we pulled out at noon when everybody in the hood was hanging around.

We laughed hysterically as I drove that ex-pimpmobile through our neighborhood. All the homies looked at us like we were crazy, but the news would make its way back to Pretty Tony and the rest of his pimp buddies. A clear message had to be sent.

We dumped the car, walked over to our fence to pick up the money for the parts, then we parted ways for the day.

As I walked home, a vision of that .44 Magnum I'd stashed flashed in my mind. I had developed a passion for guns as a kid in Mississippi, and when I got home and retrieved that pistol from its hidden place; the cold heavy steel felt good in my hands. I sat down on the floor, silent as I stared at it for a while.

I inhaled the familiar scent of gun oil, then unloaded the weapon's hollow point bullets. Even though I had grown up around guns, this was different. I wasn't out in the woods hunting. I was a young criminal-in-training and the sense of power that filled me was second only to the rush of taking that white man's car or sending Pretty Tony a message. This gun could make even the strongest person take pause.

I was sixteen and a sixteen-year-old with that kind of power was a dangerous thing.

From that point on, I carried the gun whenever we went out stealing, which didn't hold as much interest for me anymore. Now, I had visions of taking a car at gunpoint and I had that chance just a few weeks after.

The Hawthorne Mall was my target. I put the pistol in my waistband and headed to the mall on foot. Even though Mackie would be down with me, I couldn't take him. His reputation was already established; it was my time to shine.

On my way to the mall, I ran into Donnie, one of my other homeboys. He had been dying to hang out with me and asked to tag along. He had no clue what I was about to do, and neither did I - at least not exactly. Hustlers act on the instinct. Sometimes there are no definite plans.

At the mall, I went straight to the top level of the three-story parking structure – fewer people and witnesses. About five cars away, a tall, thirty-something, white dude was loading shopping bags into the trunk of a black '70 Chevy Chevelle. I had a customer who needed that car.

I scanned the area as we inched toward him, pulled the pistol from my waistband, and was in front of him seconds later. I pointed the gun right between his eyes. The barrel was the only thing he focused on.

"This is a robbery," I said, then snatched the keys from his hand.

Donnie searched the dude's pockets and grabbed his wallet and watch. We jumped into the car and the whole incident was over in less than thirty seconds. We were back in the hood five minutes later.

Donnie found three hundred dollars in the wallet and he was more excited than I was. Not that I wasn't excited; I had just experienced the power of using a gun. Mackie wasn't into armed robberies. He liked the stealth moves

— safe ones. So Donnie had just become my right-hand-man on a more serious level.

There was no turning back for me now. I just had to find a way to keep my dark side from the people who mattered.

Unfortunately, I wasn't successful, since one family member — my little sister, Sheila — had started hanging around. She became the second black sheep in the family capitalizing on my reputation, and that didn't get past my mother.

It wasn't just my sister alerting my mother to the problem. I'd stopped going to church, my teachers were calling the house about me and my sister, and by the end of the 11th grade, my grades were so bad, I was forced to go to a continuation school.

Time and time again, my mother was so disappointed and I hated that I was doing that to her. But that didn't halt my downward spiral into a criminal abyss.

It was because I loved life on the streets. I was obsessed with that pistol and Donnie and I went on a robbery spree. I never thought about getting caught or the consequences. I just believed that no one would ever catch me.

But even though I was into armed robbery, Mackie still found a way to keep up with me. It was a summer night in 1980 when I received a call close to midnight.

"Come outside in five minutes," Mackie said with so much excitement in his voice that I was outside in seconds.

The full moon illuminated the street. No breezes whipped about; there was nothing but quiet. All of a sudden "Knee Deep" by Parliament and the Funkadelics thrummed through the air.

I peered up the street and a chrome front end appeared when Mackie hit the corner in a '61 Chevy Impala. Hydraulics, which could make a car lift, lower, or dance were hooked up to that beautiful machine.

Mackie hit the switch when he pulled in front of my house, making the car dance to the music. He finished his show, then set the car on the ground.

My mouth hung open; I had definitely been outdone.

Mackie jumped out of the car. "Yeah, Brainiac, what you know 'bout hitting switches, Boy Scout?"

* * *

I would soon learn 'bout hitting switches. The guards at Eastlake Juvenile Hall hit the switch at 5:30 a.m. and I was out of my cell, another switch and I was off to breakfast, another switch and I was at school, another switch and I was out in the yard, another switch and I was doing work detail. The last switch was lights out.

Lights out. The loneliest time of the day. In the loneliest place in the world.

Chapter 6
Urban Gladiators

E astlake Juvenile Hall was the real beginning of my criminal education. Those street savvy thugs made my time with Mackie and Donnie seem pale. They sized up the mistakes I had made during the robbery attempt: I should have dumped the driver *after* I secured the truck. I should have worn gloves and a ski mask. At Eastlake, I wasn't being "rehabilitated" as the state portrayed in the media. I was being educated by veteran criminals.

Sunday, five days after I arrived, was visiting day for our unit. Visitations were held in our unit's mess hall and the whole institution shut down at noon.

I was one of the lucky inmates, since my room overlooked the whole compound. The guards kept the radio station tuned to oldies and I listened to one oldie after another as I looked out of the one-inch-thick, Plexiglass window and watched each visitor walk across the yard. The music forced me to think about things I had been avoiding all week. I dreaded facing my mother. It would be the first time I'd seen or talked to her since I'd gotten to Eastlake.

Two hours passed and my mother still hadn't arrived.

Was she that upset? Had she given up on me?

Just when I was about to give up, I spotted her. She looked out of place as she walked across the yard wearing one of her Sunday dresses.

Julia Marshall always put God first, so that meant that even her jailed son would have to wait until she gave Him the proper respect. Hopefully, she had said a prayer for my ass.

Just the sight of her filled me with comfort, but there were a few butterflies in my stomach, too. I had to look in my mother's eyes and deal with her really knowing the truth about her son.

Minutes later, one of the guards called my name, opened the door, and sent me on my way. I felt like I was walking to a funeral. I had no clue what I was going to say to my mother.

Mama turned just as I reached the table and we locked gazes. Words couldn't describe the grief in her eyes, but still, she stood to embrace me.

Right after that, she pulled out a bucket of fried chicken (parents were allowed to bring food). And as I started eating, she started preaching.

"Boy, what in the devil is wrong with you?" She didn't give me a chance to answer. "I saw you on television and those police could've killed you. You know the law says that if you use a gun, you go to prison." Finally, she paused. "Who was with you?"

All I did was bite into my chicken.

My mother continued to press me about my accomplice, but there was nothing she could say that would make me tell her who was with me. She would never understand that snitching was impossible, just like she would never understand what had pushed me into becoming a criminal. She had no clue of the anger that I felt for the world, and for my father in particular. And she would never understand the satisfaction I felt at having exacted a small amount of revenge on him - even if my revenge on my father hurt me more than it hurt him.

* * *

Now that I was hanging with Mackie, I didn't really want to deliver newspapers anymore. But it wasn't really Mackie that made me want to stop - it was my father.

I couldn't believe it when I first got the paper route and discovered that I'd have to pass my father's house every day. Seeing his house was a direct reminder that he was taking care of another family and had no regard for the family he'd left behind.

I saw his total disregard one day when I rode down his street after my paper route was done. I made it to the end of the block, where a little Dachshund always broke out and chased me. Those sharp little teeth hurt when he nipped at my ankle. I'd had enough of that shit.

This time when he ran toward me, I kicked his little doggie ass. He traveled about twelve feet in the air, landed on the sidewalk, and yelped. I laughed as I straddled my bike.

But my laughter didn't last long. Before I could sit back up on my bike, I was snatched by the collar. The material cut into my throat, causing a searing pain.

"You're gonna pay for kicking my dog, you fuckin'

nigger." The man spoke with pure rage.

He threw me to the ground and jumped on top of me, with his knees on my arms so I couldn't fight back. He had oily blonde hair, lips chapped to the point of bleeding, and he reeked of cheap alcohol. Dark red veins made his bloodshot eyes seem crazed.

I was looking into his eyes when the first strike exploded in my face. He followed with more crushing blows, calling me nigger each time. His girlfriend finally rescued me and pulled him off.

I eased onto my bike with only one thought: *This white boy done fucked up.*

I rode back down the block toward my father's house, pedaling as fast as I could. His truck was in the driveway and as I jumped off my bike, I thought, *Oh yeah, it's going to be sweet to see my dad kick that white boy's ass.*

My father answered a few seconds after I rang the bell. He took one look at my ripped, bloody tee shirt and asked, "Boy, what the hell happened to you?"

Now, I didn't stop at my father's house too often, and I never asked him for anything. So I knew that this time, he would be there for me. Through teary eyes and a bloody lip, I relayed the story.

When I finished, my father just said, "I'll be right back." He left me standing outside, then returned with a wet towel. "Put this over your lip." Still, I waited for him to let me into his house, but all he did was stand in the door and give me a boring ass speech about why I shouldn't have kicked the man's dog.

I stood on his porch dumbfounded, then just walked away. Why should I have expected anything different?

As I rode past that redneck and a friend who had joined him, crazy thoughts flooded my mind. They were leaning against a custom Baja Bug vehicle and I looked him dead in his eyes. They made sure I heard their laughter as I rode away.

I wanted to inflict as much pain on that redneck as I could, but what bothered me on a deeper level was the pain my father had just inflicted on me.

My mind was made up. That man who'd help to give me life was now my enemy. From that point on, I was only going to refer to him as Buddy, as if he were a stranger. He was merely my sperm donor; he would never mean anything more to me.

I couldn't mention anything about what happened to Mackie. I was ashamed to tell anyone that not only had I gotten beat up by a white man, but my punk ass father hadn't done shit about it.

My mother was home when I arrived, so I circled to the alley, pulled off my bloody shirt, tossed it into the trash, then cleaned up with the water hose. When I walked in through the back door, my mother was cooking dinner, so I couldn't avoid her.

"What happened to your lip?"

I gave her a story about getting beat up by some bullies and said I was done with delivering papers. I knew that would disappoint her since she depended on that little money I brought in.

I told her, "Don't worry. I have a better job cutting lawns."

Only part of that was a lie - she didn't need to worry because hustling in the streets with Mackie would give me enough money to help my mother. But, I wasn't thinking about that then. All that was on my mind for the rest of the night was that redneck and his dog.

The next morning, I ditched school, packed up a few tools and jumped on my bike. I sat across the street from that white guy's house for about twenty minutes figuring they were all at work. The Baja Bug wasn't in the driveway, but still, I first knocked on the front door. When nobody answered, I eased around to the backyard and hid my bike in the bushes.

It was easy to get inside; I slipped in through an open bedroom window and at first had to pause. The place was an absolute wreck. The sofa and love seat were filthy and covered with cigarette burns, the carpet was dingy and stained everywhere, and ashtrays overflowed with cigarette butts. A huge salt-water fish tank perched by the kitchen was filled with filmy water. White trash lived there!

That fucking dog started barking and I started grinning.

I pulled out a box cutter and sliced the sofa and love seat, then grabbed a bottle of Drano from under the kitchen sink and poured it into the fish tank, killing tropical fish instantly.

I gathered the clothes from each closet, threw them into the tub, then poured on the bleach. I plugged up the kitchen sink and both bathroom tubs, turned on the water, then left through the same window I came in.

The only other wish I had as I rode away on my bike was that I could wreak a little havoc in my punk ass father's life, too. In time. In time.

I was a professional car thief now, but also had a sideline business of stealing cases of top shelf liquor from the store where I had a part-time job, then sold them at wholesale prices to the local clubs.

But our major business was robbery. Mackie and I escalated from stealing cars to breaking into houses. We waited until the weekend after most people got paid, then we'd stroll through Hawthorne, listening as people celebrated the weekend. We had developed a good ear for quality music systems and we'd wait until Monday when people were at work. Then, we'd steal a car, drive into the driveway like we owned the joint, and as the saying goes, "we robbed 'em blind."

The money I made from selling those items went straight to my mother. Mackie's skills guaranteed that our pockets stayed full.

It was around this time that I got another car, a midnight blue '64 Chevy Impala that had been stolen and stripped, so I didn't want to keep it at my mother's. Even though I was really still upset with Buddy, I called him and asked if I could put the car in his backyard. He actually said yes and made all kinds of promises to help me to get it working.

Even though this was my second car, I still didn't have a license and I wanted to change that. I found a driving school in the Yellow Pages, paid the fee, and had my license two weeks later.

But my car sat for three whole months in my father's

driveway and Buddy didn't do a single thing to help me. Mackie and I finally pushed the car back to my house.

Once again Buddy let me down, but it wasn't long before I was able to turn on him.

One of our fences told us that he had a need for a '69 Chevy El Camino, and I knew Buddy had one sitting in his driveway - his 'baby' that he cherished like a priceless jewel.

A week later, I paid Buddy a visit and told him the news about getting my license.

He gave me the usual fake hug. "I'm proud of you."

After we talked for a little while, I asked him to let me drive his car to the store.

"Of course," he happily agreed and tossed me the keys.

The keys to the El Camino were on the same ring, just like I figured. I went to the hardware store and made a duplicate set.

The next night, I delivered that El Camino to our fence, who was thrilled. But I didn't give a fuck about that. Disrespecting my father was my ultimate goal. I was quite sure Buddy was devastated and I was happy. I wanted him to feel all the devastation I'd felt over the years.

Once again, I was forced to ask myself the questions I'd been asking for years - what would it have taken for Buddy to send my mother some money so she didn't have to work so hard? Would it have killed him to spend a little time with us? Didn't he ever think that flaunting how he took care of his "new" family would sting? Didn't he ever think that *showing* me how to be a man would have more impact than my mother trying to *tell* me how to be one?

I didn't care how hurt my father was when he discovered that his car had been stolen. He had done much more damage to me than I could ever do to him.

Chapter 7
Articulate Thugs

N ot only did I have to deal with the rejection of my father, but I experienced my first heartbreak, too. Shari Johnson was my first crush and the girl who broke my heart in three solid places.

Shari was one of a couple of black families in our neighborhood and her father was strict as hell.

Shari and her sister, Vikki, attended private school and were rarely allowed to play with the rest of us. Shari was a true square, complete with braces and thick glasses.

Because of her father, I couldn't communicate with her directly, but I wrote letters and talked to her through her bedroom window. For four months, we went on this way and I was so infatuated with her, that I was going to marry her one day. I just had to make her father believe that I was good enough.

I should have been more worried about making sure *Shari* knew I was good enough for her.

I had all of Shari's attention until Albert Joseph, one of those "pretty boys," dropped into our neighborhood and our lives. He was everything I wasn't — muscular, light skin, curly hair, and a star on our high school football team.

Shari took one look at Albert and it was a wrap for me. Things took a fast downward turn. Whenever Albert was around, Shari came outside and she looked at Albert with dreamy eyes; she looked at him in a way she never looked at me. I knew right away that I was losing her, but there was nothing I could do about it.

One day while we were playing football, Albert disappeared from the crowd of guys and slipped into Shari's backyard. Warning bells went off in my head.

I eased into my backyard and climbed the magnolia tree to get a view of Shari's home. I didn't have to wait too long to see what was going on. Seconds after I reached the top of the tree, Shari came out of her back door and slipped into the guesthouse behind their house. Albert followed her and closed the door behind them.

It felt as though someone had taken my heart out of my chest and stomped on it. I don't know how I made it down from that tree, but I went back to the front yard and did my best to hide my pain.

Albert reappeared about fifteen minutes later wearing a stupid, satisfied grin. He pulled a pair of pink panties out of his pocket like they were a trophy and while the guys laughed, I felt like passing out.

Moments later when Shari came out, my pain turned to rage. I stared at her until she looked my way, then she flipped her hair and looked right past me.

I couldn't imagine a girl being so heartless. While I was hurting, she stood there grinning at Albert with lustful eyes.

Right at that moment, I made a decision to never trust a bitch again. First my father, and now this heartbreak?

Now Shari was on my list, too. And just like my father, I was going to figure out a way to hurt her like she had hurt me.

* * *

It was hard to get Shari out of my mind, but of course, I had to keep living. And one day, school provided the perfect distraction.

I was on my way home when a huge crowd had gathered at the front gate of the school, checking out the dark blue '63 Chevy Impala Low Rider sitting at ground level. Then a big, muscle-bound, dark-skinned dude with a white tank top and a perfectly shaped Afro and sideburns stepped out. His skin glistened in the sun, every inch covered in baby oil.

Tookie Williams, leader of the Crips, had graced our presence.

The crowd treated him like a movie star, clamoring to get next to him. I was in awe at the respect people had for him.

I was unable to get the image of what I had witnessed out of my mind and before I made it home, I had a plan to get that same kind of respect. I would become a bodybuilder and assemble a badass Low Rider. And I knew just who'd help me make it happen — Mackie.

I didn't even go home, just went straight to his house. As usual, several Chevy low riders were lined up out front. Mackie was bent over the trunk of a car and after I got his attention, I told him what I had witnessed with Tookie Williams and what I wanted to do.

"I'm ready to start lifting weights and want to work on getting a solid car."

Mackie grinned. "Let's make it happen."

Two days later, we bought a cheap weight bench with weights and set it up in my backyard. I joined the bodybuilding club at school and read as much about it as possible. I lifted weights every chance I had. Mackie joined me in the evenings. Results didn't take long and my confidence began to soar. I was on my way to having the look to go along with my rep.

After just a few weeks, I had something Albert Joseph didn't have — a body that made chicks come at me from all directions. Unfortunately, because of that setback I had with my first crush, I didn't feel the same way toward the opposite sex. I developed "game" and didn't care about anyone's emotions.

That summer, I met two of the sweetest girls around — Renee and Regina, who were twins. Though my guard was up, my attraction for Renee was immediate. She was finer than Shari and was wholesome, like my mother — even with the skimpy outfit she had on when we met.

Renee was the answer to that heartless bitch, Shari! We exchanged numbers and I pursued her and treated her like she was the last girl on earth. I soon had the satisfaction of flaunting Renee in front of Shari — and watching Shari get angry every time.

Yeah, *now* Shari was interested in me. Albert had taken her virginity and dumped her the very next week. I hoped she cried about it every night and thought about how I had not one, but two beautiful girls with me.

Yes, two girls because at the same time, I started seeing a girl named Tina. Tina lived around the corner from my job at the liquor store. She was short, cute, with a super tight body and spoke so proper that I was interested in her right away. She appealed to my nerdy side.

We hung out, but didn't get to do much. Tina's mother was super strict and she scared me so much, at first I thought about leaving Tina alone.

But then one day, Tina told me she was a virgin. Why did she have to tell me that? That was when I knew that I would never stop chasing her.

I was never really serious about Tina, though. We spent all of our time flirting and doing nothing else.

But it was different with Renee. I loved being with her and her sister because the two of them exposed me to all kinds of things that I'd never done - like going to *The Rocky Horror Picture Show* and ice-skating, the kinds of things that I'd always considered "white" activities.

I had a hell of a lot of fun with Renee, Regina...and Tina. The kind of fun that should have kept me out of the California Youth Authority.

But it didn't.

Chapter 8
The Best of the Worst

So with my father and Shari as the backdrop, that's how I got to 1980, and the Viking Freight Truck robbery. I was still thinking primarily about my father, still thinking about ways to get revenge when I hooked up with my cousin, Vince. I'd asked Vince to do that robbery with me because I was in this crazy competition with Mackie and I wanted him to be impressed.

Turns out, that was a good thing for Vince *and* Mackie. My cousin was never caught and who knows what would've happened if Mackie had been with me?

That was my first big robbery and my first arrest.

And even though I was seventeen, and this was my first offense (at least as far as the system knew), I was tried as an adult under the "use a gun, go to jail" provision. That got me eighteen months in the California Youth Authority.

Because I'd used a gun, I bypassed the lower level first offenders camps, and was sent to YTS, Youth Training School, or what most criminals called "gladiator" school.

Inside, I easily completed the G.E.D. requirements before moving to learn a vocational trade, but the real education came from my peers. I was in that place with ghetto super stars like Big Diamond and Monster Kody from the Eight-Trey Gangster Crips; Fats from Piru Bloods; my sister's boyfriend, Peanut, from Black Peace Stone bloods; and King Rat from Nikerson Gardens. These guys, along with dozens of others helped to shape me into that true thug — G Man, a nickname given to me as I rose in ranks toward gangster stardom.

I was most impressed with the vets who were robbers because they made more sense than gangbangers who were fighting over territory. That never made sense to me — fighting over land that you didn't own.

But I worshipped the jewelry store robbers, like Peanut and Fats. I soaked up all the game from them that I could, even though hijacking a freight truck at gunpoint in Beverly Hills was no petty crime. Credibility was everything and the weight of my crime helped me fit in. The "upper class" felons respected me, and respect went a long way in that place.

One of my closest cohorts in YTS was my homeboy, Li'l Man from 107th Street Hoover Crips. Li'l Man was a short, light brown dude with eight-inch long braids. His full lips were darkened from years of smoking and he wore his pants halfway down his ass. But his eyes were what stood out. They cut right through you. He was a hardcore gangbanger.

Li'l Man had landed back in YTS on a parole violation and was set to be released in four months. We built a strong relationship, a sense of camaraderie that most civilians would never understand.

It didn't take me long to get used to being locked up. I had my homies inside and visitors from the outside. Renee and Regina visited me on a regular basis, along with my mother and sister. I loved it when Sheila popped up, because she always had something for me to smuggle back to the unit. We were so bold we even smoked a joint during one of her visits.

Though Tina never visited me, we actually became closer during this time. She wrote me often and I called her a few times. I was still thinking about her being a virgin, still thinking about when I was going to get a chance to hit that.

Being locked up gave me more time to lift weights and I worked out with Li'l Man who had the biggest arms I'd ever seen. I gained muscle mass easily, and thanks to Li'l Man, I ended up looking just like him.

Once Li'l Man was released, I actually started thinking more positively about my future. Maybe I wasn't destined to being a career criminal. So I enrolled in the welding class and actually imagined myself getting a job on the outside. But then Li'l Man returned on another parole violation and I lost focus again.

When Li'l Man came back, he introduced me to another dude, Big-Eyed Nate, an ex-limo driver turned jacker, who was from Black Peace Stone Bloods. Nate was a slim, brown-skinned dude, several inches taller than me. He had a suave player-player vibe, was articulate, and well-groomed and I admired his class.

During breaks, he told us wild stories about people he'd driven around and the elaborate homes they visited.

Li'l Man and Nate impressed me because they put aside their differences from being in rival gangs, and made getting money the priority.

Money was the common ground for everyone in YTS. It was why the inmates had landed in CYA in the first place, and it was the main thing everyone thought about the moment they hit the outside.

While I was doing my time, my sister, Sheila, ended up going to jail, sentenced to a few months in juvenile hall, and I could only imagine the stress that put on my mother. That's why I was determined not to give my mother any more grief once I got out.

But that turned out to be much easier for me to say than it was for me to do.

Chapter 9
Dirty Deeds Done Cheap

Parole. I'd served fourteen months of an eighteen-month sentence and now I was out. I was G Man and everyone would know my name this time around.

I had come into the California Youth Authority system as a freshman with limited understanding of the other side of the game. Now, I had graduated, leaving as a senior thug with unlimited knowledge. I'd been a caged animal and now I was being released into a city where everybody was prey.

I was one hundred times more dangerous now than before I became part of the system.

Mama took off work to pick me up and take me home. She hugged me and held me tight when I stepped outside.

"I hope you get it together this time, Grego."

Instead of agreeing out loud, I nodded. I really hoped I could, too, but I wasn't sure because I had no idea what awaited me on the outside.

After stopping first to check in with my parole officer, my mother then drove me home to the new house she'd bought in Ontario. She'd moved deep into the suburbs hoping that the rest of my siblings wouldn't get into trouble the way Sheila and I had.

When we arrived, my three brothers met me at that door. (Sheila was still incarcerated.) But my brothers were so glad to see me, giving me hugs and letting me feel their love with all of their laughter. My homecoming was a party.

After a few hours, I stepped away from everyone and stood in the doorway looking at and studying my new middle class neighborhood. This first day of freedom was good. Maybe, just maybe I would be able to get it together and stay out of trouble...this time. That was my hope.

A few days later, I enrolled in welding school in Rancho Cucamonga and actually enjoyed being around those white kids who didn't know about my background. I came to realize that I was no different than they were; I had just made a few wrong choices. Well, maybe more than a few.

Besides welding school, I kept building my life back. First, I got my job back at the liquor store as a stock boy, and my cousin Watani sold me a '71 Datsun pick-up. With a car, a job, and being in school, all I had to do was follow the script and my life would be fine.

Well, that wasn't easy. Because trouble came looking for me, and even though I was still messing with Renee, and seeing Tina, trouble came in the form of a new woman.

Three weeks after I left YTS, I was out mowing the lawn when a royal blue '79 Thunderbird rolled by. The driver, a pretty black female with a flawless almond complexion and reddish-blonde hair, almost broke her neck trying to look at me.

I stopped and watched the car come to a complete stop in the driveway of the house across the street that belonged to the only other black family on the block.

Everything was perfect until she stepped out of the car. Damn, she was a big girl! But that didn't stop me from looking until she went inside.

Then, my mother's phone rang and even though I was outside, my brother, Marvin talked loud enough for me to hear.

"Yeah, that's my brother that I was telling you about. Yeah, I'll bring him over to meet you guys. Yeah today, Sandra."

Seconds later, Marvin yelled from the front door, "Hey bro, those chicks across the street that I've been telling you about want to meet you. I've been messing with the one that owns that house. The one with the red hair is her sister-in-law."

Later that afternoon, we stopped by. Marvin introduced me to Sandra and then, the sister-in-law, Evelyn. I didn't know what it was, but even though she was a little on the heavy side, and even though there was a sixteen-year difference between us, and even though she was married, I just had to have Evelyn. Maybe it was those well-manicured fingernails or the huge diamond cocktail rings on her fingers.

"I never thought about dating a younger man," she confessed. "Hell, my oldest is a year older than you!"

"Well, we *are* going to have a relationship."

77

She laughed. "You sure sound confident. I used to watch soap operas with your Mama, boy."

Why the hell did she say that? That was almost a deal breaker!

But it wasn't. The third time after we hooked up, we had sex. It had been a nervous quickie, but from that moment, Evelyn was officially into me as her younger man.

Evelyn became the center of my world, but my woman was as crooked as they came. She ran an illegal booking operation and sold pills and cocaine, which explained her big ass diamond rings.

She drove me to and from work, took me out to eat at nice restaurants, and showed me how to live as a true hustler. She considered me a complex young thug and was patient as she let me "be" a man while schooling me, too.

I worried about Evelyn's husband, Lucky. Even though they lived out in Pomona, he complained about her being away from home too much, and I knew it was only a matter of time before something popped off.

It happened one day after he showed up at Sandra's house. I was walking out the front door as Lucky walked in and he gave me the once-over, but I didn't break stride, even as I did my once-over of him. Lucky was huge, about 6'4 and weighing nearly 340 pounds.

I made my way across the street to my mother's house, and the phone rang.

"Hi, baby," Evelyn crooned. "I'm sorry about that, but this broke ass motherfucker don't run shit. I've been taking care of his ass for the last six years." Her girlish voice was sweet as she continued, " As soon as he leaves, I want you to take a ride with me."

I hesitated. "All right baby, but you need to be careful around your husband because I ain't trying to catch no murder case." I didn't add, "Or an ass-whipping from your monster-sized husband."

After I disconnected the call, I thought, *What the fuck am I getting myself into? No pussy could be that good.*

Then it hit me: Damn, I had fucked around and fell in love with that old chick!

Chapter 10
Ain't No Fun Waiting 'Round to
be a Millionaire

The phone rang about fifteen minutes after Evelyn's call — a collect call from Arthur.

"What's up, G Man?" Li'l Man asked. "Are you enjoying that freedom, homie?"

"Hell, yeah." I laughed. "When the fuck you coming home, nigga?"

"In a couple of weeks, so don't fuck up before then." He told me that Big-eyed Nate would be paroled about the same time.

First Evelyn, now Li'l Man and Nate? I had been keeping my head out of the murky water. Why was life sending curve balls that were going to be hard to duck?

I headed outside to wash my Datsun pickup truck and thought about the fact that while stuck in that cell, I had dreamed about freedom, fresh air, and having choices. I hoped that I'd be able to stay out of trouble.

The hairs on my neck stood at attention, and when I glanced at Sandra's house, Evelyn was in the upstairs window. I threw her a kiss at the exact moment Lucky strolled out the front door. We locked gazes as he tried to figure out who in the fuck I could be throwing a kiss to.

Thinking fast, I made the same motion again, waving my arm as if I was working out a cramp. His gaze narrowed before he slipped into his car.

Lucky inched by as I bent over the hood of my truck, avoiding eye contact. He made a right turn at the end of the block and he was gone. But I knew I'd see him again.

An hour later, Evelyn picked me up around the corner and as soon as I got in the car, she gave me a passionate kiss. Then she held my face with both hands and in a half moan, half whisper said, "Damn baby, you keep my pussy sooo wet! I need you to fluff my bird tonight."

I had never heard *that one* before.

We jumped on the freeway before she told me, "We're going to meet Misty at her house up in Hollywood Hills."

So, I was finally going to meet the infamous Misty. I had heard Evelyn speak to Misty on the phone a few times and knew she was somebody important, but I didn't know details.

Evelyn began to fill me in on some details. "Misty and my mother met in jail a long time ago," Evelyn explained. "Both had been arrested for prostitution. My mother got out of the game, but Misty stayed in and she's doing very well."

We turned right off of Sunset Boulevard to Mulholland Drive. "Now, Misty wants to meet you."

The further we went up the hill, the more intrigued I became. Million dollar homes surrounded us and finally, we pulled to a stop in front of a mansion. Stepping out of the car, I felt like I was in a movie. We were still in Los Angeles, but this was a different world.

Evelyn rang the doorbell as we stood in front of the most elaborate glass and wooden doors I'd ever seen. A Hispanic maid in full uniform let us in and I followed Evelyn as she took her shoes off in a foyer illuminated by a skylight.

I scanned the place as Evelyn led the way. Almost everything was white — the carpet, the furniture, even the silk on the walls. This was the most beautiful house I'd ever been in; this is how I dreamed of living.

Then I heard a raspy, booming voice. "Is that you, Evelyn?"

The woman spoke with so much authority, I felt intimidated. I put on my poker face as we entered the room.

Misty, a plus sized woman with a light complexion and even lighter hair, sat on a white leather sofa wearing a black silk robe. I guessed that she was in her early fifties.

Her face lit up. "So, this is the young nigga that's been fluffing your bird. Is this my new son-in-law?"

Evelyn giggled. "Misty, you're too much! Why are you putting me on the spot like this?"

Misty kept her eyes on me. "Girl, you know I'm just playing. But I haven't seen you this happy in a long time. That young dick must skeet diamonds."

We all laughed and the older woman motioned for me to sit next to her. "So what prison did you just get out of?" was the beginning of an interrogation that lasted an hour.

I responded to each one of her questions with the truth. Satisfied, she finally relaxed and offered me something to drink. The maid came in with a soda as Misty left the room.

Evelyn looked at me. "She likes you. She probably already has something for you to do. Whatever she touches turns to gold, so let her do all the talking, baby."

I walked across the room on the thick white carpet that felt good under my feet to a wall made entirely of glass. Hollywood Hills had the greatest views of downtown Los Angeles. Behind me, Evelyn rambled through her purse, pulled out a stack of money, placed it on a solid glass table, and began counting.

As I watched her and then looked around the room, I realized that I was about to be groomed for what I wanted to be. I'd seen money before, but this was different. This kind of money came with its own power.

Misty returned carrying three large plastic jars. She sat next to Evelyn and recounted the money Evelyn had laid out, then smiled at her protégée.

"Damn bitch, he needs to keep on fluffing that bird if it's gonna make you hustle like this."

We laughed before she looked my way. "Son, get your ass over here and let me show you where the real money's at. I'm gonna show you how to get rich."

Misty pulled out a pill chart and explained the different types. Her main moneymaker was called Dilaudid — a synthetic heroin that didn't come cheap — $25 a pill in Los Angeles and almost twice that out of town.

I was impressed. Between Evelyn and Misty, G Man was about to move up in the world.

Chapter 11
Trouble In My Way

E ven though my mother had moved to the suburbs, trouble found me again. Bringing one of my old partners out to the house was one of my first major mistakes.

I was hanging out with Donnie one day and the neighbor across the street had a Datsun 510 that Donnie just had to have. I went against my gut and late that night while everyone slept, I helped him push the car around the corner and get it started.

My world crumpled when I got a phone call from my brother the next morning when I went to work.

"Greg!" he began, sounding panicked. "The police been here looking for you. They caught Donnie driving a stolen car and he says you helped him steal it."

Donnie had snitched on me!

There was no way I was going back to jail. After I hung up from my brother, I quit my job and was a fugitive from that moment on.

Staying ahead the cops became a family affair, since it put everyone — my mother, my siblings, and my friends — under a microscope. My mother was heartbroken when she found out what I'd done, but there was nothing that I could do to fix it.

Evelyn had my back as I hid out for a few days in a motel not far from my mother's. After the third day, I had her take me by my father's house. I wasn't sure why I wanted to see him, didn't know what I expected considering that he never gave a fuck about me. But the kid in me said that one day he might care.

I knew it was a mistake the moment he opened the door. He greeted me with the usual fake ass hug and smile and we stood outside on the front porch while he made the usual false promises. The father-son visit was over in less than ten minutes, and I was angrier when I left than before I arrived.

Now what was I going to do? I was a disappointment to my mother, abandoned by my father and I had fucked up. The police were hot on my trail. What kind of hell had I created?

Evelyn worried about me because she knew my back was against the wall, so the first thing she did was find me a place to stay with one of her friends on 104th and Prairie in Inglewood. Evelyn paid Diane well to make sure that I was hidden and safe and the whole time, I still hung out with Evelyn and Misty. It had been a couple of months now, and I was soaking up as much game as possible. But I always remembered that this was *their* hustle and I wasn't the type to lean on another person. I knew how to get money; I was just waiting on Li'l Man to get out so that we could make this happen.

A few weeks later, Li'l Man called; he was home and we agreed to meet at Diane's place. I was so excited that I couldn't even wait inside — I stood in front of the apartment until an older model white Toyota Corolla squealed its way to a stop in the driveway.

Li'l Man jumped out wearing a white tank top and jailhouse jeans. He yelled, "What's up, Cuz? They done fucked up now, nigga! Putting us on the streets together was a *big* mistake."

He had never lied.

I scrambled down the short flight of stairs and gave him a brief hug and a tight handshake. I felt like me and Li'l Man could take on the world. I nodded toward the Corolla. "Whose car are you driving, homie?"

"This is my cousin's piece of shit. But it'll get you from point A to point Z, nigga. We just got to keep putting water in the radiator." Li'l Man jumped back into the car. "Get in, G Man. Let's hit a couple of corners." After I slid in the passenger seat, he said, "There's a Mardi Gras up on the campus of UCLA. There's gonna be a bunch of bitches there."

We needed to cop some weed first, a couple of blocks away on Century Boulevard and Freeman Avenue. The place was in a huge 200 unit, two-story apartment building run by Panamanians. It was heavily gated with a courtyard in the center where they controlled all incoming and outgoing traffic. The front exit on Century or the back exit through the parking lot on 102nd were the only ways in and out.

We pulled into the back lot, walked through a 30-foot tunnel to the courtyard that was filled with kids, then scaled the stairs to the second floor and Unit 206. A Panamanian peered from behind the heavy curtains, recognized me, and opened the door. They weren't concerned about security because the sheer number of their people was enough to make jackers think twice about robbing them.

We sat on the sofa and watched the little dude as he opened the stuffed freezer, pulled out one of the black Hefty trash bags, and handed us two nickel bags of some good ass Panama Red. He said, "Come back again" before he let us out.

We made it to the car and for as long as I live, I will never forget how we looked at each other and said at the same time, "We need to get some guns," then cracked up laughing.

I told him, "I know exactly where to go."

We rolled into my neighborhood and I acquired a couple of pistols from an old connect. I preferred a Magnum, but I settled for the biggest metal they had — a .38 revolver and a .32 semi automatic pistol.

I took the revolver because I couldn't take a chance on a misfire. Li'l Man didn't give a fuck; he was so ruthless, he'd rob them with a water gun.

We made our way back to the weed house, not exchanging a single word along the way. My mind was on our next move and the gun in my hand. I pulled the hammer back and inspected the firing pin, then wiped off each shell with my t-shirt because all it would take was one hit on a fingerprint to bring everybody down.

I was calm, not worried. I was rolling with my true homeboy. We had established a bond in YTS that was stronger than my blood siblings, and I trusted Li'l Man with my life.

We stopped by my spot and grabbed a couple of shirts to conceal the weapons and tone down our appearance. Then, we sat in the parking lot going over the details.

My stomach was in knots while Li'l Man seemed so relaxed.

He turned to me with his wicked grin. "Okay, Cuz, shit might get crazy in that motherfucker. I got your back, nigga. It's do or die on mines, G Man, let's roll, Cuz!"

We stuffed the weapons and walked toward the building. There were even more kids playing outside now, but we still made it to the apartment; the door was already cracked. Two customers were in the living room, trying to get change for a hundred-dollar bill — the perfect distraction.

Li'l Man asked the dealer if he could use the restroom and moved toward the back. But then he popped a U-Turn and raised his pistol. I pulled out mine, and the customers shoved their money into their pockets, scooped up some extra bags of weed, and were ghost.

I secured the door behind them and as I turned around, Li'l Man pistol-whipped the dude. "Where's the money?" he demanded.

I unloaded all the marijuana into one big bag, then helped Li'l Man hog-tie him with the telephone cord and toss him onto the bed.

Li'l Man keep beating him. "Where's the money?"

The dude took the beating, and wouldn't answer. The puddle of blood on the bed grew larger by the second, and then there was a sudden knock at the door. Li'l Man removed one of dude's shoes, grabbed his sock and stuffed it into his mouth.

My homie moved into position as I tucked my pistol and peered out the peephole. Another Panamanian stood outside.

Li'l Man signaled for me to open the door. The dude stepped inside, and my homeboy kicked him so hard in the back that he flew past me. Li'l Man was all over him.

I took the heavy gold jewelry from both Panamanians, then tied up dude number two using the same phone cord. Li'l Man went back to pistol-whipping both of them. They still refused to talk.

"Fuck it, homie," I said to Li'l Man. "Let's go. We got enough shit."

Just as I said that, the second dude growled in a thick accent, "You niggers are fucking dead!"

He didn't get to say another word. Li'l Man laid into him hard; my homie turned into a pit bull. I tried to stop him, but he kept going until he was tired.

Finally he said, "Fuck it! Grab that receiver and turntable. I'm right behind you, homie."

I scooped up the marijuana, held the gun, settled the receiver on top to conceal the pistol, and opened the front door.

I stepped outside and navigated to the car, thinking Li'l Man was right behind me. I reached the bottom and made it halfway to the tunnel before the remaining Panamanians started to scramble, definitely moving to get guns. I made it to the car and tossed everything onto the back seat.

But when I turned around, Li'l Man's ass was nowhere in sight!

I yelled his nickname as loud as I could. After the third attempt, I went back in to get him because he would've done the same for me.

When I reached the tunnel, the courtyard was in total chaos. As someone shouted orders, I moved cautiously, edging to the opening and peeked into the courtyard— and found myself looking down the barrel of a .357 Magnum. A split-second later, the hammer fell.

My life had come to an end.

But then, I was still breathing. He had either misfired or forgot to put the bullets in.

Now it was my turn. I raised my gun to the center of his forehead. "I'm the one with the bullets, motherfucker."

He dropped his gun into my free hand, then took off running. I leveled my pistol at the small crowd and they scattered just as Li'l Man ambled down the stairs carrying his loot.

We ran through the tunnel, then I stood on point watching for any sudden movement as I waited for Li'l Man to get the car started.

Then he said words that made my heart stop. "Motherfucking car won't start!"

We had forgotten all about the leaking water pump!

He gave it another try and it turned over. I walked backward alongside the car, watching the tunnel until Li'l Man reached the end of the parking lot. We were sweating like hogs and laughing like crazy.

"Nigga, are you crazy?" I asked him. "What the fuck took you so long?"

He pulled a black leather pouch from his crotch. "The money was hanging on the bedroom doorknob the whole time, G Man."

We laughed again, but not for long. The car started smoking and choking; I don't know how, but we made it to my place just as Evelyn pulled up.

"What are you guys up to?" she asked.

I looked at Li'l Man, and then said with a straight face, "We ain't up to nothin', baby. Nothing at all."

Chapter 12
Three the Hard Way

Just a few weeks later, Big-eyed Nate contacted Li'l Man; he'd been released, so Li'l Man and I headed out to see him. Li'l Man was still driving his cousin's bucket, but at least the water pump had been fixed.

We rolled up to Nate's spot in a neighborhood called the Jungles — a part of Los Angeles that is closer to the west side and dominated by Bloods.

Li'l Man kept his eye out as we drove through. He was still a Crip, with Blood enemies. We scooped Big-Eyed Nate up and got the hell out of there.

Nate pulled out a joint, lit it up, and passed it up to me. As we rode, we formulated a game plan to do a few "follow-home" robberies. We drove to my spot to get the guns, but I was surprised when we got there. Evelyn was there, which was odd; she was supposed to be in Pomona.

In the living room, I introduced Nate to Evelyn.

Then she said, "Misty sent me." She paused for a couple of seconds. "She told me to bring you and your partners to the big house."

So far, Misty had only given me pieces of her game. But I knew there was big money at stake and I wanted to be cut in.

We jumped into Evelyn's car and set off for Hollywood Hills. Nate and Li'l Man were just as impressed as I had been on my first trip. Misty stood in the driveway with the garage door open. She motioned for Evelyn to pull inside and closed it the moment we rolled in.

She led us into her cozy den as the maid entered carrying a large tray with all kinds of drinks — except alcohol — and placed it on the white marble table.

As soon as the maid left, Misty said, "I heard y'all niggas are jackers." We didn't say a word, so she continued, "There's this so-called slick nigga that owes me thirty-seven thousand dollars. I need y'all to get what he owes me and there's a nice chunk of change to be made." She laid out the info needed to execute the move.

I listened as Misty spoke, since she looked me dead in my eyes. She expected me to make sure everything went right.

When she finished briefing us, she asked if we needed any heat. Li'l Man and I had our own pistols, but Nate was dry. She gave him a beautiful Remington 12-gauge sawed off shotgun.

Love at first sight! Cars, music, women and guns — I loved them all. I couldn't wait to wrap my hand around the grip of the expertly modified mini-cannon.

We headed back toward the garage, but Misty stopped Li'l Man. "You look like you don't play around. I got something special that I want you to do." Misty reached into a drawer and pulled out huge pliers. "Crush the middle finger on his left hand." Li'l man just stared.

"He flipped me off with a fuck-you finger," she explained.

Damn, this bitch is a true gangster.

We agreed that we would handle it that night, so Evelyn drove us back to Inglewood to get Li'l Man's car.

"Be careful," she said as we headed away to stake out our prey.

As we drove east along Century, we cracked jokes as if we were going to the movies. A few blocks later, we found a cool place to park and evaluated the scene. The house was a six-unit multiplex. His unit was in the middle, so we had to be careful because of his neighbors.

It was half-past eleven, and after midnight would be the best time. We smoked more weed and talked about the old days at YTS. At half-past midnight, I stepped out of the car to get a better feel of the situation. Four of the six units had lights on. Two had windows open. We needed to wait a while longer.

As I turned back, voices trailed me. They were talking and laughing loud and obviously drunk. Music blared from a stereo. This unit was across from our target.

Perfect!

At the car, I laid out my general observations. I had already witnessed Li'l Man in action, so I knew his capability. He became a different person, showing no emotion at all.

But how would Nate handle himself?

Under the cover of darkness, we headed down the walkway and moved in between the duplexes. The drunken neighbors were blasting the Average White Band's hit, "Cut The Cake."

I turned around, planning to tell them our next move, but all I saw were Nate's big ass eyes. But a second later, Li'l Man reappeared.

"There's a back door out of plain sight and it's thin," he said.

As we moved around the duplex, we passed our target's window; it was cracked open and the sweet aroma of cherry incense wafted out along with the soothing voice of Al Green. *Looks like ol' boy is planning on getting some pussy.*

We moved around to the back, and heard the squeaking sound of a faucet, then the shower's running water.

Li'l Man and Nate stood on each side of the door. As the biggest one of the crew, I was the kicker.

I slipped on gloves, then kicked in the door with ease. Li'l Man ran in with blinding speed and was in the living room on top of old boy in two seconds.

Li'l Man straddled the expensive leather sofa, the barrel of a pistol shoved deep down our mark's throat. Nate swept though the rest of the house and I turned off the living room lights. Li'l Man snatched the telephone cord and hogtied the dude as I asked, "Who's in the shower, motherfucker?"

He didn't respond; Li'l Man raised the pistol high and delivered a heavy blow to his face.

"It's my wife, nigga!" he snarled.

I went to the bedroom and looked for cash and valuables. A large, expensive briefcase was near the bed. I hoped it held what we'd come for. Suddenly, a female's scream cut through the air.

I rushed into the living where Nate's hand covered the mouth of a gorgeous, wet and naked female. Her hair was silky and straight — obviously a half-breed.

Nate manhandled her to the floor before he tied her up.

I went back into the bedroom to break the locks on the briefcase. We'd already been in the house too long.

I spotted a screwdriver on the dresser and worked it into the cylinder. From the living room, I heard the woman's muffled screams, along with my homies beating the man to get the location of the safe and the money.

The mark was a so-called pretty boy, but when I re-entered the living room, I didn't recognize his mangled face. Li'l Man's expression showed he was on the verge of murder, but I stopped him. With my eyes, I let him know that killing was not an option.

I turned back to the bedroom, knowing that I had to move quickly because I didn't know how much longer I'd be able to control Li'l Man. Finally, I got one lock on the briefcase open.

But then, I stopped suddenly. I heard a new sound from the living room — desperate moaning. I peered into the front and couldn't believe it.

Li'l Man had the dude's wife on her hands and knees, fucking her doggy-style. He pressed her face as close to her husband's as possible. Tears mixed with blood poured down dude's swollen face.

Even criminals had rules and rape was forbidden. I couldn't describe how angry I was.

Unfortunately though, that worked and Pretty Boy led us straight to the bedroom closet. As soon as he entered the combination and turned the handle, Li'l Man snatched him backward as Nate opened the safe. The money was there...and so was a loaded .45 semi-automatic handgun.

Li'l Man dragged him back into the living room and re-tied him. I broke the second lock and understood why dude was putting up such a fight. Large spools of gold chains were inside, along with two plastic jars full of pills. Those little powdered jewels were probably why his ass was in trouble with Misty.

We grabbed up the loot, and right before we made it out, Li'l Man pulled out the pliers. I turned my head. Even though Li'l Man had stuffed a sock in his mouth, Pretty Boy still released an agonizing wail.

We retraced our steps, and at the side of the duplex, the sounds of our victims trying frantically to get loose reached our ears. Not that we were worried. Criminals robbing criminals meant the victims couldn't call the police.

The female's sobs didn't sit well with me, though. What if that had been my mother? Or sister? Li'l Man needed to be reminded how to respect the game.

Misty had given me instructions on what to do after the hit. Evelyn had rented a hotel room where she waited. She would take everything up to Misty and bring our money back.

After we gave everything to Evelyn and waited in the hotel for her to come back, I thought again about what Li'l Man had done. I didn't know how Misty would react if she heard that piece of news.

Evelyn returned with several thousand dollars for each of us. That made me feel a whole lot better.

It was official; we were now "Three the Hard Way," and God help anyone who stood in our way.

Chapter 13
There's Gonna Be some Rockin'
(AC/DC)

After Evelyn brought the money, we laughed, drank, and smoked weed, but my little celebration was cut short when Evelyn pulled me aside.

"Misty wants you to come back to her house." She glanced over to Nate and Li'l Man. "*Without* them."

Instinct told me this wasn't good, but I had to see what she wanted. I told my homies that I'd be back, then left with Evelyn. We walked through Misty's front door at half-past two in the morning.

The house was dark except for candles placed along the hallway. But then, that raspy voice cut through every ounce of serenity the candles were supposed to provide.

"Evelyn, bring his young ass in here."

Butterflies fluttered in my stomach.

I followed Evelyn down the two steps into the sunken room, but didn't see Misty.

All of a sudden, pain exploded in my left upper arm. "Have you lost your fucking mind, young nigga?" Misty pinched the hell out of me, like some damn kid!

"I thought you were the brains, *Mr. G Man,*" she spat, her voice dripping with disdain. She was still pinching the shit out of me when she told me she'd heard what Li'l Man had done.

I wanted to slap her fucking hand off my arm, but she was right, and I knew it down to my soul. She finally released me, but continued the tongue-lashing.

"Look, if you're gonna fuck with me, you're gonna have to control your boys. Taking pussy is never part of the game, son."

Misty gestured for me to sit down next to her, then lectured me for another hour. When she finished, she turned to Evelyn. "Shit, it's too late for y'all to leave now. Take him to the guest room." Then, she waved her hand, dismissing us.

Evelyn led me to the last door down the hall, hit the switch, and the room became illuminated with a soft glow from recessed lights high in the ceiling.

I dove onto the California King bed, flipped onto my back, clasped my fingers behind my head, and took in the mural of marine life painted on the ceiling.

The old woman had class. Every single item in the room was top-of-the-line.

As Evelyn went into the bathroom, I edged off the bed, slipped out of my shoes and shirt, and walked over to the thick drapes that ran the length of the back wall. I opened them and was blown away by the breathtaking view.

Ten minutes later, Evelyn stepped from the bathroom, carrying a set of towels and a robe for me. But even though Misty's house was amazing, nothing prepared me for the huge bathroom with aqua marble everywhere. The glass shower was large enough to hold a few people and the huge window revealed a thick wall of lush, green vegetation providing privacy as well as an illusion of a rain forest.

I stepped in, took a seat on the marble bench, and let the hot soothing water cascade over my body. I was still in there when a half-hour later, Evelyn came to get me. She had changed into a sexy red sheer negligee and we went into the bedroom and laid together.

Evelyn nestled her body behind mine and whispered, "I got something for you, baby."

She rolled over, pulled something from her purse, then motioned for me to sit up before she fastened a thick gold chain around my neck. The heavy pendant — resembling a gold nugget — was designed to simulate a series of melting pieces. Huge diamonds were embedded into each "drip."

I gave Evelyn a kiss that held as much passion as I could summon. "Thank you," I said.

Standing, I walked over to the windows again. I took in the view, then glanced down at my first expensive piece of jewelry. The power of money.

"Come over here, baby," Evelyn purred. She was on the edge of the bed and I sat next to her. She held another shiny gold item in her hand — a cocaine sniffing kit, with a small white mound of powder on the mirrored glass of a gold compact mirror. Evelyn chopped the cocaine up into a fine powder and formed a few lines.

Then, she scooped her purse from the side of the bed and pulled out a 16-ounce can of Old English 800 and a pint of Seagram's Gin. She mixed them, creating a boilermaker.

As I took a sip from her cup, she picked up the gold straw and inhaled two lines. She surprised me when she passed it my way. Some of my older partners had made cocaine their drug of choice. I never gave it much thought since it was considered a "rich man's habit." My facial expression told her that I didn't know shit about this part of the game.

"It's an aphrodisiac," Evelyn said. She held the mirror, instructing me to do a one-on-one—inhaling a line through each nostril.

The high started with a head rush, then a warm sensation flooded my body. The drug's "taste" lingered in my throat.

Evelyn smiled when she passed the boilermaker. "Wash it down."

I drank, then stretched out on the bed, my head spinning as the ceiling mural came alive. The feeling was magnificent.

One hour later, we had snorted up most of the coke and my gaze landed on the thick, sexy woman in my arms. Her nearly blond hair blended with her almond complexion. In the streets, a woman with Evelyn's features was labeled a Red Bone.

Big Red rolled onto her side, placed one of those gorgeous, thighs across mine and started with a soft, sensual kiss. I responded, but she stopped me. "Slow down, baby."

I had always been the one to lead, but not tonight. By the time she made it to my nipples, I was so lost in lust, I couldn't form a thought; my dick was rock-hard.

She wrapped her fingers around my throbbing shaft. I had never let my guard down to a female before, but right now, I allowed her to have total control.

When I reached into her panties, she released an intense moan. Her pussy was soaking wet. Her warm juices enhanced my passion, and I teased her clit. Her animalistic moaning was driving me crazy.

Big Red clinched her legs shut, then her body trembled with pleasure. Hot cum flowed over my hand. She pulled her panties off, straddled me, then guided the tip of that swollen, pulsating member into her. She placed both hands on my chest as she claimed that last inch.

Big Red rode that dick, looking me in my eyes the whole time. "Don't rush it, baby," she kept saying. Every time I came close to exploding, she stopped fucking me.

"Baby, please let me cum," I begged.

But she continued to have her way for at least twenty more minutes, before she said, "Get ready to cum with me."

She fucked me like I had the last dick on the planet. Her hands splayed across my chest before those manicured nails sank into my skin.

She whispered, "Come on, baby, share your orgasm with me."

We exploded at the same time in the most pleasurable moment of my entire life.

Evelyn collapsed onto my chest, a thin sheen of moisture over her body. I couldn't say my own name, but she didn't have a problem speaking.

"I hope you don't think we're through, G Man."

Damn!

As she sauntered to the bathroom, I managed to scoot to the edge of the bed and take this all in. I was nineteen years old and on the run from the law, yet I was sitting inside a million-dollar house. I had just been rewarded for committing a violent crime and introduced to a new drug. A real woman had just fucked me senseless.

This was the life.

Chapter 14
The Next Level

Only one word could describe Evelyn — insatiable. Twenty-four hours had passed, and the woman had taken me to school. Youth and the determination to prove myself worthy were the only reasons I made it through that first night, the next day, the next night, and the following morning.

Big Red had finally fallen asleep. I was exhausted and couldn't wait to get some shut-eye, too. But ten minutes passed and I was jerked awake. Evelyn was snoring like a lumberjack! I stayed still, hoping to catch a wink between the chorus line of hog-calling and chainsaw sonata.

Finally, I rolled out of bed and closed the drapes. With darkness covering the room, she finally toned it down. But not even five minutes passed when there was a knock on the door and then, "Okay, you love birds. Rise and shine."

Evelyn rolled over and grinned at me. "She's ready to go to work."

I wanted to tell the old woman that after being with Big Red all day and night, I had put in enough work already!

We showered, dressed, then walked into the kitchen where ham and cheese omelets awaited. Misty laid out the day's itinerary and I was pissed. I didn't recall telling her I was available, but I didn't say anything.

After breakfast, Misty spread huge jars of pills over the table. Wearing rubber gloves, she counted the pills like a precision machine, slipped the pills into plastic bags, then slid the bags into large mailing envelopes and addressed them.

She instructed Evelyn, "Run down to the post office and mail each overnight. I'll be ready to go when you get back."

Just before we left, Misty eyed my new chain. "Red, that young dick must be damn good."

They had a good laugh, as we gathered the envelopes. I pushed my chair back and spotted a roll of 100-dollar bills under the table. I passed it to Misty and walked out the door, knowing I had just passed a test.

In the garage, Evelyn unlocked the door to a brand new Cadillac Fleetwood. "Get in, baby. We're taking the Caddy."

That expensive leather was ice cold, but I couldn't have cared less. I couldn't believe this shit was happening. I was on my way to cutting into Misty and her empire.

After we hit the post office, I told Evelyn to stop by the hotel for just a minute. I used my key to enter the room and she waited right by the door as we stepped inside.

Nate and Li'l Man were passed out and I reached to shake Li'l Man awake; his pistol was in my face the second I put my hands on him.

"It's me! G Man, nigga!"

He pulled the gun back, but the commotion woke Nate.

The first thing they noticed was my chain. "Damn, homie! Where the fuck did you get that piece?"

Evelyn, who still stood near the door, replied, "I bought it for him."

L'il Man didn't respond to that. Instead he asked, "So what time are we going to the mall, G Man?"

A span of silence followed. I took a quick glance at Evelyn, then explained, "I have a few errands to run for Misty first. We can hook up later, though and —"

Li'l Man looked me dead in my eyes. "Check this out, G Man, it's bros befo' hos, homie."

Talk about being caught between the two. He was my homie and our bond was sealed. But then, I reflected on what I had experienced in the past few days. In this game, if you're around money, you'll have money. Misty and Evelyn were rolling in the kind of money that didn't have an end in sight.

The kind of cash that Li'l Man and I brought in needed replenishing weekly, if not daily. Three the Hard Way acquired money in a way that left us open to getting shot, killed, or jacked.

Misty's pill program was high profit with minimum risk. Rolling with my homies might land me in a coffin that very night.

But unfortunately, that damn loyalty overrode common sense. I turned to Evelyn and saw the uncertainty in her eyes.

I parted my lips to give her the answer she dreaded, but Li'l Man interrupted, "Look homie, go ahead and take care of your business with your people. We'll hook up tomorrow." He gave me a wink and a wicked grin, then lit a joint, hit it, and passed it to me. I took a deep drag and passed it to Nate. Evelyn inched forward and made eye contact.

Shit, I was fucking up.

That quick, I'd forgotten that Misty was waiting on us. We hit the door, but Li'l Man grabbed my arm before I stepped outside.

He spoke in a whisper, "Don't ever let this happen again, G Man."

Evelyn made tracks, driving fast as hell to get us back to the big house. When we got there, Misty was standing outside, hands on her hips, with her dark brown eyes flashing.

As soon as the car stopped, Evelyn hustled to the back seat and Misty slid into the passenger side and I went to the driver's side. I put the car into gear and that was as far as I made it before Misty's death pinch gripped my arm.

"Have you lost your fucking mind?" she said through clenched teeth. "You can't work while you're high."

Damn, this bitch didn't miss nothing.

Misty made me go back into the house and take a cold shower, but that wasn't enough. Her sermon started the moment we were out of the Hills. "Look, son, there's a lot you've got to learn. Never mix business with pleasure."

I glanced at Evelyn through the rearview mirror; she was laughing. If I told Misty what Evelyn's freaky ass was doing last night, I bet she wouldn't find a damn thing funny.

I navigated that Cadillac through morning rush-hour until we reached the east side of Los Angeles in an area known as the Low Bottoms.

People pushed shopping carts containing all their worldly possessions, some with mangy dogs following behind. Homeless people huddled around fires burning inside 55-gallon trashcans behind every liquor store or abandoned building.

We reached a vacant lot where a passenger van awaited. Misty and Evelyn got out, but Misty instructed me to follow her. A bum appeared from under a makeshift cardboard shelter. Misty handed him four small yellow pills. Clutching those Dilaudids like jewels, he scurried back to his shelter.

She explained, "He's now responsible for watching the van." It wasn't long before a crowd built in the parking lot. Misty had everyone's attention. "This man right here," she pointed to me, "this is my godson. From now on, you'll answer directly to him." She pulled out a list and started a roll call.

Evelyn handed each two pills as they entered the van. Soon the van was loaded with close to fifteen people.

Evelyn and Misty jumped into the Cadillac, while I took the driver's seat in the van and trailed them. I cracked the window because the stench in the van was overwhelming with all of those homeless people.

The first stop was a McDonald's parking lot. Misty walked over to the van and instructed four of the passengers to exit.

She handed one of them a small plastic bag of cosmetics. "I told y'all about coming to work funky. Y'all got five minutes to bird bath before the van leaves."

The four went into the fast food restaurant and they were out in three minutes. Then, our workday began.

Throughout the day, I ferried my passengers to several doctor's offices, where they used medical cards to obtain prescriptions for Dilaudids. At the end of the day, Misty handed each passenger fifty dollars and they each placed the prescriptions in her hands. At twenty-five dollars a pill, no wonder the woman was rich.

We left the van there and I jumped into the Cadillac with Misty and Evelyn. We headed to the mall and the moment we stepped inside Nordstrom's, all the sales girls flocked to my "godmother" as if she were royalty.

I was taken on a shopping spree where Evelyn and Misty picked out all my clothes. Then, we headed back to Mulholland Drive to shower and change since Misty wanted to go out for dinner. When we were ready to leave, I went straight for the Cadillac, but the maid strolled past me to the other car and removed the covering.

A beautiful eggshell Carniche Rolls Royce was revealed in all its glory.

I rubbed my forefinger across the silky smooth paint.

Misty said, "Get in son, I'm hungry."

I climbed into a back seat that had room for at least five or six people. Heavy doors closed behind us.

As we rolled westbound on Sunset Boulevard, I thought about my homies.

Bros befo' hos.

By enjoying my time with these women, was I betraying them? I would give them a call first thing in the morning, but for the moment, I was rolling in the back seat of a Rolls Royce.

Power. Money. Pleasure. Loyalty. Well, not exactly in *that* order.

Chapter 15
Predators and Prey

We returned home hours later after having the best steak and lobster in Hollywood. Misty went toward her bedroom, and Evelyn and I went to the guest room, picking up where we had left off.

This time, a new lesson awaited. She instructed me in the fine art of a giving head. Evelyn taught me where her most sensitive areas were.

She explained, "No two women are the same. It's your job to explore a woman's body and pay attention."

Evelyn said she was going teach me how to eat pussy better than any bitch. "Touch is most important. It has to be featherlike," she said, guiding my fingertips across the smooth expanse of tender skin. "Foreplay is important. Take your time and bring her to the brink of ecstasy." Evelyn smiled down at me. "Make her crave that orgasm like it's a drug." Then, she broke out that gold aphrodisiac coke kit.

That night, I flipped the script. All it took was that bit of instruction and I used it to please and control Evelyn.

At thirty-five, she was a sexual beast, but at nineteen, I was the one with stamina. Control was my goal, and as I watched her body convulse time after time, I knew I had reached my goal and then some.

* * *

The clock struck three before Evelyn passed out. I threw on my robe and went to my favorite spot — the window. I was fascinated by this lifestyle, but I also wasn't used to taking orders — especially not from a female. I was a leader, not a follower.

Did they think I could be bought? Or manipulated? Could I trust them?

I couldn't let Misty think she had that kind of control. How much respect would she have for me as a man?

It was the middle of the night, but I called Li'l Man and told him I'd be there shortly. Then, I grabbed my pistol, gathered the rest of my belongings, and woke Evelyn. "Get up, Red. I need you to take me to the hotel."

She raised a single brow, but didn't part her lips to ask the question I knew was in her mind.

We were on Sunset Boulevard when I managed a calm, "Listen, baby. I don't mean any disrespect, but my loyalty lies with my homies first. Tell Misty that I've got a few things to square away and I'll be in touch."

I gave Evelyn most of my money and jewelry before she dropped me off.

With tears in her eyes, she said, "Just be careful."

"I will," I promised before I slipped into the hotel. Only after I entered did I wonder how Evelyn would explain this to Misty. That old woman wasn't used to rejection, but that was her problem.

I was in the hotel room for only two minutes before Li'l Man, Nate and I picked up where we left off — plotting the next move. We waited for daylight, then struck out for Hollywood Hills.

We started the day at Norm's Restaurant, then Nate took us on a tour of his old limo routes in the Hills. There was no shortage of potential victims in this area.

I sat in the back seat as Li'l Man scanned everything with the eyes of a predator. We pulled into the Westwood area and something caught Li'l Man's eye. I followed his gaze to a Rolls Royce two lanes over. An older white couple in the car wore matching white mink coats. I took my eyes off Li'l Man for two seconds to tap Nate's shoulder so he could check them out. The door opened, closed and Li'l Man vanished. That motherfucker was crazy!

Nate scrambled to get our car into the far right lane. Li'l Man was nowhere in sight and the Rolls Royce had disappeared, too. We circled the block, frantically looking for our homie.

I finally spotted him just as he opened the door to jump back into our car, laughing as he said, "Damn! They got away, G Man!"

I didn't bother to tell him how stupid that move had been. It wouldn't have made a difference.

Nate maneuvered away from the traffic, hitting the backstreets so that we were in the Hills in no time. We parked and waited for our prey. Several cars went by before Nate pulled out behind a shiny new midnight blue BMW.

The personalized license plate said something like "Daddy's Rich." We followed the BMW up the winding road through the Hills until it turned into a long driveway.

Nate stopped the car. Li'l Man jumped out, and Nate was on his heels. He told me, "Find a cool spot to park."

I went further up the hill and attempted to make my way back. One slight problem — I couldn't remember which driveway. Every residence was elaborate with the same dense vegetation and cobblestone walkways. A sudden muffled female scream gave me the answer to my question.

I followed the sound until I came upon an open front door. I entered and closed the door behind me, spotting Nate first as he checked the house to make sure it was clear. I almost didn't want to know where Li'l Man was.

A tall tree stood in the middle of the house. A small stream ran through the foyer with Japanese Koi fish swimming underneath. I walked up the spiral staircase to a loft where I found Li'l Man tying up a young woman with a telephone cord.

Li'l Man pulled me aside. "Homie, we done struck gold! This white bitch has two roommates and all their parents are rich. The chick told me where all the loot is. Even her roommate's shit."

What he said next sent chills through me.

"Cuz, I think the bitch is liking this shit."

Nate came in carrying a loaded pillowcase. That's when I said, "Let's roll, homies. We've already been here too long."

Li'l Man said, "Go get the car and we'll be right behind you."

I hesitated; why didn't they follow me out?

I ran out, got the car, parked in front of the house, and then five minutes ticked by. Finally, I pulled into the driveway.

My worst fears were confirmed when I entered the front door. That familiar sound of a woman's muffled groans filled the air. I took the stairs two at a time and was blown away. This time Nate had joined Li'l Man.

We were pulling a major robbery in the heart of white man's land, and these niggas wanted to get some white ass? We could land in jail for that alone.

"This shit ain't cool at all, homies." I turned to leave, but took one last glance back. That crazy chick had a smile on her face!

When we got into the car, I jumped into the back seat. We rode in silence before Li'l Man finally spoke up.

"Check this out, G Man, you need to get up off that sensitive ass shit, nigga. We're straight up gangsters, Cuz, and we ride our own beefs."

I acted like I hadn't heard him. I only thanked God the hit wasn't for Misty. She would have ordered me to kill them both.

Now I knew that Nate was just as much of a wild card as Li'l Man and I had to take into consideration. I had to make a decision. . . and soon.

Chapter 16
Decisions

Everybody was in high spirits. Well, everybody except me. I tried my best, but I was troubled by that rape shit.

We were sitting around, smoking weed and bragging about our crimes like they were a legal sport. I caught Nate looking at me and I didn't look away. For him to go down like that meant one thing — he was intimidated by Li'l Man.

Nate was weak. I couldn't hustle with a dude like that.

But with Li'l Man, I was just too damn loyal. I was as much of a thug as he was. The difference? I drew a line when it came to morals. Rape was immoral. As many women who were giving away pussy, there was never a reason to take it.

It was an hour before midnight when I called Evelyn and told her to come get me. I didn't even think about her husband until I hung up. He was probably lying right beside her. I'd never wanted to put her in a dangerous situation, but that night, I didn't give a shit.

Evelyn pulled up in thirty minutes. I grabbed my things and told my crew, "I'll hook up with you in a couple of days." As I reached the door, I glanced back at Nate, looked him straight in the eyes, then walked out. Was he sharp enough to get my message?

Once we hit the freeway, I told Evelyn what happened. She was as disappointed in me as she was with them.

"You were just as wrong as they were if you *allowed* it to happen. You're the thinker. Li'l Man is a straight up gang-banger. He needs you, you don't need him." She left it at that and moved on. Evelyn schooled me in a cool kind of way.

Evelyn was quiet for a minute, then said, "Your mama's been asking about you." I knew she meant Misty. "She says she's gonna kick your ass when she sees you."

I laughed, having the feeling the old woman could back up that threat.

I didn't know where we were going, but I didn't ask. We traveled east on the Pomona Freeway, out of my parole zone. Not that it mattered. I was on the run from my parole officer and it was a fucked-up feeling. Constantly looking over my shoulder had to be one of the most stressful ways to live. But, there was no turning back for me.

Of course, my father was always the first person I blamed when I thought about my situation. The system was always second. And third was society; society didn't give a fuck about me, so why should I give a fuck about society?

Evelyn took me to Pomona, an area so far away from the heart of L.A. that I had never ventured into the city before.

She pulled into the parking lot of the Tee Pee Motel. Evelyn paid for the room and I checked out the Indian theme. Each room looked like a teepee, and there was space between them, providing privacy. This was what I needed — to get away.

Over the next two days, Evelyn went back and forth between the motel and her house. Even with her husband and four kids, she made time for me. Now *that* was a true hustler — working between a family and a young lover.

On the third morning, the phone rang, startling me. I picked it up, but didn't say anything.

Then, that familiar voice barked, "Son, where the fuck have you been?" Misty started the conversation like she usually did. "You need to get your ass over here ASAP!"

For the first time in days, I laughed. I didn't mind Misty talking shit. My defiance was what got her attention.

When she allowed me to get a word in, I said, "I have a couple of things to take care of, and then I'll holla at you."

Evelyn picked me up and drove me back to Los Angeles. Li'l Man had checked out of the hotel and was staying at his grandmother's spot. I wanted to see him, talk to him, and I hoped that he had calmed down.

We parked in front of a single story brick house, where an elderly black woman sat on the porch. A walker hung next to her chair. Her hair was completely white and the navy blue robe she wore needed washing — like months ago.

She had to be pushing 75, and was glaring at my unfamiliar face through tired eyes as I approached. The strong jaw line, keen eyes, and prominent nose were family traits she shared with Li'l Man.

I put on a good ol' boy smile. "Is Li'l Man here?" She frowned, so I amended, "Is *Arthur* here, Ma'am?"

She finally smiled, showing nothing but gums. "He's back in his room." She pointed toward the end of the driveway.

Music blared from the garage loud enough to be heard halfway up the driveway. I reached to knock on the door and froze when that familiar song hit me — the O'Jays "For the Love of Money." The song meant it was not the best time to have a conversation with my homie.

I turned to exit, but the wooden door swung open. Music vibrated all the way to my toes. I couldn't see his face through the wire mesh screen door, but then he opened it.

Even from where I stood, the room was hot and stuffy; the stale air was trying to make a break for it. Dingy white sheets covered the windows and a cheap mattress was on the floor. A small folding table and two folding chairs were the only other furniture in the place.

The whole image gave me pause. I had no clue Li'l Man lived like this. With as much cash as we raked in, he could afford to do better.

We shook hands and embraced as usual. "What's up, Cuz?" Li'l Man gave me a once-over. "I need to hit a lick, G Man." Then he opened the door wider as I stepped in. "I hope you done got enough pussy, Cuz."

That was the opening I needed. "Speaking of pussy," I said, "your ass is gonna stay broke if you plan on hustling with me. I can't fuck with that rape shit, homie."

We sat down and had our first serious homeboy discussion. He told me that he understood and gave his word that it wouldn't happen again.

When we finished, I scanned the room again and saw the reason why Li'l Man was so hungry for money. A pair of blue dice was stashed under all the trash on the table.

My gaze locked in on the brand new pair of black Dickies on top of the pile of dirty clothes. The knees were dirty and scuffed, which confirmed my suspicions. He was spending his loot shooting craps. This was going to be a problem.

"I have to go see what Misty has planned for us. I'll call in about an hour."

I was lying. From that point on, I would keep my dealings with Li'l Man and my godmother separate. Just like in military covert operations, he was now on a need-to-know basis.

He walked me to the car and the moment Li'l Man passed his grandmother, she said, "I hope you cleaned your room."

He didn't say anything and she shook her head. "That's why your sorry ass don't have the key to the house." Then she hit him with a barrage of insults that ended with, "Yo' parole agent done been by here."

Li'l Man's next words blew me away. "Granny, you need to take your old ass back in the house," and he laughed.

I was raised to respect my elders. This was just another big difference between me and my homie.

Just before we pulled off, Li'l Man asked to borrow a few dollars. I passed him two crisp hundreds, then told him, "Call Nate."

Li'l Man paused. "I forgot to tell you. Nate called and said he had to go out of town. Had a jewelry store move he had to do with his old homies."

As we pulled off and rode toward Misty's house, I grinned. *Nate wasn't as dumb as I thought.* Li'l Man would be much easier to handle by himself.

The next several days were crucial as I sat in the hotel and figured things out. Maintaining a relationship with Misty was a no-brainer. Hustling with her brought in serious money and she gave me a couple of assignments.

But one thing haunted me about Misty — she had a dark side. When someone crossed her, she always taught him a cruel lesson, and I wondered what she would require me to do.

Two days later, I told Evelyn I was ready to see Misty and we arrived at Misty's house in the early afternoon. As soon as we pulled up, Evelyn muttered, "This bitch," as she took in the shiny black Jaguar with Oregon plates that was parked in the driveway.

I didn't have a clue what that meant, and I didn't find out until we went inside. When Evelyn and I stepped into the house, we heard the female chatter, but once we entered the kitchen, it all stopped. All eyes were on me.

A chubby little girl, about ten years old and wearing braces stood in a chair next to Misty. There was also a stunningly beautiful woman there, with exotic hazel eyes, light skin, and dark, straight hair. She wore a form-fitting navy blue dress that ended right above her knees. The matching four-inch heels made her stand at about 6'2".

She was draped in as much jewelry as Misty, and like Misty, she was in her early 50's. Everyone in the room, even the little girl, was counting pills from two plastic jars.

Misty perked up. "Hey son, it's about time."

Then she introduced me to the sexy female, an old friend named Regina, and she shocked me when she said the girl was her daughter, Hope. I didn't know Misty had kids.

Evelyn and Regina exchanged half-hearted greetings as Misty motioned for me to follow her to the den.

There she explained, "Evelyn and Regina don't care for each other. They're competitive when it comes to young men." Then that fast, she switched gears. "There's a doctor I want you to hit. He owns a pharmacy in Compton and owes me and Regina a large sum of money." She ran the whole plan past me and wanted only specific pills; we could keep any cash. At the end of my briefing she asked, "Are you gonna have that crazy nigga with you?"

I said yes, knowing she meant Li'l Man.

"Make sure he works the doctor over. Now get Evelyn out of the house to keep the bullshit down."

Despite her words, I hung out in the kitchen twenty extra minutes, trying my best not to look at that sexy ass woman. I could feel the heat of her stare, but I couldn't afford to make eye contact. I knew she was doing her best to flirt with me and mess with Evelyn.

Finally, Misty walked us to the front door. Regina followed and her expensive perfume seduced my senses.

We exchanged goodbyes and before I closed the door, Regina said in a sultry voice, "Bye, G Man. I'll see you when you get back."

Misty closed the door before she could say anything else.

We took off and no words were exchanged for several miles. I could actually see the hair standing up on the back of Evelyn's neck, but my thoughts were on Regina.

I was flattered and intrigued. That was the kind of company I wanted to keep and it seemed like Regina was dealing in big money like Misty.

I finally broke the silence with Evelyn. "I didn't know Mom had children."

She didn't take her eyes off the road. "She's got four between ten and twenty-three; three girls and a boy." Then she grinned. "Her *real* son is named Greg, too."

Wow! I wasn't sure why, but that made me feel jealous. Evelyn went on to tell me that Misty's Greg was off at college getting the best education money could buy.

Seemed like I was just another tool for her game. I was the son that he wasn't, the self-educated street thug.

I asked Evelyn to swing by Li'l Man's house. I was only there long enough to run him through the moves about the doctor. Midnight was our time.

Chapter 17
Mama Don't Cry

I had hours before Li'l Man and I would see the doctor. So, I decided to do what I'd been dreading — I wanted to see my mama.   It was late afternoon when Evelyn and I made the trip to Ontario, but I wasn't worried. Parole agents rarely came looking for violators that late in the day. And I was willing to take the risk. I missed my mother and siblings and just wanted to spend a little time with them.

When we reached the house, I had Evelyn pull a thousand dollars from my stash. "Okay," I said. "Wait for me at Sandra's. I'll call when I'm ready."

I took a few moments to compose myself before I opened the front door. My brothers were in the living room watching television. They looked up, shocked, then jumped up, so happy to see me. As they embraced me, the wonderful smells of dinner wafted into the living room and I walked into the kitchen. My mother had her back to me as she handled her business on the stovetop. A sense of security filled me anytime I was in her presence.

Mama turned around just as I reached out to her. Our gazes locked for a brief second, and it was like looking at a mirror image when I saw the same pain in her eyes.

"Boy, get over here." She enveloped me in a warm hug, then grabbed my arms and pushed me back two feet. Her piercing brown eyes scanned every inch of my body and lingered on the expensive jewelry.

"Grego, where in God's name did you get this stuff? And why are you throwing your life away?"

We both knew that I couldn't answer the first question, and didn't have an answer to the second one. So, I remained silent.

She dabbed the sweat from her forehead. "Sit down and eat."

After she fixed our plates, an awkward silence filled the room when we sat together. Then, my mother said, "Your parole officer calls here every day. Why don't you turn yourself in, son?"

I wasn't used to disobeying her, but I avoided her eyes as I said, "I can't do that, Mama," even though I knew that decision would pain her.

But once we got that out of the way, the mood turned festive. My brothers and I enjoyed the pork chops, rice and gravy, and cornbread. And of course, the glass of Kool-Aid — red.

When I hugged my mother to say goodbye, I slipped the money I had into one of the pockets of the robe she wore. Then, I hugged my brothers and slid a hundred dollars to my oldest brother, Marvin. He knew to split it among all of them.

I phoned Evelyn to let her know that I was ready and then my mother walked me out.

She said, "That white man across the street stares at me so hard it scares me. I don't know what would make you steal his car, boy. I think I'm gonna have to move."

I really didn't need to hear that, a harsh reminder of the damage I caused my family.

"How did you get out here?"

I didn't get a chance to answer. Evelyn pulled in front of the house, and Mama looked toward her, then back at me, her eyes wide with disbelief.

She shook her head. "I know darn well you're not dating that old woman. We used to watch soap operas together!" She spun around and went back into the house, slamming the door behind her.

We pulled off, but I spotted that neighbor across the street in his garage. He looked in my direction with that same stare my mother mentioned. I told Evelyn to stop and park directly in front of his driveway.

I rolled the window down so he could see my eyes. So what, he knew I was the one who stole his car. Him fucking with my mother was not an option. I tried my best to make him feel my rage. It took only two seconds for him to get the message. He rushed and lowered the garage door.

By the time we were on the freeway, my thoughts were on the midnight job. I hoped the doctor didn't resist. I was ready to pistol-whip anything that moved. God help that poor man if he fucked up and gave me a reason.

Chapter 18
The Last Dance

Traveling westbound on the freeway back to Los Angeles, Evelyn stole a glance in my direction. She talked, but I tuned her out; I was too deep into my thoughts to hold a conversation.

I opened the glove compartment and grabbed the heavy pistol. Its power flowed through me. I rubbed that smooth wooden handle until it reached the same temperature of my body — hot and angry.

Evelyn knew that I was in a dark place. She switched on the radio, and the soulful sounds of Luther Vandross filled the car.

Music always calmed me — especially that smooth crooner. I finally sat back and relaxed.

Two hours later, Li'l Man was with us when we pulled into a motel in the heart of Compton. The two-story place was a dope fiend's paradise. Addicts everywhere.

The stench hit us as I searched for the light switch in our room. With the lights on, things looked worse. The carpet which was once bright red, was now closer to dark brown. The red velvet bedspread was filled with cigarette holes and the nightstand told a story of its own. Thankfully, we weren't there for pleasure.

The doctor's office was across the street and the view from this room gave us the opportunity to check out the activity.

It also gave me the chance to check out Li'l Man, who'd been acting strangely since we picked him up. First, he wasn't at his house when we arrived, and when he jumped into the car twenty minutes later, he was sweaty and musty. All the signs pointed to him having been up all night shooting dice.

Still, we were here, so I explained the game plan to Li'l Man—more than once. Too much was riding on this. I had to make sure this went down as planned.

I cracked the curtain enough to see the back door of the pharmacy, which led to the alley. The doctor had parked a brand new white Mercedes Benz back there, probably purchased with Misty's money.

It was getting close to the time when Misty told us the doctor left, but we still couldn't make a move. The pill heads roaming the parking lot could be possible witnesses.

As I stood at the window, the motel's door slammed behind me. Li'l Man was on the prowl. He reached the alley, made it to the doctor's car, and stooped down where I couldn't get a line on him. Soon the right rear corner of the car tilted when a tire deflated. Though I was pissed that he had made a move without waiting for a signal, I was impressed.

Admiration turned into shock, though, when one of the doctor's assistants walked up on Li'l Man. There was nothing I could do to warn him.

Li'l Man stood just as the dude passed. The man took a second glance back toward the car as he walked to the door. Li'l Man tried to play it off by pretending to tie his shoes, but he had been exposed.

When he came back to the motel, all I could think was, *What in the fuck am I gonna tell Misty?*

Li'l Man knew I was upset. "Don't worry, everything's still cool."

That reassurance dissipated when a black Cadillac pulled up and a burly black dude stepped out. He scanned the area before he went through the back door. Then not long after, he left carrying a money bag along with another bag in his left hand. The right hand held a huge .45 semi-automatic at his side. He jumped into his Cadillac and pulled off with two things — the loot and possibly my future with Misty.

I sat down on the bed next to Evelyn as Li'l Man paced, talking plenty shit, as if this wasn't his fault. Then, he went into the restroom.

Evelyn didn't say a single word. She didn't have to. Even though we were homeboys I had to accept that having him around wasn't gonna work. Misty was too strict and my credibility was more important.

We left, and I barely kept my anger in check. Evelyn had already stopped at a phone booth and called Misty. Even in the back seat of the car, Li'l Man wouldn't stop moving.

He probably owed somebody, so I told him, "I'll loan you a few C-notes to hold you over. But I have to go to my spot to get it."

We rolled up Century Boulevard and I told Evelyn to turn into an alley so I could take a piss. We were directly behind Papa Bears, a popular gay club.

Li'l Man followed me and we started to take care of our business. But then, two men came out of Papa Bears, embraced, and then kissed passionately.

Li'l Man stopped pissing, almost midstream. He ran back to the car, grabbed his pistol, and walked back to the alley. I had no choice but to follow him.

Before I could step away, Evelyn gripped my hand. "What the fuck are y'all doing?"

"We'll be right back, baby."

A couple of other dudes had come out of the back and Li'l Man walked right up to the small crowd of about five, pulled out his dick, and finished pissing on everyone's shoes. All I could think was, *God help the first one who says anything.*

In a high-pitched voice, the tallest one said, "What the fuck is your problem?"

Li'l Man hit him in the mouth with the pistol. Several bloody teeth fell to the pavement. Then Li'l Man grabbed his long ponytail, and literally dragged him to the back door of the club. I pulled my pistol, instructing the others to follow.

Li'l Man yanked open the door and we made our way through the hallway. "It's Raining Men" pounded from the speakers and drowned out the whimpering of our victims. I didn't know what Li'l Man had in mind. His crimes unfolded as they went along.

We reached the doorway to the dance floor; it was early, so there were only about fifteen people dancing and a few dudes at the bar.

I scanned the area as Li'l Man moved to the center of the dance floor. The tall punk with the ponytail stood next to him, with a bloody mouth and rigid with fear.

Li'l Man's pistol was in plain view, but nobody noticed. He looked confused, and I couldn't afford to let him to make the next decision. My ass was on the line, too.

I climbed into the D.J. booth, stuck the pistol right in the D.J.'s face, and motioned for him to move. I lifted the needle off the record, and the whole world stopped. I turned on the bright lights, then tapped the mic with my pistol.

Li'l Man's voice sounded menacing as he said, "All right you faggots, this is a robbery. The first motherfucker that moves gets shot."

I held my gun on the crowd as he herded everybody to the middle of the floor, taking off their jewelry and emptying their pockets. Then he cleaned out the cash register before he led the manager to the back.

I filled the awkward silence with, "All right, get those fucking clothes off, punks! Everything but your underwear!"

Seconds later, they were standing in a variety of panties and G-strings with polka dots or hearts. Two of them didn't have on underwear at all.

I instructed everyone to throw their clothes into one pile, and then, I focused on our getaway.

Li'l Man's hysterical laugh echoed as he came back. "This is some crazy ass shit, homie." His wicked grin was a signal. "Let's go."

In less than ten minutes from when we left, we were back at the car, startling Evelyn, and laughing like kids on Christmas.

Evelyn didn't hide her disgust.

We jumped on the 405 North and drove for about twenty minutes before taking an exit to the nearest motel to drop Li'l Man off. He insisted that I come upstairs to divide the loot, but I told him to give me a grand and make the rest last him until we hooked up again. We embraced and parted ways.

On the freeway again, Evelyn still didn't say a word. And that was fine. I was more worried about having to face Misty.

Finally Evelyn's voice broke into my musings, "Baby I can't tell you what to do, but you need start using your head a little more."

That was the same conclusion I had already reached.

***

Evelyn picked me up from my motel early the next morning to take me to Misty's. I didn't take three solid steps into the house before that signature pinch latched onto my arm. I actually felt like crying!

Misty led me down the hallway to the den. "What fucking planet are you from, son? How stupid are you?"

I caught a glimpse of Evelyn smiling. She was glad that Misty checked me the way she wanted to.

My affiliation with Li'l Man was officially over. I just had to figure out a way to tell him that.

Chapter 19
Divine Intervention

Two more weeks of hustling with Evelyn and Misty was an education. Misty showed me how her operation worked and Evelyn enjoyed watching me learn.

Li'l Man called every day and had left several messages with Diane. He was probably broke again, but it was his kind of desperation that got people killed or back in jail.

After a couple of days, I called Li'l Man back and he told me he'd bought a '67 Impala. "I need money to fix it up," he said.

We agreed to meet up at Diane's apartment around noon. Evelyn went with me, though she waited inside while I stood outside. The sun was beaming down rays of warmth — the kind of day that made me wish I wasn't on the run.

Noon came and went — no sign of Li'l Man. Another fifteen minutes, then the sudden screech of tires filled the air.

A dark blue '67 Chevy flew down the street with an Inglewood Police car in pursuit. The car went by so quickly I didn't get a good look, but I knew it was Li'l Man.

I ran back into the apartment to get Evelyn. As soon as we ran to the end of the block, I looked to my right. Several police cars surrounded the Chevy.

The police had a black male in handcuffs bent over the hood of the car.

Li'l Man looked up just as we passed and we stared at each other. I saw a pistol on the hood, but there was nothing I could do for him. That robbery at the gay club was our last dance.

Fate intervened; I didn't have to have that "we can't hang out anymore" conversation that I was so dreading.

Chapter 20
Under Pressure

I was still handling business for Misty, but I wasn't about to become anybody's yes man.

Eventually, I made a few calls to put another crew together. When Evelyn overheard one of my calls, she didn't hide her alarm. "Baby, you're moving fast, slow down and let the game unfold for you."

"I got this covered," I told her, and then I asked her to be at my motel room early the following day.

She told me she'd be there by nine, but the next morning, she wasn't there. That was unusual; she was never late. I did push-ups to pass the time, but as hours went past, irritation set in. I didn't play that late shit and she knew that.

I was pacing when she knocked and walked in wearing dark oversized sunglasses.

When she sat on the bed, heavy tears started flowing and I saw the scratch marks on her neck. She sobbed and mumbled something about Lucky choking her.

I removed her shades and exposed a right eye that was purple and swollen shut.

Lucky had put his hands on *my woman*! She might have been his wife, but she was my woman, and that superseded any legal document.

She explained that he was upset because she was away from home too much, and he accused her of having an affair with "that young nigga."

I took domestic violence seriously, always thinking about the abuse that had been inflicted on my mother. A man who hit a woman was not a man. He was a bitch and deserved to be treated like one.

I opened the drapes, allowing the sunlight to flood the room. The sun's rays gave me the energy I needed to think about the ways I could inflict pain on Lucky.

When I turned from the window, I asked, "Do you guys have any kids together?" This was a question that I'd never asked her.

She whispered, "No, baby." But her expression changed — from sadness to worry.

I turned back to the window, looking out at everything and nothing, building a scenario in my mind. With no kids, he'd be the only one to feel pain. I wished that it was my father instead of Lucky — but then again, I could always pretend.

Evelyn cleared her voice. "Uh, baby. He's in jail. The neighbors called the police."

And just like that, I smiled. "He's a lucky man," I said, "and I don't mean his name, either."

She told me that Lucky couldn't make bail and she wasn't fronting the cash.

Evelyn stayed with me for the next few days. Two of her kids were grown and were used to running the household. But after a few days, she convinced me to go home with her to meet her kids. She'd told her three boys and one girl all about me, though I never asked her too much about them. I did know, though, that she already had a grandchild.

It took a while, but I finally agreed and we took the forty-five minute ride to Pomona. As we rode through the city, I opened the glove compartment and took a glance at my pistol, also making note of every significant landmark, a trait that remained since my mother taught me to do that. The part of town where Evelyn lived was called "The Islands."

We passed Winchell's Donut shop, where a small crowd had gathered out front — pimps and whores!

Evelyn grimaced. "Yeah, this is our whore stroll, but don't get any ideas, G Man."

I kept my gaze on the street, but thought, *Shit, Pomona might not be too bad.*

We parked in front of a not so impressive house — one of six located in a cul-de-sac. There was a huge tree in the front, dead leaves were everywhere, and the grass was in need of mowing.

Loud music reached us the moment I opened the car door. Prince was crooning "Soft and Wet" but he had company on the vocals. And whoever was singing with him was doing a good job.

The screen was locked, but the wooden entry door was wide open and the smell of fried chicken and marijuana flowed outside.

Evelyn screamed, "Reuben, open this motherfucking door and turn that bullshit down!"

A slim figure, about my height, appeared. Evelyn yanked the door open, and her twenty-year-old son stood there, wearing a pair of tight Jordache jeans. His complexion was much darker than Evelyn's and showcased a major acne problem. His hair was about fifteen inches long and styled in a press and curl. A white headband matched his tank top.

It didn't take much for me to sum up his status. G-a-y. Evelyn introduced us and his handshake was warm and sincere.

The house had a cozy feeling, but the place was nothing like Misty's. The furniture wasn't expensive, but it wasn't the cheap motel stuff either. In the small kitchen, a young female fried chicken, as a toddler rested on her hip.

Arlene was Evelyn's seventeen-year-old daughter, and Evelyn's four-month old granddaughter was named Lovely. Arlene came across as friendly and accepting.

"Would you like a beer and fried chicken?"

She held out a can for me. I took the beer and had a seat on the couch.

"The chicken'll be ready in about ten minutes, y'all."

When Evelyn disappeared into the back, I looked around. The place was clean, with the exception of a few pieces of clothing strewn about. A pair of bright red Converse All-Stars were parked in the corner, a bright red jogging suit hung on a kitchen chair and two red bandanas lay on the armrest of the love seat.

Warning bells — I was in Blood territory!

The hairs on the back of my neck stood up. I wasn't a gang member, but I was from a rival neighborhood.

And my pistol was locked up in the car!

Evelyn appeared from the back with two other young males in tow.

The taller one was eighteen-year-old David. He had a red bandana tied around his neck. The other was thirteen-year-old Lamont.

David sized me up as he shook my hand. Lamont gave me a half-hearted handshake and turned to leave.

I realized Evelyn had an open relationship with her kids when David asked me, "You wanna smoke a joint?"

All eyes were on me until I said, "Yeah."

I followed David down a dimly lit hallway to where a single red light bulb hung from the ceiling and the smell of marijuana reeked even more. He stopped at the second door and opened it to a flurry of activity.

The air was stuffy and hot, reminding me of Li'l Man's crib. Eight young dudes and a couple of females were crammed into the bedroom. A Run DMC rap song blared from a ghetto blaster. Several dudes were on their knees in a dice game.

Two females sat on the edge of the bed, with dudes between their legs while they braided their hair. A huge red bandana covered the whole bed. The red attire was everywhere.

A cheap card table was perched up against the far wall, where two more thugs rolled some joints.

I was probably only two years older than any of them.

David, obviously the shot-caller, turned the music down and introduced me to his homies.

A familiar voice interrupted with, "What's up, G Man?"

I scanned the room and a dark-skinned dude with a medium build stood up from his spot. Snoop from YTS!

His gaze narrowed. "Didn't you used to kick it with your homeboy Li'l Man from the 107th Hoover Crips?"

The radio switched off and the room became deadly silent.   *Ain't this a bitch! These niggas probably think I'm a Crip.*

I kept my expression solid. "Yeah, he's my homie, but I don't bang."

David glared at Snoop. "Fuck that dumb shit. This is my Mama's boyfriend, blood, so kill that noise." David finished the introductions with no further comments from anyone.

Minutes later, I was sitting at the card table with a joint in one hand and a forty-ounce in the other, blending in easily. We were all thugs, no matter the gang affiliation.

A few minutes later, Evelyn opened the door, looked at me first, and said to everyone, "The chicken is ready, y'all. Come on and eat."

David reached for her shades. "Mama, let me use these to take one last picture."

He had them in his hand before she could stop him. Her swollen, black eye was exposed.

For the second time, every gaze was on me. I'd been given a pass on the affiliation issue, but putting my hands on their mother would not go unanswered.

I frowned, and Evelyn quickly said, "Lucky did this, David. That's why he's in jail."

I let out a long, slow breath. I would have hated to be in Lucky's shoes right then.

The whole house now accepted me, but I was playing with fire. Evelyn's house was the neighborhood hangout and a Blood stronghold, and that could only lead to trouble.

But for the rest of that day, I chilled. We ate fried chicken, partied late into the night, and I eventually passed out in Evelyn's bedroom, resting on the bed that she shared with her husband.

I had retrieved my pistol before I'd laid down, though. Not that I gave a fuck about Lucky, but I had to cover my ass. Somebody could help his ass make bail, and the first place he would come was home. Actually, I *wanted* a confrontation with him. And with my pistol, I was ready.

I awoke early the next morning and felt I had entered the twilight zone. Evelyn was still sound asleep with her granddaughter in her arms. This woman was my girlfriend, yet she was lying next to me with her grandchild.

My life was more complex than any nineteen-year-old's should ever be.

Chapter 21
The Wasted Years

For the next several years, I disappeared into the shady underworld of cutthroat criminals, where we had our own rules, never involved the police, and used street justice that often led to death. But that was the choice I made; I didn't want to go back to jail, so that's how I had to live — underground.

Living that life meant that my relationship with my mother was not the same. Not only could I not see her because I never knew when my parole officer would show up, but I couldn't stand to see the pain that I caused in her eyes. So I avoided her.

But I still hung out with Evelyn. Being with her had matured me beyond my age. She was my lover and teacher, and it really didn't take long for me to fall in love with her.

But I never told Evelyn that I loved her. I wasn't man enough to step up that way. I was still holding onto having my heart broken by Shari Johnson, who I still called that heartless bitch. And I'd vowed that I would never let that happen again.

And then, there was Misty. I still hustled for her, sucking up all the game I could. But I knew my days with her were numbered. Not because of her, but because of me.

I never wanted to just be her yes man, her henchman, and I knew she was only going to let me make a certain amount of money. She knew that I was a true thinker, so she wasn't about to let me get the best of her.

I stayed for as long as I could until I stopped fucking with her altogether.

But it wasn't just the relationships that made my life complicated. It was being on the run from the law that was hard, that was taking its toll physically and mentally. I was agitated all the time and just wanted this nightmare behind me.

One summer night, I asked Evelyn to take me down to my favorite spot — the beach. We rolled up to the beach at Playa Vista.

This place was like heaven to me; here I could think.

Rolling the window down, I took in the salt smell in the misty air, then turned the radio off so I could hear the waves crash.

Evelyn sat next to me in total silence. She knew.

I leaned back and got lost in my thoughts of my life.

My crimes had escalated. Now I was doing home invasions, armed robberies, and car jackings. I was completely out of control, wearing the title of ex-felon that would be mine for life.

I knew that prison was going to be the next chapter of my life, but I no longer feared that reality. There was life after prison, parole after prison, another chance to get my life together after prison.

That was when it hit me — I was ready to go to prison.

I left the beach that night feeling a calm that I hadn't felt in years.

And then as if I had willed it to happen, it happened.

I was at Evelyn's house feeling a little bored. So, I took a walk to the liquor store, just two blocks away. It was only two blocks, so there was no need for me to carry my sawed-off 12 gauge double-barreled shotgun.

But I had it when the police rolled up on me. I was arrested for carrying that concealed weapon. Then, of course, they found out that I'd been on the run. I was in violation of my parole, and now had a charge for carrying a weapon.

This led to the next phase of my criminal career, a phase where I was in and out of prison. I went away for eight months on that charge, but then, I was home for only four months when I was picked up again. This time it was for robbery with the use of a firearm and I was sentenced to eighteen months.

That became my life. For the next twelve years, I was in and out of several prisons.

Evelyn really did her best to stand by me, but eventually that relationship had to end. How could you build anything with a person who spent more time in prison than out on the streets?

But once she was out of my life, women just became a tool for me. I never connected emotionally, not really, though I was conscious about one thing — I didn't want to bring a child into this world.

It wasn't that I didn't want to be a father, but I'd made a promise to myself back in juvenile hall that I would never let my child go through what I'd had to go through. So, I was careful. Always careful.

Beyond that, I was all about the streets. My education was in full swing. I'd grown up as a gangster and now my education to be full-fledged criminal was in full force.

If this was all I could be, if being a criminal was all that was ahead of me, then I was going to be the best at it. It was going to be me against the world! And I had every intention of winning.

Part Two

The Education of a

Criminal

Chapter 22
Kiss the Ground

On April, 1, 1993, karma gave me another opportunity to get my life right. I had been locked up for seven years and three months in Chuckawalla Valley State Prison on an attempted murder charge. That case — well, it's a long story. Let's just say that there was no way I was going to let anyone get away with disrespecting me, my family, or my girl.

But original charges of murder-for-hire were changed to attempted murder and I was set to be released when I was 31 years old.

On my last day in prison, I walked the jogging track. Two of my right-hand men flanked me — Peanut from the Schoolyard Crips and Big Boo from Original Valley Gangsters. I now weighed 290, with biceps measuring 22 ½ inches. I was the biggest convict on the yard and the strongest, bench pressing 475 pounds. But I was humble and carried my size with grace.

As we made our way around, "jailhouse politicians" came out to greet me. I had established a lot of power; hustling in prison was no different than on the streets. Just another city within a city.

A shot-caller from each clique (the lower level foot soldiers weren't allowed speak to me directly) approached me with words of wisdom. The power and respect I had didn't stop with the inmates; it extended to staff members, too.

After my walk, the three of us headed back to my cell, and ran into the program administrator. Mr. Hadley was a power hungry dude with an ulterior motive for his every action.

"Well, Mr. G Man, are you ready for the streets?"

The better question was: *Were the streets ready for me?*

Mr. Hadley was a step below the Associate Warden, but was a hands-on kind of guy who knew everything happening in "his yard," including that I sold drugs.

We shook hands and he wished me good luck.

At the housing unit, butterflies fluttered in my stomach. The State of California had warehoused me for seven years, and other than the master's degree I'd earned from the most ruthless criminals in America, I was returning to the streets without a trade or degree. I was an angry, muscle-bound black man with a felony record and zero options. The California prison system had created me and was releasing me into the free world.

And they were releasing me to my family. Even though I had tried to be careful, I now had children.

I'd finally hooked up with Tina (my girl who I'd met all those years ago at the liquor store.) Once she told me she was a virgin, I was never able to leave her alone. It didn't take long for her to get pregnant.

But the timing was bad. Not that there's ever a good time to be arrested, but my son was born a few weeks after I was arrested for assault.

So now, I had a seven-year-old son who I'd never seen without a barrier between us.

Then, there was my four-year-old son, Julius, or should I say, my alleged son? Julius's mother was my ex-wife, Precious, who I met in 1985. I married her in 1990, purely a marriage of prison convenience. Smuggling drugs into prison and conjugal visits were a must for a convict.

But Precious' lies and bullshit made it hard for me to manage her from behind the walls. And when she claimed to have gotten pregnant by me, I had a gut feeling that child wasn't mine. But even though I claimed him, I divorced her and married my current wife, Debbie. I also met Debbie in 1986 as I was fighting my case in county jail. She was so beautiful, I couldn't pass her up.

She had a daughter, Hernicka, who was only a couple years older than, Greg Jr. Her father wasn't in her life, so I accepted her as my own.

So that's where I was going when I left prison — to be with my wife, Debbie, and her daughter. It was ten o'clock when Big Boo picked up my cardboard box with my possessions and we started the slow walk to the yard gate. I was supposed to be happy, but it felt like a death march to the gas chamber. Would I know how to live on the outside?

I approached the gate and took one glance back at the place. Then, I gave both my homies a hug before the guard patted me down and sent me on my way.

"Hey, G Man, tell Tupac to keep his head up!" Peanut shouted out.

I chuckled. I had never met Tupac in person, but we were friends. We'd been introduced by my baby brother, Anthony, who we now called Serge. Tupac and I had talked on the phone while I was in prison more than a few times.

I sat in Receive & Release with five other inmates. The guard took his time processing us and I smiled at his attempt to inconvenience me. All I could think was, *Mister, I've got all the time in the world.*

The guard called my name last, and I stepped to the property cage. He took my fingerprints, returned my street clothes, took a Polaroid picture, and gave me the standard $200 gate money. The prison van escorted us off the property. I looked out the tinted window and saw my sexy, high maintenance wife standing next to a bright red Nissan 300ZX in the parking lot. The van's door opened, and the heat hit me like a huge blow dryer. But still, I stepped out into freedom.

I took four or five steps, stopped, lowered myself, and kissed the scorching pavement.

My wife looked better with each step I took. I even picked up a little swagger between the van and her car. I hadn't even left the prison grounds, and I was already starting to feel invincible.

My wife wrapped her arms around me, our first touch in the free world. I loosened my grip just enough to give her a passionate kiss and get an immediate hard-on.

I tossed my box into the back seat, then looked out of the window as we pulled away from "Chucky's house."

On the highway, my wife ran her mouth, and about six exits later we stopped for gas and food. The gas pump looked alien to me and an anxiety attack set in; beads of sweat covered my nearly bald head.

"Greg!" Debbie called out. I held the nozzle, feeling vulnerable, like I was standing there butt ass naked.

Debbie showed me how to work the new design gas pump, and then we drove to a Guess clothing outlet.

Debbie told me, "Start looking for something while I go to the restroom."

Over at the shirt racks, from my peripheral vision, I saw people staring at me. Bulging muscles were a good indication that I'd just been released from the nearby prison.

I took one shirt off the rack and stared at the tag for the size. For the last seven years, all I'd known was small, large, and extra large. But these civilian clothes had actual sizes.

Thank God Debbie came out of the bathroom and was right behind me. As quietly as I could, I asked, "Baby, what size do I wear?"

My wife plucked off a few items, and I didn't say a word. I was more than ready to leave.

Finalizing the purchase should have been the no-brainer part. Counting money was something I knew all too well. The cashier rang up my total while I reached into my pocket. I broke out in another cold sweat. Panicking, I checked my other pockets.

"Come on! Don't tell me that you lost your money?" Debbie snapped.

I had and she was not happy. We had planned on sitting down to eat a nice meal, but I settled for a Whopper from Burger King.

We arrived in North Hollywood three hours later, and pulled into the underground parking garage. I grabbed my bags and followed Debbie. As soon as we stepped inside, a dozen red roses and an assortment of "Welcome Home" balloons greeted me.

Moving into the living room, I checked out the classy, expensive sofa and chairs and paintings on the wall.

My wife had excellent taste, and not just in men.

I slipped off my shoes and went onto the balcony. I looked past the Universal City sign to the skyscrapers of downtown Los Angeles. My old neighborhood was out there and I couldn't wait to go home.

The telephone rang just as I stepped inside. Debbie answered, then smiled. "It's your crazy ass little brother."

Serge was the only one who knew my release date. As soon as I said hello, an explosion of voices signaled that my mother's living room was packed with my homeboys, making me feel instantly better.

I hung up, telling my brother and my boys that I'd see them soon. My wife returned from the kitchen with a chilled bottle of Remy Martin. A couple of fat joints rested on the edge of the ashtray on the glass coffee table. All I needed was some pussy, and I would be straight!

I poured myself a stiff drink and settled on the sofa.

"Relax while I take a shower," Debbie told me.

The moment I heard the water running, my dick got hard. I picked up a joint and fifteen minutes later, I was already past high. My system was too clean for all this.

Debbie appeared, wearing sheer white bikini panties and a bra, hands on her hips, and feet spread apart. She looked like a sex goddess.

Slowly, gracefully, she walked toward me. I was so high and horny, I could've passed out. The scent of sweet, expensive perfume enveloped me and I placed a soft kiss on her stomach. She took my hand, led me to the bedroom, and we made love like I was going back to prison tomorrow.

* * *

I walked back into the living room just after 8 o'clock that night. I'd been satisfied by my wife, but there was another woman I wanted to speak to. I needed to hear my mother's voice. But when I called, Serge picked up the phone on the first ring.

"Nigga, we're on our way to come scoop you up." He didn't give me a chance to say otherwise.

My mother must have grabbed the phone away from him because then, I heard, "Hey, Grego. How does it feel, son?" Her voice was comforting and right then, I made plans to see her the next day.

I went back into the bedroom, not knowing how to tell my wife that the crew was on their way.

But then, Debbie said, "Listen, baby, I don't mind you going to hang out with your people. As a matter of fact, you *need* to. I want to hit the mall."

She pressed a key into my hand, dressed, and left. I made a few more calls to let people know that I was home before the bell rang. I buzzed them in, and while I was putting on my shoes, Serge and my O.G. homeboy, Country from Nine Duce Gangster Crips, blasted through the door and bum rushed me.

"Come on, big bro, 'Pac is waiting on your ass. As a matter of fact, he's around the corner."

Man, it felt good to be home.

We drove three blocks over to Lankershim Boulevard and pulled into a lot next to a brown, windowless building with expensive cars parked outside.

Serge rang the buzzer as I glanced at the security camera. A burly guard opened the door and we walked into a dimly lit recording studio. The odor of marijuana overpowered every other scent.

Familiar voices shouted over the music. Tupac's voice stood out as he rapped over a track.

"How long will they mourn me. . . "

My eyes adjusted to the dark and there stood 'Pac wearing his handkerchief tied around his head. He wasn't a hardcore gang member; he'd change the color of his rags according to his mood and attire. But he'd sport the blue more often because my neighborhood provided his security.

'Pac was shirtless, the huge *Thug Life* tattoo on his stomach was prominently displayed.

The engineer grinned at me. "Motherfuckin' G Man! You done made it home."

The music came to a halt as I embraced my homies.

'Pac came out of the booth and lit the room with a warm smile. We embraced.

"These white folks done fucked around and released an O.G. thug to the streets," he said.

Everyone laughed.

'Pac was a lot smaller than I imagined, but his charisma was overpowering.

Alcohol flowed. 'Pac held something that looked like a cigar. He lit it and passed it to me.

I said, "No thank you, I don't smoke."

Everybody cracked up.

"You been gone too long. This is a blunt—weed, marijuana, nigga."

I tried to play it cool, grabbing it and taking a pull. I immediately knew I was in trouble. I coughed violently; they got a big laugh from that, too.

The recording session turned into a party and as we all sat around, I evaluated the scene.

The men in the studio wore as much elaborate diamond-encrusted jewelry as 'Pac and I was sure those were their expensive cars in the lot. These were my people. Most of them had once worked for me. Now they were big time hustlers in their own right.

But now, G Man was back. I just had to find my own place in this new game.

Chapter 23
The Cost of Freedom

Five o'clock the next morning, Debbie was still asleep. I made coffee, turned on the news, then reviewed a list in my head. First things first: My parole officer was going to be visiting me at my home this morning.

Making it off parole and discharging that prison number would be the challenge. Fewer than twenty percent ever made it because there were so many dos and don'ts. Until I got off parole, I was still in prison, just a prison without walls.

With no one to talk to this early, I called Misty who was always up at the crack of dawn. We'd kept in touch all these years and she really took care of me while I was in prison. Because of her, I never had less than one thousand dollars on the books.

"What's up, Mom?" I said the moment she answered the phone.

"Hey, son! When did you get home? And when are you coming to see me? I got a couple dollars to put in your pocket," she said all in one breath.

"I'll come see you tomorrow."

She gave me the address of her store, which was really a front for her business. Next, I called Tina. I couldn't wait to see my son and so I asked Tina to bring Greg, Jr. by my mom's house a little later.

I was in the middle of my calls when my wife, still groggy, staggered into the living room. "What the fuck are you doing up so early? Are you still on the prison clock?" She shook her head, then made breakfast as I continued calling, waking everybody up.

My parole agent showed up at my apartment at 8 o'clock sharp. To my relief, she was a sista girl and made it clear that she wouldn't be petty.

"All you have to do is avoid trouble and contact with the police, all right?"

I nodded, not telling her that with the crowd I hung with, that was going to be hard as hell.

After my PO left, my wife dropped me off at my mother's house before she went to work.

I stood outside the house and just stared at it for a moment. My mother was at work and I was sure my sister, Sheila and brother, Serge were asleep.

I still had the key, so I let myself in and taking a running start to my brother's room, I threw all 290 pounds of me on top of Serge.

He gasped, but it turned into laughter. Minutes later, we were outside on the front lawn smoking a joint. It didn't take long for people in the neighborhood to find out I was home. About fifteen of my homies gathered around to greet me. Everybody was taken aback by my size.

My homecoming turned into a small block party. Before I was sent to prison, I was a hustler who wasn't selfish with my game. I had been good to these dudes.

Of course, a few envious folks and backstabbers turned up, too. . . people who had talked shit behind my back. I gave those dudes an extra firm hug that spoke volumes and screamed, "Yeah, I'm back; watch your step!"

Some of my guests slid folded stacks of crisp hundred dollar bills into my hand. Others offered drugs to get me on my feet.

Right then, any chance of going legit was gone. I was a ghetto superstar, a role model for all the wrong reasons.

Then, I sensed something happening as bodies shifted, conversations halted, and the air became tense.

Somebody hollered, "Watergates, Cuz!"

A succession of safety latches clicked. Young Gs barked out orders to lower level foot soldiers. Unarmed homies ducked for cover. Armed soldiers slid into position. They all moved with military precision within a matter of seconds.

An older model, four-door Cutlass Supreme drove by slowly. The tinted driver's side window rolled halfway down and the huge barrel of a sawed off shotgun was pointed right at me!

I braced for the explosion, but there was only menacing laughter as the car sped away. That was just a warning.

I glanced around me and the ground was littered with bodies. Everyone had dropped to the ground. I was the only one standing in harm's way.

Clearly, I had been in jail too long. Reflexes for protection inside prison were different than what was needed on the streets.

But one thing was clear during those moments — the leader. A young homie really stood out; he seemed to be in charge of most of the younger foot soldiers.

He'd introduced himself as 'L' and I was impressed by his leadership and the respect he commanded. I made a mental note to find out more about him.

Soon, I cleared the front yard; I didn't want my mother to come home to a welcoming committee of thugs.

Once everyone was gone, I asked Serge and my homeboy, Big Country, to give me a ride. Before I took a seat on the passenger side, I asked Big Country, "Do you have *any* contraband in your car?"

Just coming in contact with illegal substances was a violation of my parole.

Big Country hesitated before he said no.

I shook my head. "God help you if your lie costs me my freedom."

Twenty-five minutes later, we pulled up in front of Misty's store on 35th & Central Avenue. She was outside and I saw seven years hadn't changed her too much; she still looked like a million dollars, especially with the huge diamond rings on her fingers.

She smiled as I stepped out. "What in the fuck took you so long, son?" she said as she led me inside.

She was just talking shit since I'd told her this morning that I wouldn't see her 'til tomorrow. I followed her past the two-inch bulletproof glass and into the back room. Once we were alone, I gave her a tight hug.

"Look at how big you've gotten, son." Then she reached into her bra, pulled out a thick roll of one hundred dollar bills, and popped off the rubber band. Without counting, she peeled off several bills and stuffed them into my pants pocket.

When she took a deep breath, I braced for one of her lectures, grateful that at least she wasn't pinching my arm. But she kept the conversation light and we chatted for a while before she turned the conversation to Evelyn.

"She's up in Sacramento getting her life together," Misty told me.

I didn't say anything, though I knew what Misty was talking about. After we broke up, Evelyn moved up North and started using crack. That was back in 1985 when a serious crack epidemic was in full swing. She lured me into the drug business with talk of the substantial profits that came with selling crack. I formulated a plan and put together a new crew to hit Sacramento. I was successful, but Evelyn got caught up.

Walking me back to the car, Misty said, "Take your time, son; let the game come to you. Call me if you need me."

The moment my brother, Big Country and I turned the corner, I pulled out the cash. Misty had dropped four thousand dollars on me. Now I could take care of a couple of things: get some cheap transportation and have money to throw a birthday party for my son in a couple of weeks.

Back at my mother's place, a euphoric feeling filled me when I saw my mother's car in the driveway. A few neighborhood homeboys were hanging around the front porch, and I embraced them before I moved into the house. My mother was in the kitchen frying chicken. I snuck up behind her and kissed her neck. She was already laughing as she turned around.

"Oh my Lord! Look who's finally made it home." We embraced and she stepped back to take a good look at me. "Boy, you've gained weight. I know you're hungry."

We shared a good laugh before I strolled back into the living room just as Sheila came through the door. Her eyes lit up. "Oh shit! What's happening, Bro?"

We hugged, then not too long after that, all sat down to dinner. Afterward, my sister and I went into the front yard to smoke some weed.

But just as I pulled out the joint, Tina pulled up with Greg Jr. and I put it right away. I grinned hard. This was truly the highlight of my day. I would finally get to hold my son.

He opened the door and scrambled from the car before it came to a full stop. Li'l Greg ran at full speed, jumped up into my arms, and I hugged him so tight I probably cut off his circulation.

Tina embraced me while my son was still in my arms.

Tina went into the house, but Greg Jr. stayed outside with me, as if he didn't want to let me out of his sight. But when my homies showed up, I sent my son into the house so we could smoke weed and talk shit. I'd only been outside with them for about twenty minutes when Debbie's sports car hit the corner. She stepped out wearing a tight purple leather miniskirt with a jacket, and classy hat. As she moved toward us, I thought, *she has one of the sexist strolls I've ever seen.*

Debbie sauntered past everybody, making eye contact with only me. She gave me a peck on the lips, then went inside.

My homies looked at me with disbelief and admiration. She just added to my ghetto stardom.

The next morning, Debbie dropped me off at my mother's house again, my unofficial headquarters. But I knew I didn't want my wife driving me everywhere. I needed my own car. Although I had a nice amount of cash, I didn't want to spend it. I wanted to finance a car. That meant I had to find someone with good credit since Debbie's credit was as jacked up as mine.

I had a victim in mind: my ex-wife, Precious.

I called her and told her I wanted to see "my son." She agreed to bring him by and I figured that would be the perfect opportunity to talk to her.

While I waited, I checked out the messages my mother left for me. These were calls I had directed to my mother's house, rather than to the apartment that I shared with my wife.

One of the messages stood out — it was from Susan. She had been hired by my lawyer as a private investigator when I was facing that murder case. Susan was about fourteen years my senior with shapely legs, but her greatest physical assets were firm 38D breasts. She'd been married to a black man when we met, and that made it easier for us to relate.

She was a no-nonsense kind of chick and was well respected by all the major shot-callers and murderers I was housed with.

In the beginning, I was a little intimidated by her, but we stayed in touch through letters and phone calls after I was sent to prison. I had fantasized making love to that woman for seven years.

So, seeing a message from her made me smile. I took a seat on the living room sofa and called. Her voice was confident, yet playful when she realized she was talking to me. "Hey, you. I better not be the last to know your ass is home."

She was divorced now, so I nervously asked her to come see me, and she agreed. This day was going well.

The front yard was filled with family and friends when Precious showed up. I stood in the living room window as she and Julius walked past my people. The contrast between how everyone felt about Precious versus Tina was stark.

No one paid much attention to them, but regardless of how I felt about Julius's questionable parentage, I couldn't stop being a father until I could prove otherwise. Especially since Precious had gone so far as to name him after my mother, Julia.

I spent a little time with Julius; he was only three and I wasn't sure if he really understood that I'd been away and now I was home. But I wanted to get to know him. Then, I talked to Precious like I really cared about her before I told her that I needed her help getting a car.

"No, problem," she told me.

The next day, Precious picked me up from my mother's house with a plan.

"I know this spot we can check out in Torrance."

I made sure to look her in the eyes with sincerity. "Thank you, baby, you don't know how much this means to me." I followed up my words with a passionate kiss.

About two hours and two thousand dollars later, I left the used car lot with a burgundy 1988 Chevy Celebrity — a popular cop vehicle, of all things.

On the way home, I paused at the end of my mother's block. The front yard was still full of my homeboys.

I punched the gas pedal and the tires squealed as I tore down the street. Like a scene from "Starsky and Hutch," I slammed on the brakes just as I reached the front of the house.

Everybody scattered like roaches. As I stepped out of the driver's seat, I doubled over with laughter. What I had done was considered a cruel joke in the hood, but as an O.G., I could get away with it. They regrouped and laughed with me.

Now, all I had left to do today was connect with Susan. I called my wife, telling her the good news about my car and that I would be home later. With my special guest on the way, I didn't want Debbie showing up here.

I waited with anticipation and a few hours later, a late model dark blue Toyota Camry pulled up and parked across the street. A white female opened the driver's side. She was dressed in Levi 501 jeans, a solid dark blue blouse, and white Nike tennis shoes. Her straight blonde hair with highlights hung to her shoulders.

Susan walked through the crowd with the same confidence as my wife. She smiled, and I couldn't keep the corners of my lips from turning upward.

She stopped two feet in front of me. "Get your ass over here and give me a hug, Mr. G Man."

We embraced as though no one else was around. Serge and a couple of my homies already knew Susan from back when she worked for my lawyer.

The rest of the guys stood with puzzled expressions. First Debbie, then Tina, then Precious, now this beautiful white woman.

I made quick introductions, then pulled her to the side.

"So how does it feel to be in the free world?"

"Great," I told her, always mindful of how lucky I was to be out.

"Let's go grab a bite to eat."

Ten minutes later, we were on Crenshaw Boulevard. But we were so busy talking that getting something to eat was all but forgotten.

"Hey, you wanna see my house? I live up in Baldwin Hills."

"Sure," I said. A million thoughts flooded my mind as we drove from Crenshaw up Stocker, through the affluent neighborhood. Excitement and anticipation flowed through both of us. I grabbed her hand just to make sure this was no dream.

Susan must've read my mind. "No, you're not dreaming, dude."

She pulled into the driveway of her two-story home at the top of the hill. Just like my godmother's, this house had money written all over it.

Susan opened a heavy wooden door and a Siamese cat sprang out. She introduced me to Anne as if she were an actual person, before we walked inside. We didn't stop — we headed straight to her bedroom and she turned on the light, proudly displaying a master bedroom that was huge and immaculate.

"Take off your shoes and relax."

Without my shoes, I waded through the plush carpet to the sofa in front of the window. I sat and gathered my thoughts as the sweet scent of mango suddenly filled the room. Looking up, I saw that Susan had lit candles that were placed about the room. A fifth of Hennessy chilled in an ice bucket on the table.

Susan poured two drinks, then turned off the lights and switched on soothing R&B music. She once again excused herself and I stood to survey the space. I passed her desk, then did a double take. The jailhouse pictures I'd sent her were in picture frames, along with family photos.

The door to the bathroom opened just as I picked up one of the pictures. "Don't let that go to your head, Greg, I had nowhere else to put them."

I grinned. "Yeah, whatever."

We laughed as I took a good look at Susan, whose hair was wet and face devoid of makeup. She wore a white silk pajama top that reached just above her mid-thigh; she looked sexy as hell. I wondered if she was wearing any panties. The question gave me a super hard erection.

We sat, had a drink, and smoked a joint.

By the second drink, the effects of alcohol, marijuana, and lust kicked in. Thanks to Evelyn's teaching, I was confident that I would blow Susan's mind.

Susan stroked my hand and waves of passion flowed through me as we kissed.

She pushed me back onto the sofa and settled between my thighs. Susan sucked my tongue into her mouth and I stopped her long enough to unbutton my shirt. Her pajama top had inched up, revealing smooth, athletic legs. I grabbed those firm ass cheeks. No panties!

She pulled away and took a sip of Hennessy, then pressed her lips to my nipples, sucking them. A moan rumbled in my throat as sensations — cool and hot — shot from my head to my toes. I surrendered to her, once again being schooled by an older chick.

Susan unbuttoned my pants and pulled them off; my boxers and socks were next. She locked gazes with me as her top flowed open, revealing her firm breasts; the hard nipples were the size of pencil erasers. She pushed me onto the couch, straddled my thighs and leaned forward. Her chest felt good next to mine as we locked in for a long sensual kiss. My dick couldn't get any harder.

I glanced down, taking in her neatly trimmed bush and lightly flicked my finger across her clit. The smooth texture of her hair was so different than the wonderfully kinky hair on a sista's vagina. This aroused me even more.

Susan's warm hand wrapped around the shaft of my dick. Her touch was soft, almost delicate as she stroked it. I don't know how much time passed before I felt my swollen tip entering her soaking pussy. Her head tilted back as she clasped her hands behind my neck.

Since my reputation and pride were at stake, I resorted to an old trick and forced myself to think about something non-sexual so that I wouldn't cum. It worked. Susan took her time lowering herself onto my dick, squeezing me like she didn't want to let me go.

We established a smooth rhythm. She moaned and talked me through every stroke as sweat drenched us. Her voice was low and sultry as she teased, "Can you handle this pussy, G Man? Is it worth the seven years you waited?"

I couldn't manage a single word.

She smiled. "It's just you and me, baby. How does this pussy feel to you?"

She was driving me crazy! I took a deep breath, and whispered, "The game ain't over, Susan, we're just getting started."

She ground her pelvis against me, then increased her rhythm. She moaned, her fingernails dug into my shoulders. Those golden words finally escaped her lips. "Oh shit! I'm cumming, baby! Can you feel my juices on that big black dick?"

She had turned this into a black and white thing, which turned me on more. Her body shuddered as an orgasm ripped through her. She lowered against me, and I felt the rapid beat of her heart.

I wrapped Susan's legs around my waist with my rock hard dick still inside her. I lifted us off the sofa and placed her in the middle of the king size bed. Then, I fucked her, nice and slow at first.

I taunted her. "Is this what you're looking for, baby? Is this dick worth the seven years *you* waited?"

She arched her back and met every thrust. I was in pussy heaven.

She worked up to her fifth orgasm and all I could think was, *Greg, don't come too soon.* But then she pulled me down to her body and her hot tongue went right to my nipple. No trick would help now.

"Aw, fuck, Susan! Cum with me, baby."

We both exploded at the same time.

Susan and I laid on our backs and I tried to get my breathing under control, I took a good look at her.

Just two days before, I was in prison. My only escapes were my fantasies. I couldn't help the huge grin that spread across my lips.

"What are you smiling about?"

"Shit, life."

"So, what are your plans now, G Man?"

"I think I'm going to check into becoming a personal trainer, or maybe even go back to school."

"That sounds like a plan, Greg, just make sure you stick to it."

Susan dropped me off at my mother's house, and we agreed to have lunch in a couple days. Then, I called my wife to let her know that I was on my way home.

As I drove through the streets, I put in a Tupac classic, "Thug Life."

I went North on La Brea toward the Valley, smiling and bobbing my head, even though this stereo system was a piece of shit. I would upgrade as soon as possible.

La Brea eventually turned into La Cienega, the same street that I viewed from Susan's bedroom. I glanced up the hill toward her house. I was on my way to my wife, but didn't feel guilty about being with Susan. I'd known her long before my wife. Plus, Debbie had done her fair share of fucking around on me while I did my time. Our mutual interest in hustling is what sealed our bond.

Unfortunately for Debbie though, I had a taste of Susan and now I was hooked.

Chapter 24
Satellite Niggaz

The game had changed in the seven years that I'd been gone; getting money in the streets was much harder. So that meant I had to hustle everywhere and that's what I did. For the next three years, I became a Satellite Nigga; I hustled not only in Los Angeles, but I set up a satellite operation in Sacramento and a few other cities.

Times were good. Even though I had to be away from home a lot, Debbie didn't care. Often, I'd come home from my out-of-town trips and leave five or six thousand dollars on her nightstand; that's what she cared about.

But things weren't always steady. If someone got caught and went to jail, or if there was a cocaine drought, things could slow down real quick. And that's what happened to me.

Suddenly, I was an out of work thug with a wife and my two sons and Debbie's daughter to support. The bills were piling up and I hoped to find something before desperation kicked in.

My high maintenance wife didn't seem to notice; she kept her hand out for mall money. She was still as sexy as a motherfucker, but there was nothing Debbie loved more than money.

I was thinking about all of this as I sat on Serge's living room sofa. My brother rolled a joint, took a couple of deep drags and passed it to me. I let the smoke ease from my lungs and opened my eyes to a picture of my mother on the wall in front of me. After the thick haze of smoke cleared, the solution came to me!

Mama had moved back to Natchez, Mississippi two years ago. It was time to pay her a little visit; maybe being away would help me figure out my next moves.

I wanted to go right now and I needed someone to travel with me, so I called Precious since she had relatives in the same area. And of course, she agreed to go. "Just give me a couple of hours."

Next, I called Debbie. "I'm about to take a road trip to Mississippi."

"Today?"

"Yup."

Then, shock went through me when she said, "I'm going, too."

Thinking quickly, I said, "I'm riding with Jerome."

She hesitated for a moment, then said, "Okay, but promise me that you'll see me before you hit the highway."

Four hours later, Precious, my son Julius, and his thirteen-year-old sister were packed into a Lincoln Town car. We jumped on Highway 10 and kept rolling. I never stopped to see Debbie; I would deal with her later.

I'd purchased a cell with an illegal chip inside so that I could talk for unlimited hours for free. To keep my wife happy, I called her from every stop. After about the third time, she got crafty and asked to speak to Jerome.

"He's fighting with his wife on the phone right now," I told her. "But I'll have him call you as soon as he calms down." I hoped that would keep her settled for a while.

When we entered Louisiana, I was at the wheel. I thought Precious was asleep, so I called Debbie. Out of the corner of my eye, Precious stirred under the blanket. I needed to get off the phone, but Debbie hit me with, "Tell me that you love me."

Damn! The oldest "caught you slipping" trick in the book.

"I love you." Then, I hung up.

Precious pushed the blanket away as tears streamed down her face. That didn't bother me; she should've been sleep instead of ear hustling. Plus, Precious knew that I was married; what did she think? That I would leave my wife?

I would never leave Debbie for Precious. First of all, I would never trust Precious. Many people, including Debbie, tried to give me reasons why Julius wasn't my son. Besides the fact that she'd had numerous affairs while we were married, Debbie asked why Precious hardly brought Julius around my family.

As I drove, I thought about these things and I looked over at my ex, who was asleep once again. For a few minutes my gaze went between the road and looking at Precious. Back and forth. And, I had only one thought: *I pray to God this bitch isn't lying to me.*

Chapter 25
Mama Knows Best

We made it to Mississippi, a place I hadn't set foot in for seventeen years. But everything looked the same as we drove through town toward the country where I grew up. I observed the people along the route, hoping to see somebody I recognized. I didn't see a soul!

Our property was at the very end of the road and the further we drove in, the worse it was. Young dudes were hanging out with pit bulls and sagging pants, just like in L.A. When some saw our California plates, they threw up the signature West coast "W" hand sign. I found the influence of the West coast all the way down here amazing.

We reached the gravel road that would take us onto my family's property, and it brought a smile to my face.

My mother was out the door and down the stairs to greet us before the car stopped. It felt so good to be in her arms, even though I was a grown ass man.

My mother hugged my ex-wife before she turned to Julius. She wasn't as warm to this "grandson" as she was to Greg Jr., who looked so much like me.

Then Precious asked, "Is it okay for me to take the rental car?" She had made plans to visit her relatives in Vicksburg County, about twenty minutes away.

I had so many relatives in the area that transportation wasn't a problem, so I let her have the car. After Precious drove off, I sat and talked to my mother for a while before I gave her a goodnight kiss. It had been a long trip and I was tired as hell.

* * *

I awoke to the smell of bacon and the sound of the washing machine.

"Greg you need to come on and eat. I've got to go to work in a little while."

At first I thought I was dreaming, but then, I laid in the bed for a while with that dreaded question hanging over me: *What the fuck was I going to do next?*

But then, I told myself that I was in Natchez to relax and enjoy some time with my mother. Figuring out my next hustle could wait.

I hit the shower before walking into the kitchen. My mother made a good ol' Southern breakfast: yellow grits, deer meat, and biscuits.

Damn, it's good to be back in the country.

Even though my mother had retired from Northrop Aircraft in California, she wasn't the type of woman to sit around. Now, she worked as a nurse.

Before she left, Mama gave me my cousins' phone numbers, but it had been so long since I had been in Natchez, I didn't know who was "cool enough" to hang out with me. I reached back in my memory bank, thinking of who would most likely have become the black sheep since I had been gone. I needed to find that person because I needed to get my hands on some good weed.

But before I went in search of my cousins, I went outside and strolled our property. As a kid, I felt like this place was in a world all our own. There was only one way in and one way out with a bayou surrounding the entire area of land. My grandmother's old house was across the road.

The memories settled in as I scanned the familiar landmarks: the garden and plum trees, the barbed wire fence where we once stored the hay and feed for the livestock and the barn, which was in pretty bad shape.

Next, I headed up the road to my Aunt Lena's brand new double-wide trailer. Just like my mother, my aunt had retired

and returned to Mississippi. The only thing was, tragedy struck my aunt shortly after she arrived. She had a serious stroke and was placed in a nursing home, so now her trailer was empty.

The key to Aunt Lena's trailer was with the keys that Mama left me, and when I went inside, I was surprised at how nice the place looked. But it was hard to enjoy the space; as I looked around, my heart hurt for my favorite aunt. I decided right then to definitely go and see her.

When I walked back to my mother's house, a black Ford F-150 truck was parked in the driveway. A young dude stepped out of the truck and smiled as he approached.

"Hey cousin, Greg. It's me, Opey. Uncle Ernest's son."

Wow! The last time I saw him, he was just a little boy.

"Your mom called and told me to give you a ride into town," he said.

After we hugged, I thanked him, then ran into the house and changed.

Visiting my Auntie Lena was top priority and Opey took me there first. When I walked into her room at the nursing home, I couldn't believe it.

My aunt laid there in the bed, hardly able to move since the stroke paralyzed her whole left side. All I could think about was the last time I saw her, vibrant and totally independent.

"Hey, Auntie Lena," I said as I approached her bed.

Her eyes brightened when she looked up at me and I took her hand. She could hardly talk, but I talked to her. I told her about what was going on in California, my two sons, and then I promised that I would visit her every day while I was in Natchez.

But as soon as Opey and I left and jumped back into his truck, I said, "Where can I get some weed?"

"I don't smoke, but Cousin Cowboy would know. He's into everything under the sun."

As Opey drove to hook up with Cousin Cowboy, I tried to remember him. Even once I saw him when we pulled up to his house, I didn't get any memories. But based on his appearance, I knew we could hit a few street corners and do some damage.

Cowboy was a high yellow nigga, a pretty boy. He wore the latest gear and a few oversized pieces of some bullshit silver jewelry, fake diamonds and all.

But after hanging out with him for just a few minutes, I could tell that he was cool as hell. He'd lived in L.A. with his wild ass mother and father for a couple of years, so I figured he would be a little sharper than the rest of these dudes in Natchez.

Cowboy was a unique kind of country boy who spoke in his own hip, country, slick-city language and said, "True dat" to damn near everything.

He gave me a playful hug. "I'm glad you came to visit, Big Cuz. Now let's get some bud."

We walked toward a '86 Cutlass Supreme, where a little wanna be homie waited. When we reached the car, the homie was bumping Tupac's "All Eyes On Me." The trunk was rattling like hell and damnation.

Cowboy wanted to make an immediate impression, so he yelled, "Fool, turn that shit down!" then jumped into the back seat. "This is my big cousin from Cali."

The youngster shook my hand. "My name is Damian."

Cowboy instructed him to take us to the weed house. We came up empty, so we hit the next road over and couldn't find any there either. We looked for the next three hours and we ended up with was some shit that tasted like hay.

I turned to Cowboy. "Homie, I thought you were the man! You can't even find a decent dime bag of weed." Then, I grinned. "I think you need to get out of the game, little Cuz."

We cracked up before heading to visit the rest of my relatives.

One paved two-lane road took everyone to and from town. It was once Pine Ridge Road, but was now called Martin Luther King Jr. Boulevard. Three little mom and pop stores were along this road, spaced about two or three miles apart.

Dude didn't have air conditioning in his car and I was sweating bullets and shells. We stopped and bought a twelve-pack of beer, each took a can, and then put the rest in the chest. The humidity made me appreciate that Budweiser.

As we rolled down the road, gang graffiti was spray-painted on walls, blue and red bandanas hung everywhere, and dudes threw up gang signs as we passed by.

We'd only driven a few miles when we rode up on a few trucks parked, looking like they were having a tailgate party.

Cowboy said, "Hey, mane, dat's some of yo' cousins right dere."

We pulled over and I hugged everyone. All the talk was about how big I'd gotten. I guess I did look big to them. These cousins were square dudes who believed in work and an honest lifestyle. They didn't know anything about prison life.

Cowboy was the exception. Everybody knew that when Cowboy was around, trouble was right on his heels. Hanging out with him automatically labeled people around him.

I normally didn't give a fuck about what people thought, but since my family roots were deeply implanted in the area, I had to be careful. I would never intentionally tarnish my mother's name.

We had a few beers and bullshitted for a good while, waving to every damn vehicle that went by. Then another pickup truck parked behind us and as soon as the dude stepped out of the truck, Cowboy yelled, "What's happening, Vince?"

My cousins greeted Vince warmly — which was different from the way they had greeted Cowboy.

I did a quick scan of Vince. An old hustler taught me that a person's shoes told a story — from crackhead to lawyer. Vince wore work boots that didn't seem like they had seen much work. He had the same light complexion as Cowboy, but was soft-spoken, younger, more handsome and very likable. He did more listening than talking, always a good sign. It meant he was a thinking man like myself.

My overall evaluation of Vince was that he probably was a hard-working man who had a little side hustle to get him through.

I tossed back the last of my beer. "I'll holla at y'all later. I'm only gonna be here for a few days and I've got more relatives to visit."

My cousin Jeff intercepted me on the way to Cowboy's car and offered to give me a ride, even though it was out of his way. He didn't want me hanging out with Cowboy.

Vince said, "I'll give him a ride. I'm going that way."

I got Cowboy's cell and said, "I'll call you later," then tossed him the rest of that bullshit weed.

Vince pulled off with Tupac thumping through the speakers. Everybody seemed to be into my boy. He pulled over to the side of the road, whipped out a baggie with a nice amount of weed inside and tossed it my way. "Check dis' here dank out, Big Homie."

When I opened the baggie, the scent alone let me know this was quality shit.

He pulled out a Swisher Sweet cigar from the glove compartment, rolled a perfect blunt, and passed it my way. The sweet taste of the marijuana was pleasant, but my lungs expanded too fast and I coughed.

Vince grinned.

"Where you get this shit at, homie?"

He told me he could get it anytime. "But it ain't cheap. An ounce costs about a hundred and fifty."

Damn! It was only about thirty dollars for an ounce back in L.A.

Then Vince made the wonderful mistake of saying, "If we had pounds of this shit down here, we could get rich."

His words were confirmed by the fact that everywhere we went, dudes were looking for weed. The dealers ran out faster than they could re-up their supply.

By the time we got to my mother's house, I couldn't push the thoughts of hustling from my mind. I called Precious and asked when she was going to bring the car. She told me would in a little while, but after two hours passed, Vince and I headed back out in his Chevy.

As we rolled around town, everywhere we went people were saying the same thing: "Mane, there ain't no weed down here."

I couldn't stop my wheels from spinning if I wanted to.

"You want to go to a club, Cuz?" Vince asked me.

That sounded like a good idea; I needed to check out the social scene if I was going to hustle down here. The club was all the way in the boondocks, but when we got there, the place was packed. It was definitely too hot to go inside.

"Hang out here," Vince said, and ten minutes later he returned with two ice-cold beers. He shook his head as he passed the beer. "Big Homie, you ain't gonna believe who's inside da' club."

I didn't wait for him to tell me. I walked through the door, and squeezed my way through what felt like hundreds of sweaty bodies until I reached the bar.

Precious was sitting there snapping her fingers, enjoying herself like she hadn't lied to me. I pulled up a stool and sat next to this female who right away started trying to talk to me. But, I kept my eyes on Precious.

It took about twenty minutes before Precious felt my eyes burning a hole in her. She turned and saw me looking dead at her. I didn't say a single word. I turned to my right and talked to that country ass female sitting next to me. Then, I took her hand and walked right past Precious and out the door.

Yes, it was going to be a long ass trip back to L.A., but that was all right; I could play the game better than anybody.

All Precious had done was put herself in a fucked up position. She didn't bring the car like she said, so she would end up footing the bill when we got home.

Chapter 26
Thinking of a Master Plan

My little vacation had come to an end, but I already knew that I would be back. I told Cowboy and Vince that I would formulate a plan and get back with them.

The hardest part of leaving was my mother. She fried up some chicken and made sandwiches for the road, but as we were packing up to leave, I really watched the way my mother interacted with Julius. Grandmothers knew their grandchildren — and it was obvious that despite the ploy of giving the boy her name, my mother did not feel Julius was mine.

When we hit the road, Precious drove the first leg. I curled up in the passenger seat with a blanket draped over me and through half-open eyes, I looked at her for a long time. I realized that I didn't know the woman. She came across as Sweet Polly Purebred, but she was trying to play me, she'd always been trying to play me. Didn't she realize that I was the master of the game? I couldn't be played.

I made her ass drive damn near to New Mexico before I took the wheel. And to make matters worse, I talked to Debbie on my cell almost the entire way home.

* * *

Back in L.A., Precious dropped me off at my cousin's house in Inglewood. I tossed my luggage into the bed of my Toyota truck and Precious turned up her lips. "What about the money for the rental?"

I answered with a solid look in her eyes and a lie in my heart. "I'll bring it to you in the morning."

On the 110 heading toward North Hollywood, my mind was consumed with the decisions before me. There was a lot of money to be made down in Natchez.

At home, my wife was waiting for me with her hands on her hips. "When the fuck did you get back?"

I had learned to keep every response vague and tried to remember the lies I told. My wife was as effective as a seasoned prosecutor.

I didn't say a word, just dug in my pocket and pulled out a few hundred bucks. That satisfied her. . . for the moment.

Debbie heated up some leftover tacos, taking her sweet time. I was dying to get to the phone, but instead, I took a shower, changed into sweats, and tried to look like I wasn't up to a damn thing.

We played this cat-and-mouse game all the time. Finally, Debbie got ready to leave and right before she closed the door, she gave me that special "prosecutor" look and said, "I'll be back to finish where I left off, honey."

As soon as that red Nissan 300 ZX pulled off, I took a seat on our black leather sofa and made my first call to

Althea, one of my hustling chicks who worked for me in Sacramento. I still had a bit of business up there and some dudes owed me money.

Althea had collected two thousand dollars and I told her to keep three hundred and send the rest by Western Union.

Then I called Serge, who now had a barbershop in Inglewood, and told him I was coming in to get a haircut. But I was also going there to see what kind of hustle I could stumble upon.

Before I left though, I made a few more calls, contacting a couple of people with weed connections. Unfortunately, there was a drought, but everyone promised to hit me up the moment some came in.

I dressed in what my wife described as my "kit" — a full range of jewelry. Hustling in L.A. was all about presentation. Depending on the situation, it didn't hurt to have a few classy pieces of jewelry.

On the way to Inglewood, I picked up the money from Western Union, then at the barbershop I scanned the parking lot to get a line on who might be inside. One car belonged to Big Syke, another to Spray-Paint from East Coast Crips, and the last one to Big Russ.

The barber section was located in the back and I walked in, taking stock of the scene. I hugged my brother and whispered my usual, "I love you, little bro."

Then I hugged Big Russ — a 5'8, 240 pound bruiser with a bald head and strong Belize accent; he was *the* weed connection.

Over his shoulder I saw two other dudes who looked familiar, but we had never met. Serge introduced them as

Kurupt and Dazz Dillinger from the Dogg Pound. Both were big name rappers, associated with Snoop Dogg.

Big Russ sat next to me. "What the fuck is up, G Man? I know you got something going on, Big Homie."

I told him that I'd just returned from Mississippi and how there was a shortage down there.

Big Russ said, "I have five pounds and can get at least twenty pounds up front if you have an outlet."

I never liked to hustle that way — accepting a deal where I would be responsible for the product and the cash. Anything could happen. The package could get lost during the process and the connection expected his money regardless. According to street rules, the matter had to be resolved.

I thought about it for a moment. "I'm not sure I'm gonna even hustle down there. But when I leave here, I'll stop by to check the quality."

Big Syke was in the corner on his cell and when I walked toward him, he held up his finger, asking me to wait. Not five minutes later, his raspy voice yelled, "What's up, Big Geezee?"

I embraced him in the same manner as Serge because he was family, too.

I slipped into Serge's chair after everyone was done. I told him about the trip to Mississippi, and he gave me updates on the California end of things.

"You just missed Jay. He asked about you."

That statement made me curious and a little bit excited. Jay was Serge's partner and he didn't fuck with nobody. Jay wore confidence and smelled like money.

I asked my brother a couple of questions about Jay and then when Serge finished my hair, he spun me around in the chair. "Bro, you're slippin'," he whispered. Then, he spun the chair again so that I faced a gorgeous female with an olive complexion and a tight body.

Serge said, "Nigga, she's been trying to get your attention since you came in the shop."

Lashawn and I had an undercover relationship since I'd been released from prison. The first time I looked at her working in Serge's shop, I had to have her, but Serge was the only one who knew that she and I had hooked up.

I gestured for her to call me on the shop phone and we carried on a conversation cell-to-phone while looking at each other from across the shop. As I talked to her, I took the opportunity to admire her natural beauty; she didn't wear make-up. She had a flat stomach, even after having a baby. She wore her hair in two long braids that hung to her waist.

Lashawn was married to a Satellite Nigga who was always out of town, and treated her like shit whenever he was home. We made plans to hook up later that evening.

Debbie was as beautiful as Lashawn and I loved my wife, but when it came to women, I couldn't help myself. I loved the thrill of the hunt.

When I went to my truck, my pager was vibrating like crazy. Cowboy and Vince had been trying to reach me.

I called back and Vince said, "I have dudes lined up for a minimum of five pounds apiece!"

Cowboy didn't have pound sales like Vince, but it still amounted to quite a bit of business. Between the two of them, I would be able to build one hell of a satellite and one hell of a clientele.

"I'm on my way to check out some shit in a few minutes. I'll call you back." I still felt torn between hustling and not hustling in my hometown, but it seemed like it was taking on a life of its own, leading me there.

So, I headed over to Big Russ'. The quality of the weed was perfect and so was the price. Then Big Russ gave me the downside, "I can't get it in large quantities on a consistent basis."

That wouldn't work; consistency was the key to winning the game.

Big Russ saw my hesitation. "I've got another plan to get all we need. Why don't you send your boys a couple of pounds and see how it goes?"

He tossed two pounds of prime across the room before I could protest. That moment right there sealed my fate.

I had heated things up in prison, hustled my way through Los Angeles, Sacramento, a bunch of other cities, and now Natchez, Mississippi was my next town.

Big Russ only paid 350-dollars apiece for the bags and we agreed that we would split the profit. I was on my way.

On the freeway headed home, I was bumping Tupac on the stereo and glanced at my pager. I had several more missed pages from my wife, Cowboy, and Vince.

I called Vince first and told him of the plan. "Get me a reliable shipping address and don't tell Cowboy until the product arrives."

I didn't want Cowboy to know because I could already tell that he talked too much. He could fuck around and get us caught up before we even got started!

"I'll ship the product without anyone needing to sign for it," I said, finishing up with Vince.

All Vince would have to do was lay back in the cut, watch the package being dropped off, then wait until it was cool and pick it up.

It was after ten o'clock when I made it home where the "warden" was waiting.

Debbie didn't give me the opportunity to get in the door. "I've been paging you all day. Why didn't you call me back?"

I placed the bag on the sofa. She looked inside, then glared at me. Before she could gear up to preach, I said, "I have a migraine. We'll talk about it in the morning."

I wasn't exactly lying; I did get debilitating headaches from time to time. I just didn't have one at that particular moment.

Debbie went into the bedroom, came out with some blankets and pillows and tossed them onto the couch. She spun around in front of the bedroom door and said, "If you think you're going back out of town again, you better get ready for a motherfucking divorce," then slammed the door so hard, it sounded like a 12-gauge shotgun.

I sat on the sofa and watched the news for awhile, then crept up to the bedroom door and turned the handle. She had locked me out.

My wife didn't mind me hustling, but she told me she was getting fed up with that out of town shit. She complained that I spent too much time away from her and my kids.

I trudged to the sofa and pulled out the cell, but before I could make a call my pager went off. Precious had hit the line about ten times. I knew she was calling about my half of the money for the rental car. I erased her calls, then made my calls before I rolled up a fat-ass joint and went out on the balcony.

I took a few moments to focus on every aspect of the plan I was about to execute in Mississippi. A while later, I stretched out on the couch and closed my eyes.

To me, this was the most important part of the day. This was when I went over every event and tomorrow's game plan frame by frame.

* * *

When I woke the next morning, my mind was clear; I knew what I had to do.

But before I could get my day started, Serge called and said, "Jay wants to talk to you ASAP. He's got some major legal problems going on."

I told Serge to have Jay hook up with me later, then I made breakfast, showered, and got dressed in a square outfit — a pair of Dockers, a flannel shirt, and casual shoes. Before I left the house, I called Vince just to make sure that everything was still a go and told him I would call him later with the package's tracking number.

My first stop was Home Depot for rubber gloves and duct tape. Then back home at home, I used one of Debbie's shoe boxes and wrapped the product, making sure that I didn't touch anything with my bare hands. At the post office, I spent the few extra dollars to send the package overnight, then called Vince and gave him the info along with instructions. This was a test to see how well he could handle business. I had a lot of faith in Vince; Cowboy was the one who worried me.

Right after I hung up from Vince, I got another page, this time from my cousin Watani, who now lived in Atlanta. Watani was a big time manager, handling a couple of rappers and people like Monster Kody's (from Eight Trey Gangster rips) speaking engagements.

"I need you to do me a favor," my cousin said. "I need you to locate Monster Kody for me, then pick him up and take him to Ruthless Records for a meeting before you get him to the airport for me tonight. He has an engagement here in Atlanta, and I don't want him to miss his flight or his meeting."

"Sure," I told my cousin. Not only didn't I mind helping Watani out, but Monster Kody and I were cool. As I navigated my way down to Long Beach where he lived, I reflected on the days that Monster and I spent in the hole at Chino in 1991.

Chino was a disciplinary housing unit, the place for the worst of the worst offenders. I was in for selling heroin; he was waiting to be transferred to the most secure prison in California—Pelican Bay.

Monster, a shot-caller and educator, was a natural leader with a wealth of talent and power. He was the most intelligent convict I had ever encountered. As our relationship evolved, I gained more respect for him than any man on the streets, with the exception of my cousin, Watani.

When I arrived, he came right downstairs since Watani had called him and told him I was on my way. I was taken aback by his appearance. He had lost a great deal of weight, but still had that familiar thousand yard stare of a complex criminal.

I stepped out of the truck to greet him, and heard the words, "Habara Gani, Fati."

Even though he spoke Swahili, I greeted him in English. "Good morning," I said, because I'd forgotten most of what he'd taught me in prison.

We embraced; it was great to be in the presence again of a true and proven solider.

I called Debbie and asked her to leave work because I was bringing home a guest. I rarely brought anyone home because of the basic rule, "you don't shit where you eat," so she knew this was important.

On the drive to my home, Monster and I caught up before he asked, "What's up with Tupac, Fati? Isn't Watani still his manager at Interscope Records?"

I brought him up to speed on 'Pac's situation at Death Row Records. Tupac had recently been thrown into jail to serve a short prison sentence for sexual assault in New York. He had a million dollar appeal bond pending.

My mind drifted as I drove and we chatted. Back in prison, though we were caged and treated like animals, we were feared by most and respected by many. We were two intelligent, but prison educated black men — a threat to society. We were the kind of men they never wanted to release.

We had both faced attempted murder charges, but there wasn't enough evidence, and we were now free.

We walked into my apartment where Debbie was at the stove frying up chicken wings. She warmed up to Monster immediately. Despite being a ruthless criminal, Monster was a gentleman.

I called Watani and let him know that I had Monster with me.

"Put Sanyika on the phone," he said, calling Monster by his Swahili name. They talked for a few minutes and Monster wrote down his flight information.

While we ate, Debbie's gaze narrowed at our guest and I watched Debbie as she took stock. Later, I would ask for her opinion. A woman's intuition was a motherfucker and Debbie had it in spades!

Monster helped clean up and volunteered to take out the trash, which gave my wife an opportunity to question me.

"Isn't that the same guy that was in prison with you? Didn't he write that book about street gangs?"

I nodded and told her I'd fill her in when I got back.

Monster thanked Debbie, then we made a trip to Inglewood to the house where I grew up. Serge had rented it from the new owner, and it was still the major hangout.

About twelve dudes were standing in front and as they greeted us, I heard their whispers. "Ain't that Monster Kody from Eight Trey Gangster?"

Once I introduced Monster to Serge, my brother began cracking jokes as usual.

"Ain't you *Big* Monster Kody? Ain't you the same dude that's on the cover of that book holding an Uzi? What did you do, join Jenny Craig?"

The whole house erupted with laughter. Serge could talk about anybody and all they could do was laugh. We sat around the living room smoking chronic and laughing our asses off as Serge held the floor. He made his way around the room, cracking jokes on anybody.

Eventually, Monster came off the sofa and stepped to Serge. "Yeah, you pretty funny with them jokes, Serge, but can you fuck with me on some freestyle rapping, homie?"

Monster didn't know my brother, because if he did, he wouldn't have put Serge on the spot that way. Monster always loved a challenge, but so did Serge. They went back and forth for about five minutes before Serge took control and had his way with Monster. An explosion of laughter rocked the living room the moment Monster finally called it quits. It was time for us to leave for his appointment at Ruthless anyway.

Big Russ called right as I slipped into the driver's seat and said he wanted to ride with us up to the meeting. He only stayed a couple of minutes from Serge, so it didn't take us any time to get over there.

When I parked my truck in front of his house, the three of us jumped into his Toyota Corolla to travel the rest of the way to the meeting.

While we were driving, Big Russ inquired about the package I'd sent to Mississippi.

"Everything's cool. It'll be there tomorrow before noon." I gave him the tracking number so he could keep tabs on it.

I sat in the meeting with Monster, Big Russ, and the executives from Ruthless Records while they laid out the terms of the deal they had for Monster, which included a music video and possible movie deal.

But then in the middle of the meeting, Big Russ received a call from Jay, Serge's partner, and I could tell that this was a serious call. Big Russ stepped into the hallway for a few minutes, then poked his head back in and motioned for me to join him.

"Listen," he began, "Jay needs my help." He told me that the Feds were looking for Jay, so he couldn't go back to his hotel and he needed Russ to retrieve some important items. "So, what do you want to do? I have to make that run."

I didn't hesitate. "I'll roll with you."

The meeting was just ending when we walked back in and, I pulled Monster aside. "We have to take care of some business, homie. You'll have to drop us off, then meet us back at Big Russ's house."

We gave Monster Kody anything that would identify us: Big Russ gave him his ID since I'd left mine in my truck. I gave Monster my illegal phone.

On the ride over to the hotel, I analyzed the whole situation. I was going to a hotel room that was probably under surveillance. The Feds could be in the room waiting. I was on parole and could get a violation just for coming into contact with the police.

But this was also an opportunity for me to cut into Jay's line of business, so I was going to take my chances.

We reached the lot where Jay told us his rental was parked with the keys to the hotel under the mat. I scanned the lot for any red flags. Under my instructions, Big Russ circled the hotel a couple of times and I still didn't see anything unusual.

We pulled up next to Jay's rental and turned the Corolla over to Monster. As Monster pulled off, I felt a gut check. Rumor had it that Monster was using crack and the temptation to fuck up was always great. I was just glad that my phone was the only property that Monster had in his possession.

I stood a few cars away scanning the parking lot as Big Russ retrieved the keys from the rental. We entered the hotel lobby as if we belonged there and then took the elevator to the fifth floor. Everything looked good so far. We still had to enter the room and I thought of the worst-case scenario — a bunch of cops aiming guns at my head screaming, "Freeze, motherfucker!"

Big Russ slid the card key into the lock and slowly opened the door. The room was empty and we both sighed with relief.

I told Russ, "Hurry up so we can get the fuck out of here." I stood close to the door listening, careful not to touch anything. But something on the nightstand caught my eye — a newspaper not from California.

The words *MURDER* and *DRUGS were* splashed across the front page. I rolled the paper up and tucked it under my arm. Big Russ and I carried out three suitcases of expensive clothes and shoes. I didn't relax until we pulled out of the parking lot. And even then, I kept an eye on that rearview mirror.

We made it to Big Russ's house, but Russ's car wasn't there and neither was Monster Kody. Big Russ called Jay to give him an update, then rolled a fat-ass joint and we relaxed since Jay was on his way.

The newspaper I'd swiped was from Atlanta, and I read the story detailing a thirty million dollar cocaine ring. It described how the dealers used computers to ship drugs across the United States. It also detailed a story about the murder of a young, black female who was killed for stealing money from the dealers.

Jay, along with his cousin, was named as one of the main suspects.

"Shit," I whispered. "What the fuck have I gotten myself into?"

Chapter 27
Chain of Events

After a few hours had passed with no sign of Monster, I called Watani. I explained the situation and I was concerned that if he didn't return soon, he wouldn't make his flight.

Watani said, "Li'l cousin, don't stress yourself out. There's only so much you can do."

Watani told me he would get in contact with Monster Kody's younger brother, and see if he could fill in, but he asked me to keep him posted.

Jay showed up about an hour later, and I was impressed by the fact that he walked in with his normal big, confident smile. Of course, he didn't know that I'd read the article, but he carried himself like he didn't have a care in the world.

As soon as he came in, he extended his hand and thanked me for going with Big Russ. Then Jay turned to Russ. "Hurry up and roll me something to smoke. You know my nerves are bad right about now."

We sat around making small talk, but I knew Jay was checking me out the same way I was checking him out. As we talked, I learned that Big Russ had gotten those few pounds of weed he'd given me from Jay.

The moment Russ left the room I slid Jay the newspaper and looked him straight in the eye. Neither one of us said a single word, but that moment established a bond that no one else had with him. He had no choice but to trust me.

Then we started talking about Mississippi and the weed he'd gotten for me. I broke the numbers down and could see his wheels turning as I spoke. He shot questions my way, and I answered every one.

He said, "This Mexican will give me any amount of pounds at dirt-cheap prices as long as I can move them."

I learned that at $250 per pound, Big Russ was fucking me without grease. With that information, Russ was now out of the picture as the middleman; I was going to deal with Jay directly.

Jay then changed the subject on me. "I know you have a DMV hookup. I need a new I.D., and money is no object."

I had no idea how he knew about my connection, but before we got married, Debbie used to fuck with a trick named Big Al. He was the ID man and because he was still lusting after my wife, she could get anybody a whole profile — for the right price.

I told him I would get on that, and then Jay asked me about Mississippi again. "When is the money supposed to come back from Mississippi?"

I couldn't give him a definite time because this was my first experience sending something down there. But I told him, "Probably in a couple of days."

Jay said, "Keep that money. You don't owe Russ anything." He continued, "And, if everything goes all right in Mississippi, my connect will drop at least twenty pounds on me. If you're serious about hustling down there, I'll front them to you just as long as the turnover's quick. I'm talking about moving some serious weight as soon as possible."

Shit, I was getting in deeper and deeper by the hour. But I was excited as hell.

I called my wife right then, and put Jay on the phone. She gave him her word that she would have his new I.D. within a week.

But right when Jay disconnected from Debbie, Big Russ busted into the room. In his deep Belizean accent, he said, "Yo! G Man, you ain't gonna believe what the fuck just happened, homie. I've been trying to call Monster on our cell phones and some other Crip answered my phone talking 'bout, 'what's up, Cuz? What you need?'"

In other words, Monster had already sold our phones to some hustling bangers in his hood!

All Jay and I could do was bust up laughing. Big Russ didn't find a damn thing funny, though.

Jay and I exchanged numbers and agreed to hook up in the morning. When I finally slipped into the driver's seat of my truck, my pager was vibrating again.

The first five pages were from Precious, the next eight from Debbie, a few from Althea (my connect in Sacramento), and the last two were from Vince and Cowboy.

I usually made my "slick" calls while I was stuck in freeway traffic, but Monster had sold my phone. Now, I'd have to figure out a way to make those calls from home, a difficult process since the warden/investigator/prosecutor was going to be posted up on my ass.

Luck was on my side. When I got home, Debbie was asleep. I closed the door to the bedroom and made my calls from the living room.

First Vince and Cowboy told me that the demand for the weed hadn't changed.

Next I called Althea, and found out that she had only collected a few hundred dollars. I instructed her to send that money first thing in the morning.

I grabbed the blankets and pillow from the closet, then rolled myself a joint, stepped out on the balcony, and took a couple of deep tokes. As I looked out over downtown L.A., I thought about my mother. What reason was I going to give her for returning to Mississippi so soon?

When I stretched out on the sofa and closed my eyes, thoughts of what kind of lie I could come up with swirled in my head. I must've fallen asleep right away because the next thing I knew, Debbie was standing over me and light filled the living room.

My wife didn't even say good morning. She just went in. "Greg, I talked to your cousin in Mississippi. He said he didn't see Jerome the whole time you were down there. So who did you really go down there with?"

I narrowed my gaze at her, and put on my best poker face. "Well, call *my cousin* and let him tell *me* that shit!"

She glared at me, and stormed out of the house. I had won that round, but all I had done was put a Band-Aid on a cut that was bound to bleed again.

I went to the window because my wife was not beyond doubling back on my ass to get something that she had left, on purpose.

When I was sure that Debbie was gone, I made coffee, rolled a joint and turned on the news. The news was a valuable tool for a hustler. I was addicted to finding out about current, national, and international events.

After I watched the top stories, I checked my pager and Precious was still blowing it up. It was time to formulate a good lie so she could back off.

Then I saw a number I didn't recognize, but when I saw the code—007—that Jay said he would use, I knew it was him.

I returned his call and he just wanted to get that money to my wife as soon as possible. I gave him her pager and then he said, "So what's up this morning, G Man? I'm just sitting here smoking a blunt, watching the news, and drinking some coffee."

By mentioning the news, he'd just gone three for three on my ass. I told him that I was doing the same thing.

We set a time to meet at Big Russ' house later.

Next, I called the 800 number and checked on the package. Mississippi was two hours ahead of California, so it wasn't expected to arrive for a couple of hours.

I took a shower and dressed, though my mind stayed on that package. Even though I'd been through the process many times, I'd be anxious until that package reached its destination.

Once dressed, I called the overnight shipping company again and the automated operator stated the package was en route, so I called Vince to give him a heads up. I instructed him to page me and put the number seven as the code when the package arrived.

The number seven was for the number of years I'd spent locked up. I already had two strikes under California Law, and was looking at twenty-five-to-life for just about any crime now. No hustle was worth that, so I vowed not to take too many risks.

Before I walked out, I called Russ. "Have you heard from Monster?" I asked.

"Big Homie, all kinds of motherfuckers are answering our phones! But I ain't tripping off the phones, I just need my fucking car back." Russ let out a long breath and asked, "Yo son, do you know where Monster be hanging out at?"

"Shit, your guess is as good as mine, homie."

"Nigga, I can't even call the police on this dude because I know he's a killer."

I told Russ to calm down until I arrived. I grabbed a CD that fit my mood — Outkast's new album.

Coming up with a plan to return to Mississippi would be no easy task. First, I'd have to explain it to my mom, because the town was small as hell and everyone gossiped.

As soon as I pulled onto the Hollywood Freeway, I lit a joint and turned up the volume.

The more tokes I took, the better the bass sounded. Then it came to me: My mother knew that my wife and I argued. I would tell her that Debbie was stressing me out and I needed a break for a month or two. Now all I had to come up with was an income alibi. I couldn't hang out in

Mississippi paying bills with no job to explain the cash flow.

A few miles down the road, the second big thought slammed into me: I would tell everybody that I had just settled a nice-size lawsuit.

I smiled, turned the music up a little more, and got lost in the rhythm of that pounding bass. The pager vibrated on my hip. It was Vince's number, followed by a seven.

My smile widened as I released a deep breath; I was in business. When I pulled up in front of Big Russ's apartment, Jay's car was already parked outside. I heard Russ' booming voice all the way out on the sidewalk. The smell of chronic — good ass weed — seeped outside, too, along with Reggae music so loud that Russ couldn't hear me banging on the door. I walked around the side of his apartment and peered through the window. Jay sat on the edge of the bed. Russ had his back to me as he ran his mouth.

Jay and I made eye contact. I put a finger to my lips, then I banged on the wall with all my might.

"Freeze, motherfucker!"

Big Russ spun around with a startled look, but then relaxed when he saw me. "Yo son, why the fuck you gotta blow a nigga's high like that, Big Homie?"

Russ opened the door and passed a blunt as we strolled to the bedroom. He let me use one of his "chipped" phones and I stepped into the kitchen to call Vince.

"Hey, Big Cuz, what took you so long to answer my page? That shit done come and gone."

Only four hours later and the weed had made its rounds!

"I tried to tell you that shit was already sold before it got here. So what you want me to do with the cheese?"

It was hard to wrap my head around this news. That fast? "Hold tight. I'll call back in thirty minutes."

I slipped into a chair at the kitchen table. Avoiding a Mississippi hustle was unlikely now. The potential profits were too great and overcame any common sense.

I walked my ass right back into the bedroom and told Jay the news, knowing he'd be impressed. His pleased expression told me that it was all a done deal.

We were all happy then, not knowing that the hustle in Natchez, Mississippi would prove to be the biggest mistake that either one of us had ever made in our lives.

Chapter 28
Executing the Satellite Formula

Pulling away from Big Russ's spot, the first call I made wasn't about business. I had to call Tina.

"What's up, G?"

I always enjoyed the sound of her voice. Even though we weren't together, she would always be a special part of my life.

"I want to come by and see Greg," I told her.

"He hasn't made it home from school yet, but he should be here any minute."

"Okay," I told her, then rolled toward Hawthorne.

I was excited to go and see my son. Greg Jr. was ten years old, and he and I shared a special bond. The fact that he admired me was dangerous, though. Any young black male in the ghetto who looked up to someone who was as deep in the game as I was, was setting himself up for the same end.

The last thing I wanted was for my son to emulate me. That's why I made sure he never wanted for anything from the very first day I came home. I knew money couldn't buy love, but I dangled expensive carrots in front of him as an incentive for him to get good grades. I went the extra mile to encourage him to complete his education so he could become everything that I wasn't.

So far, it had worked.

Greg Jr. was waiting outside on his porch when I pulled up. A warm sensation flooded my body every time I laid eyes on him. When he saw me, he ran to me and jumped into my arms.

We embraced for what seemed an eternity. As always, I told him, "I love you, son," since I knew that tomorrow wasn't promised. Then, I went right to the same question. "How are your grades?"

"Pretty good, Daddy."

We had a "no secrets" pact. We talked about damn near anything, so I didn't have to worry about him lying to me. I didn't lie to him either. When he posed questions to me about the illegal side of my life, I answered, but I still steered him toward staying in school and as far away from street life as possible.

I hung out with Greg and Tina for a few hours while Tina cooked some of her famous tacos. After we ate, I gave Greg Jr. a hundred dollars, even though I was damn near broke. I then sent him back out to the truck to look for something that wasn't actually there.

When he went outside, I strolled into the kitchen and grabbed Tina from behind before moving my hand around to the front of her tight ass shorts. She wore them on purpose. Tina was the biggest tease and she knew it.

A small moan rumbled in her throat before she caught herself and said, "You need to stop, G. Your son is here."

I turned her to face me and planted a passionate kiss on her lips as my fingers eased under her panties.
I played in that wetness for a brief moment. Then, I released her, gave her a peck on the lips, and strolled out the door to hug Greg, Jr.

"I love you, son," I told him, before I left.

Heading toward the Valley, I placed a call to Vince. "Send the money Western Union. I'll need all of it. I had to put all this shit together on limited funds."

Before I could finish my little speech, in that country drawl of his, he replied, "Hey, Big Cuz, you ain't even got to go into all dat shit. I got yo' back, I know dat it's gonna be greater later."

With that, Vince proved to be the perfect foundation for me to build on. He could very well become my right-hand man.

Next I called Cowboy, and when he answered the music was so loud I couldn't hear a damn thing.

"Turn that shit down!" I shouted.

Cowboy was the complete opposite of Vince. Before I could even get a word in, he said, "Mane, what's cracking wit' you, Big Homie? Sheeeiitt!! Mane, all we did down here wit' dat teaser was stir up a bee's nest. These square dancing ass wannabe ballers done lost dey minds behind dat West Coast fire you sent down here. Dees dudes is blowin' my pager out da' water fo' sho."

I held in my anger. "You're talking way too much over the fucking phone."

"True dat, Big Homie. My bad."

I blasted him with, "Check this out, Cowboy, you need to calm the fuck down and start thinking or I'm not gonna fuck with you, Cuz. I hope you ain't telling motherfuckers down there that I'm the one sending this shit."

His silence was my answer.

I gave him a tongue lashing. "Never let your left hand know what your right hand is doing. Meaning, the less people know about your business, the better. Never let anybody anticipate your next move. Meaning, if they know which way you're headed they can a) set you up b) use it against you to hone in your business and take over c) get you busted by letting the info drop to the wrong people at the wrong time.

"Never shit where you sleep. Meaning, don't do business on your home turf. The way you start off is the way it'll end. Meaning, if you start off sloppy — such as the way you had just handled your business, then things will end up sloppy.

"And I don't handle my business sloppy. I can't fuck with anyone who could fuck up my game. So, just keep your mouth shut and wait until you hear from me."

Schooling Cowboy was going to be a job, but I needed him —for now.

I walked into my apartment to find that the warden had posted up on my ass again.

"Yeah, you slid by me last night, sweetheart, but you need to tell me what the fuck is going on. I know motherfucking well that you're not thinking about going back down to Mississippi," Debbie said. "I'm not bullshitting with your ass this time, Greg. And who the fuck is Cowboy? And why in the fuck has he been calling the house all day? Look at the caller ID! He's called here at least ten times."

Damn, that Cowboy had fucked up again!

"You probably got some bitch down there waiting on your silly ass."

I did my best to duck the barrage of questions. After about an hour of getting nowhere, Debbie went to the bedroom and once again, slammed the door behind her.

I picked up the phone, but before I dialed out, the door swung open and she growled, "Here's Jay's shit."

She tossed his new social security number attached to a printout from the DMV, and slammed the door again.

I watched the news until I thought the coast was clear, then made the first call to Jay. He agreed to come first thing in the morning to get his profile.

Next, I called Cowboy's silly ass. "Quit calling my fucking house!"

213

"True dat. My bad, Big Homie." I then called Precious and explained that I would give her the money, but, "I've got to put some shit together, so lay off."

Before I hung up, I had her put Julius on the phone and I told him that I loved him.

After all of my calls, I did my favorite thing — I walked out onto the balcony and lit a joint. Looking at the city lights calmed me; this was a nightly ritual I looked forward to.

My lungs expanded from the potent marijuana and I tried to keep from coughing and waking Debbie. Marijuana had a way of enhancing the senses. The lights I took in a few seconds ago now looked animated and dreamy.

I went back inside, put out the joint, closed my eyes and visualized my next day. I was asleep within minutes.

Chapter 29
Deadly Premonitions

I woke up early the next morning soaking wet. I had tossed and turned all night and I tried to remember the dream that had caused me to have such restless sleep.

I turned on the news, made some coffee, and rolled another joint to kick the morning off. The alarm in the bedroom sounded, giving me fifteen minutes or so before my quiet time would end.

Grabbing a joint, I went out onto the balcony. The morning's smoggy haze rested over L.A., and I stood there, staring at downtown for awhile. When I heard the shower in the bathroom turn on, I hit the joint again and exhaled.

Then my mind filled with the dream I had last night. It was a nightmare, really, something that had been haunting me since 1986 when I was charged with attempted murder.

In this crazy ass nightmare I was given a choice to choose which limb I would rather lose — an arm or leg.

I chose the arm every time; I'd rather be able to walk. Each time I had that dream, I woke up sweating like a research monkey, wondering what message was being sent to my subconscious.

"Greg, do you want me to make you breakfast real quick before I leave?"

I'd expected a question from my wife, but that wasn't it. Her pleasant attitude threw me. What had changed?

I didn't ask her, though. The peace offering to make me breakfast was refreshing.

Debbie woke my stepdaughter for school, then she made grits, eggs, and bacon and went on about her day without talking shit.

The moment Debbie left, my pager vibrated. I thought it was Jay, but it was Misty.

I hated when Misty paged me. No matter where I was or what I was doing, she expected me to call her back. And it was hard not to because of the way she'd taken care of me when I was locked up. Plus, there was always the chance that she was calling with a big money job set up — something that would keep me from going to Mississippi.

When I called her back, she answered in that raspy voice, "Hey, son, what's going on? Why the hell haven't you called me, boy?" Before I could get a word in, she said, "Come up and see me today; I need to see you."

Misty never asked if I was busy; she just told me what to do. I was tired of that old rich bitch calling the shots.

But as usual, I asked, "What time do you want me up there?" "As soon as possible."

I told her I would see her later.

I waited for Jay. He'd insisted that he come to my place to pick up his new profile to take to the DMV — a test if I had ever heard one. I would have done the same thing. Hustling meant knowing where a dude laid his head. You had to evaluate the other person's lifestyle.

Just like when I took that trip to Li'l Man's house and saw his living situation. Not only did I understand his position of not giving a damn about where he lived, but it clued me in to his issues — gambling and his lack of self-restraint.

Jay wanted to make sure that everything added up before making that final commitment to me. All my shit was in order, so I didn't worry.

As I waited, I made another cup of coffee and glanced down at a single piece of paper on the kitchen table with figures that I had put together concerning potential profits from the new hustle.

When I fell asleep last night, the paper was on the living room table and now I knew why Debbie was so cool. She'd seen the paper and the figures and my wife was no dummy when it came to money; she was going to let this trip to Mississippi ride.

Now that it looked like this was really going to happen, once again, I went over every detail of the plan, this time including other factors: the police, the haters, the postal system, the overnight delivery system, the jackers, airport security, Greyhound bus security, snake bitches and anything else we could encounter. Organizing a major operation was worse than being the CEO of a large corporation.

Especially since nobody played fair. We made up the rules as we went along. And unlike in Corporate America, lawsuits didn't level things out; street justice was the call to order. Murder was always a possibility and that alone added a stress factor.

I decided that I would fly into Jackson, Mississippi and then get a ride into Natchez, which was just under two hours away. Good ol' cousin Opey was square enough, so I called him right then.

"Hey now, Big Cuz, what's going on out there in Hollywood?"

Opey had never been to Cali, and he, like most country folk, thought movie stars walked the streets or lived next door.

Opey's fascination with L.A. made it easy for the lies to roll off my tongue. "I'm coming back. I'm looking for new talent for Watani's entertainment production company." I went on to tell him when to pick me up from the airport, with instructions not to mention my visit to a soul because I wanted to "surprise my mother."

Minutes after that, the buzzer sounded. Jay had arrived. I greeted him at the door, then watched him as he scanned the living room. Approval flashed in his eyes.

"Do you want some coffee?" I asked.

He nodded, and as we both sipped our cups, I slipped the paper with the figures in front of him.

He gave it a brief once-over.

"Okay, Big G, I'm gonna drop you five hundred bucks. Let's make a list of supplies that we're gonna need to do this shit right. A top of the line vacuum sealer, latex gloves, lead paper, and a commercial scale that could weigh up to at least a hundred pounds."

I scribbled that list down as he gave it to me. He said, "I'm waiting on my people to drop twenty pounds. By the time you set up shop, the shit will be there."

We talked for a couple of hours, solidifying the plans, and then agreed to hook up later.

When he left, I got ready to see Misty. She didn't play that flashy shit, and I didn't feel like hearing a lecture. So, I threw on some sweats and a white t-shirt.

I loved her beautiful million dollar home, but I hated the drive because the traffic was always so fucked up. A one-hour trip could easily turn into three. I couldn't even smoke a fucking joint on the way there; Misty would surely know that I was high and she didn't play that shit either.

I slid in a Kenny G CD because jazz was what I needed to evaluate the situation from beginning to end once again. I had pulled off some hustles in my time, but this one was the motherfucker of all hustles. Cross country, new players, new employees, new shipping system, hometown relatives — one hell of cash cow if it was handled right. Twenty-five-to-life if it wasn't.

I arrived at Misty's house and found Mexican workers on a landscaping project out front, two others were waxing and detailing cars in the driveway, and another was loading supplies into a van. Two Chevy low riders sat among the rest of the expensive vehicles.

The whole scene was disturbing. Misty's house stood out and she was committing the kinds of mistakes that she warned me about: a) Don't call attention to yourself; b) Never expose your hand to your neighbors and c) Never get comfortable.

I shook my head as I made my way to the door; her Spanish maid of twenty years answered. The woman still couldn't speak a lick of English, but she greeted me with a smile and I moved past her to the office that Misty had set up.

As I approached, I heard her voice. She was on the phone, but she ended the call the moment she saw me.

"Hey, son," she said, giving me a hug. "What took you so long to get your ass up here?" She didn't give me time to respond. "I finally got that shit you were asking me about. Come on out to the garage and let me show you something."

I followed her and she opened a cabinet to display ten kilos of cocaine stacked along two shelves. Wow! I couldn't believe it. Misty had violated another major rule: Don't shit where you eat. Keeping the drugs in-house was asking for trouble. Possession was nine-tenths of the law. Her house. Her drugs. Her felony. Her time. Bottom line.

I locked gazes with her. "Mom, what the fuck are you doing?"

Before she could tell me, her young boyfriend walked into the garage.

And this was one of the reasons why she and I weren't as cool as we used to be.

She'd been fucking with this young dude on her payroll. It was hard to accept her being a sugar mama when she was a true gangster.

Dude wore a diamond encrusted Rolex on one wrist and the matching bracelet on the other. He had the "full kit" that flashy, high rollers wore — big neck chain and all.

I looked him dead in his eyes and shook his hand only out of respect for Misty. A moment of awkward silence followed when I didn't take my eyes off of him. He looked away, then turned his back to me as he walked out of the garage.

"So how many do you need, son?"

"Shit, mom, I ain't in Sacramento anymore. I'm on my way to Mississippi now."

Misty didn't miss a beat. "Well, I'm pretty sure they smoke crack down there."

I explained the operation I was about to get into and all Misty said was, "Well, how many pounds do you need to get started?"

I said, "I'm cool for right now, Mom. My partner's got me covered, but if I need you, I'll call." I hugged her. "I still got a lot of shit to do in the next few days."

She warned me to "be careful around those country dudes because they're hungry down there."

I could have told her that she was already housing "hungry," and his young ass was going to eat her alive.

Instead of going back through the house past her stud, I opened the garage door.

Misty pointed to one of those Chevy Low Riders. "Greg's got about a hundred grand into these damn cars."

Yeah, her young stud was named Greg, too; another reason not to like his ass.

"What the fuck am I supposed to do with all this shit you had me get?" she asked, trailing me to the car. "Tell your boys that I'll give them a cool deal if they buy more than one kilo."

I couldn't wait to get in my car and light my joint. With what I had just witnessed, it wouldn't have mattered if I had showed up to her house as high as a motherfucker. That day, I lost a great deal of respect for Misty.

My mind was back in Mississippi as Kenny G belted some soulful jazz. I called Jay to give him my flight plans and he told me he had been to the DMV and had to stick around until his I.D. came.

Jay then asked, "How are you going to get the 'mail' to Mississippi once we're both down there?"

I answered, "My wife always handles my mail and business when I'm out-of-town."

That was cool with Jay and I hung up. But I had barely put the phone down before Big Russ called.

"Yo, Big G. What's up, Big Homie?" he asked, his voice sounding so loud, it was like it was coming through a bullhorn. "Have you heard from Monster yet? I can't hustle without my wheels, son."

"Quit crying, homie. You act like I keep him in my back pocket. All you can do is wait and see what the fuck happens."

He was still whining when I hung up.

My thoughts were back on my business. We needed a mule to bring the first twenty pounds to Mississippi. I couldn't risk an outside source on that kind of weight and my mind went straight to Cheerio.

Cheerio was a crackhead, but he was the best at transporting dope. He'd worked for me before when I had out-of-town hustles and he was petrified of me, so I didn't have to worry about him running off with my shit. I would have Serge locate Cheerio for me.

I treated this like a complicated game of chess; all the pieces had to be in place before the first move could be made. Cowboy and Opey were rooks. Vince and Jay were knights. Debbie was the Queen. And I: Grego, Braniac, G Man, Big Homie, Big G, Big Cuz, Son, was the King himself.

On Jay's personal chess board, things might have been a little different — I might be considered a Knight, while he anointed himself the King. But the truth was, it was my plan, my outlets, my people, my risks, and my ass.

Bottom line — I was the master of the game.

Chapter 30
No Turning Back

Two weeks later, I was on a DC-7 plane looking out the window as it barreled onto the runway at Jackson Memorial Airport. The flight went by quickly because I was mapping, remapping, weighing, analyzing and mentally moving pieces on the board.

As the wheels hit the ground, the potent odor of weed jarred me and I tapped my shirt pocket. I had picked up a half ounce of chronic before I left L.A., stuffed it into a balloon, compressed it to the size of a golf ball, and tied it twice. I'd hidden it in my pocket, just in case I had to swallow it.

I know it was a stupid risk, but I had to have some good ol' Cali weed. But it seemed like this Cali weed was a bit too potent.

As I exited from the plane, I put on my game face. I strolled through the airport and didn't look anybody directly in the eyes. I had to be cool, just in case my moves were being watched by an undercover cop.

Dockers, prescription glasses, low top Timberlands, a fisherman's hat, plain shirt, and a USA Today newspaper was tucked under my arm. I had to blend in with the crowd.

I walked at a brisk pace, stopped to get a cup of coffee, and looked at my watch every three minutes just like the rest of the squares.

By the time I grabbed my luggage, good ol' Cousin Opey was waiting for me curbside. We jumped on the highway headed to Mama's house.

I kept my game flowing with small talk — shucking and jiving as it's called. I reached into my carry-on, pulled out a couple of Tupac's CDs and handed them to Opey,

"Here you go, little cousin."

His eyes lit up. "Hey now, Big Cuz! That's what I'm talkin' 'bout." Cousin Opey spoke in a slow country drawl just like his father—my Uncle Ernest. "Straight up, Cali style. Thanks, mane! I sho' 'nuff ' preciate dis here. Let me put one of these CDs in."

Opey chose my favorite, "Me Against the World." There was silence for a moment before the intro faded in, the volume increasing with the words, *"At twelve twenty-five a.m. Wednesday, Tupac was on his way into a Times Square building to record at an eighth floor studio with another rapper, but in the lobby Shakur was shot several times including two graze wounds to the head. . ."*

By the time the song started I was in deep thought. 'Pac's music did that to me. The first song, "If I Die 2nite," had lyrics that burned into my soul.

Cousin Opey was bobbing his head and singing along with Tupac. I gazed out the window as we traveled along the two lane highway and nervousness set in. I was about to look my mama right in the eyes and tell a bold-faced lie. Shit, I needed a joint!

But there were three reasons why that wouldn't be a good idea: a) I needed to be on top of my game, b) my Uncle Earnest just might be there and he could smell a lie from damn near a mile away, and c) the weed would make me think too much.

Tupac crooned, "So Many Tears. . ." The bass line pounded.

"I shall not fear no man but God. Though I walk through the valley of the shadow of death. . ." and he went on to tell how he had shed "So Many Tears."

Opey reacted to the song. "Damn Cuz, dat's the shit right der, mane."

That country ass dude ruined a good song by trying to sing along with it. But, I gave him some dap — and let him enjoy the music while I tuned him out. The drive down the highway to Mama's house was one long ass ride.

* * *

A mile away from my family's property, the sky turned pitch black. A lone street light illuminated our property through the tall pine trees, giving it a halo effect. This visual was soothing and welcoming.

I grabbed my luggage from the bed of the truck and paused at the front door. Inside, my mother was humming a gospel song. Now that was music to my ears!

She sat at the kitchen table, curlers all over her head as she paid bills. She was draped in a worn out light green robe and had reading glasses perched on the tip of her nose. There was a low fire glowing from the fireplace behind her and the smell of fresh burnt pinewood filled the warm room.

Her head snapped up. "Grego, what on God's earth are you doing back down here, boy?"

I was at a loss for words for all of maybe a half second. "Mama, I got homesick."

Well, that wasn't a lie. Then I followed with the "other" lie "Debbie and I. . . we're having some problems."

I was glad that my Cousin Opey was there. With him being a complete square, he was the credibility that I needed to pull this off. As soon as I was convinced that my mother bought it, I told Opey, "I'll holla at you in the morning," translation: I'm tired of your country ass and it's time for you to leave.

Dakari's high pitched voice carried into the house as Opey walked out. When my nephew walked in the door, I gave him a big hug. It was good to see Dakari. I hadn't had the chance to spend time with him the last time I was here.

My nephew was what many considered a hood baby. Yes, my sister's son had pretty much been raised on the streets of Los Angeles.

Even though Sheila lived with my mom after Dakari was born, she was out of control and my mother had no say in how her grandson was raised.

But when my mother moved to Natchez, Sheila sent Dakari to live with her, putting another burden on my mother. I'd heard how Dakari was disrespectful and was really more than my mother could handle. That was one good thing about me being here for an extended period of time. I was going to put him in check.

Dakari stepped back from our hug. "Hey, Unc, what you doing back down here? You just left, mane." It hadn't taken him long to take on a Southern country drawl.

But right then, I wasn't thinking about his accent. I gave Dakari a hard look and didn't say another word. Even though he was only nine, he had been around long enough to know that questioning me was not the thing to do.

My stare made him nervous and he giggled a little, then looked away in a move that was nothing but respect. He respected and idolized my high-risk lifestyle. I hated that.

My mother turned to me. "Grego, are you hungry?"

"Heck, yeah, I'm hungry, Mama."

It didn't take her long to whip up smothered pork chops, vegetables and cornbread. Before I could even finish my plate, I heard Uncle Ernest's truck pull up. My mother's place was so peaceful and quiet, I could tell whose car or truck was coming down the gravel road — even from a half-mile away.

I wasn't ready to deal with him — my Uncle Ernest had always been a father figure for me from the time I was little. But now, I felt like he was the cop of the family.

I had come prepared for this meeting. Before I left Los Angeles, I stopped at a surplus store and purchased the best pair of overalls they had in stock. I quickly laid them across the back of one of the kitchen chairs before my uncle came in.

My uncle's giant frame filled the doorway and his weary eyes focused on me. His heavy, deep voice filled the room as he spoke in the slow, country drawl. "Well, look at wat da devil done sent us." Then his gaze shifted to the coveralls. He walked across the room, picked them up with his huge leathery hands, and said, "Looks like Santa done come a little early for me."

I smiled.

He joined my mother and me at the table, but even though my uncle was smiling, fear churned a hole in my stomach. These were the two most important people in my life and I was sitting across from them, lying.

That's why I didn't stay out there long with them. I kept the visit short, told everybody good night, and rushed to the room that I was sharing with Dakari.

"Hey, Unc," Dakari said. "Vince and Cowboy done been down here today looking for you." He gave me a sly smile letting me know that his little ghetto-to-country ass had already put two and two together and come up with five.

"Take your ass to sleep. And for the record, you ain't seen shit and you don't know shit."

229

"Unc, you already know I know what time it is."

I took a quick shower, then turned the lights out and lay there evaluating the day's events. I had managed to make it by my mother and uncle — at least tonight. Tomorrow held a whole new set of challenges.

I closed my eyes and began my nightly ritual of visualizing my next moves.

Then, Dakari's squeaky voice interrupted my thoughts. "Hey Unc, now I could be wrong, but I think I smell some chronic."

Damn, I had forgotten about that! But it was tucked away. How in the hell did he smell it?

"Nephew, take your little ass to sleep."

This time I closed my eyes and listened to the surroundings. Unlike Los Angeles, the place was nothing but peaceful. The chirping of crickets was like music.

A flash of light outside my window startled me. I jumped out of the bed and Dakari roared with laughter.

"What the hell you tripping on, mane? Dem ain't nuttin' but fire flies. You sho' nuff been gone too long."

He was still laughing as I grabbed my pillow and banged him up a little. He returned the attack and we kept at it until my big ass got tired and called it quits.

Damn it felt good to be away from Los Angeles. Even with what was ahead of me, my stress level had been reduced by at least half.

We settled down and I went back to my thoughts. How was I going to get those twenty pounds down here? How was I going to slide Jay in town?

I finally drifted off to sleep with the smell of cow manure and wild grass in my nose and Dakari's snoring in my ears.

* * *

The next morning I woke up feeling like I was in a twilight zone, until I glanced over at Dakari. Then I smelled it: the wonderful aroma of breakfast calling out to me.

I sat up and made a quick call to Vince, giving him two instructions, to come in about thirty minutes, and act totally surprised to see me.

The first order of the day was to make the rounds and get my own story planted about why I was in town before something else circulated. With the high unemployment, there was plenty of time for folks to sit on the porch and gossip. The story could end up that I was about to run for Mayor or something.

My nephew was still sound asleep and I snatched all the covers off his skinny ass.

He jolted from the bed, shrieking, "Hey, Unc, what's up wit' you, mane? It's cold as heck in here!"

"Get your punk ass up and help your granny with anything she wants you to do. And you better not let me find out that you're giving her any problems."

I hit the shower and by the time I finished eating breakfast, Vince walked through the door. He locked a gaze on me for a split second, then rolled the rest of the way into the kitchen.

"Hey, Big Cuz, when you make it back down this way, mane?"

I rolled with his play and made small talk, then went to the bedroom and left a list of chores for Dakari to finish by the time I got back.

Before I left, I kissed my mother. "I love you, Mama."

My first stop was to see my Aunt Thelma, my grandmother's sister. Aunt Thelma was the shot caller; she was a small confident woman with a lot of power who had earned the right to hold the Matriarch title of our family ever since my grandmother died in 1977. Seeing her would be the biggest test of all, especially since I hadn't seen her when I was here last time.

But this time, it was imperative that I visited her. She was a very wise woman and like a human polygraph machine. She had a special gift of being able to "read" people. So if I could get past my mother, my uncle and Aunt Thelma, I'd be home free.

Vince and I pulled up in front of her house and the squeaky screen door announced our arrival. We ventured into the kitchen, where she usually was during that time of the day.

When we walked in and I didn't see her, I called out, "Hey, Aunt Thelma, where are you?"

Her voice rang out from some other place in the house. "Grego, is that you? Have a seat in the kitchen and cut yourself a piece of cake."

A few moments later, Aunt Thelma appeared. A petite woman with silky, salt and pepper hair that complemented her smooth, olive complexion, she already had me sweating and she hadn't even asked me a question yet.

"I heard you were here. What happened? You changed your mind about going back to California?"

She knew damn well that I had gone back. I kept my composure and ran my well-rehearsed lines past her. We sat there for a good hour, and everything was cool. I got past her! Now all I had to do was let the country grapevine take its course. It was only a matter of time before I would be "officially" cleared by the family.

Now it was time to put the next phase into action. I found the closest juke joint, which was on the next road over. Black Dot's was a wooden shack nestled in a group of family homes, with a pool table, a jukebox, a makeshift dance floor, and a steady flow of alcohol. The place was named after the owner who was short, fat, and black as tar.

Security was unheard of in that two-sheriff town. The laws made it legal to carry a weapon just as long as it was visible. Packing a pistol was like carrying a cigarette lighter —potentially deadly, but necessary.

Vince opened the door to the joint. The place was dimly lit so I moved slowly, allowing my eyes a few moments to adjust from the bright April sunlight. I scanned the room, paying close attention to everybody's position.

I'd worn a few pieces of simple, but expensive diamond-encrusted gold jewelry and I laid them on the edge of the pool table before I picked up a pool stick. My body language told everyone that I was not from the area.

The whole time I played, I looked around without ever really looking around. I was scoping out three things: the haters, the hustlers, and the females.

Over the years in the game, I realized that females were the key to any city. Pillow talk was priceless. The woman had to be street savvy, not a real looker, someone with low self esteem. She also had to work a 9-to-5, have her own place, a car, and have no more than two kids.

But there was one most important question that I asked a woman...and it was either a deal maker or deal breaker: "Do you have a diary?" If she said yes, it was a wrap. A diary was worse than a confession.

The first impression is a lasting one, so I made sure that onlookers saw at least one hundred-dollar bill in my bankroll, no matter how broke I was. I paid for the pool games, beer, and chicken wings. I made sure that we looked like we were having a ball, while my peripheral vision kept me on top of who was taking it in.

I really paid attention to what the chicks were playing on the jukebox. Heartbreak music conveyed that either a man had just left her, she was looking for a man, or her man was cheating. I had to be careful because dudes down there would do a nigga real harm for fucking with their women.

After a few games, we headed into town to find Cowboy and we saw him right away. I spotted him first, wearing fake ass jewelry and holding an animated conversation with some other wannabes.

When he laid eyes on me, he jumped right into his usual hustler Cowboy role.

"Aw shit, it's on and cracking now, pardners. My big cuz done touched back down in dis bitch fo' sho', mane."

"Get your silly ass in the car, playa, and shut the fuck up."

He gave me a head nod. "True dat, Big Cuz. Let's hit some corners and smoke some of dis' fire I'm holdin'."

As we pulled off, I said, "Don't even pull that bullshit out. I brought y'all some real shit from Cali. Let's hit the store and grab a few blunts."

We stopped at the mom and pop store and Cowboy rolled the blunt as we drove away. He inhaled, then coughed so hard his whole face turned red. Vince and I laughed all the way back to Black Dot's.

There were a few more cars than before, as people were getting off from work. I ran the game plan past them. Vince and Cowboy were two different kind of hustlers and that meant they had separate tasks.

"Cowboy, I need you to peep out all game. Let me know who's who, while Vince and I continue to shoot pool."

Before we went inside, I took off my button down shirt and sported the white-tee underneath. My size would make my presence felt without me saying a single word.

We made our way over to the vacant pool table and I gave Cowboy a hundred-dollar bill to buy beer.

Vince and I started the game, but I caught a chick over by the jukebox checking me out. She made a selection and Anita Baker's "Same Ole Lovin'" blared through the speakers. She had my attention already!

She wore a navy blue school bus driver's uniform. Her body was kinda tight and her nails were done. My luck couldn't be this good.

She took a seat at the bar and continued drinking. Anita was followed by Earth, Wind, and Fire's, "After the Love Has Gone," along with the female now taking a shot of hard liquor instead of beer.

Cowboy was talking to some dudes sporting gold teeth and thick gold chains. I kept my eye on him as Vince and I started our next game.

Then music selection number three hit the air. Al Green's, "How Do You Mend A Broken Heart?"

Damn, three for three!

I looked up at Vince. "Hey, young homie, do you know who home girl is over there?"

"Naw, but I think Cowboy used to fuck wit' her cousin."

I made eye contact with Cowboy and motioned for him to come over. When he stood next to me, I asked, "What's up with home girl over there? Don't you know her?"

Cowboy's gaze shifted to the woman. "True dat, I still be fucking wit' her cousin. I peeped game, she been checking you out, Big Pimpin'. She cool as a motherfucker, too. But she be having big time attitude problems."

I chalked the attitude issue up as confidence. Some dudes didn't know the difference. Before I finished grilling Cowboy, one of my cousins walked in.

"Hey, big boy, yo' mama told us you was back. We knew that we'd catch your ass over here."

Minutes later, six of my cousins were hanging out with me, drinking and having that good old down south family fun shit. My stock value had just increased. Anyone trying to scope me out would see that I had a strong family presence.

The chick I had focused on walked right past me while making her move toward the exit, allowing me a better look at her. She had dark skin, wore prescription glasses, and was very tall, at least six feet tall. I made it a point to make eye contact with her, long enough to acknowledge her. My gut told me she held the key to the city, but until I got her in bed, I wouldn't know for sure.

We hung out there for a few more hours until I felt I had just about everything I needed to know. As Vince drove me home, I asked him to pull over.

"I need to call my wife," I told him.

I couldn't call Debbie at my mother's house. If my mother heard me, that would expose part of my lie. I dialed her number.

"Where in the fuck have you been, motherfucker?" my wife shouted into the phone. "I've been paging your ass all fucking day! I know your pager works, so go ahead and think of another lie. That's why I hate it when you take your ass out of town. You think you can do whatever the fuck you want."

The moment she let me get a word in, I said, "Baby, I left my pager at my mama's house and I just got home. You know I've got a lot of family down here to visit."

Her tone didn't change. "That's the first thing you know how to do is tell a lie. I just talked to Jay. He said he talked to you a couple of times today."

Damn, the warden had pumped another rookie friend of mine for info. I forgot to warn him. At this point, all I could do was stick with the original lie. I hurried off the phone with a promise to call her in the morning.

Then I called Serge. "What's up, little Bro? Have you located Cheerio for me yet?"

"Yeah, I told him that you want him to stop by and check in with me every day. He's ready."

The plan was coming together!

I finally made it to my mama's house and brought Vince in with me, making sure Mama saw me with the "right" company.

"Thanks for the ride, man. I'll see you in the morning."

As soon as Vince left, I went to the bedroom to check on Dakari.

"Did you help your Granny out today?"

"Yeah, Unc, I told you, I always help her out."

"I'm going to check it out myself. Don't make the mistake of lying to me."

Mama heated some leftovers and we watched the late news together.

During one of the commercials, Mama said, "Thelma called. She said you'd been by."

I waited to see if she would make any other comment. When she didn't, that reconfirmed that I had made it through the toughest part of my return.

But there was still my uncle to deal with and he showed up around midnight. When I saw him wearing the new coveralls, I smiled.

I had a feeling Uncle Ernest was there to check up on me, so I sat with him and my mother around the kitchen table for another hour, though it felt like at least three.

It seemed like I was passing the test with my uncle too, and for the next few days, I just hung out with Vince. He picked me up and took me everywhere I needed to go, including going to visit Auntie Lena. While I was there talking to her, she told me that she was concerned about the note on her trailer home. That gave me an idea.

I didn't say anything to my aunt, but as soon as I left her, I called Watani.

"I'll take over the payments on your mom's trailer as long as I'm in Mississippi."

Watani agreed that was a good idea, taking some financial stress off of him. And that worked for me; I wouldn't be under my mother.

That afternoon when I spoke with Jay, he told me, "I'm having a little problem getting that twenty pounds. I'll send five to get things rolling."

"Okay, I'll have Cowboy find an address to use and I'll call you later."

I put in a call to Cowboy and when he answered, he started talking too much. "Mane, what's cracking, Big Homie? I got all dees cowboys on deck and ain't nuttin' out there right now and —"

"Listen, playa," I said, trying to keep my frustration in check. "You have to stop talking on this fucking phone. This is the last time I'm gonna speak on this." When he remained silent, I added, "Check this out, I need a cool address. Find one and hit me back. Pay attention to what the fuck I'm saying to you, Cowboy."

"True dat for realz dis time, Big Homie, it'll never happen again. Word is bond."

It would happen again and I knew it. But, he had that address in less than three minutes — one of the reasons for taking a chance on him.

When Cowboy called me back with the address, he also told me, "Ol' girl has been asking about you through my girl."

I knew who he was talking about and I had anticipated that move. The last few nights I'd seen her at Black Dot's. Though we still hadn't exchanged a word, I made sure that she saw me with plenty of money and I made sure that I selected the same kind of music that she did — the same artists, different songs.

Cowboy had also given me what I needed to know about her. Her name was Vikki, she had no kids, and lived alone in an apartment that charged according to a sliding scale.

The most valuable information that Cowboy had given me was that her boyfriend had just dumped her for a light-skinned chick.

It didn't get any better than that. Her self-esteem had taken a beating.

I told Cowboy, "Cool, I'll take it from here."

First, I called Jay with the address, then I called Vince to take me to Black Dot's.

As soon as we got to the juke joint, I scanned the room, but didn't see her. Vince and I shot pool for a while before Cowboy showed up and I moved to the jukebox.

I could feel the heat of someone's stare, and though I still hadn't spotted her, I selected The Temptations' "How Could He Hurt You?"

When I turned around, Vikki was only a few barstools away.

I walked past her, getting as close as I could without actually touching her. In an almost whisper I said, "What's up Vikki?" without breaking stride to the pool table.

"How you know my name?"

Whatever else she said was drowned by the music. The lyrics of the song did the rest of the work.

How can he treat you like that?
'Cause if I had your love I'd never let you go
How could he cheat on you...

I returned to the pool table with Vince and before the song was even halfway through, he said, "Mane, you's a bad motherfucker. Your girl's on her way over here right now."

She walked up to me as though she had all the confidence in the world. "I need to talk to you. Outside."

I laughed. "What did I do?"

She responded with a country drawl, "Don't worry 'bout what you did, jus' meet me outside in five minutes."

I hadn't realized that she had such a strong country accent; it was sexy as hell.

She turned and walked away. Vince shook his head and smiled.

I walked to the parking lot, already impressed. She could have scored some points by walking with me through the club. Instead, she chose to be discreet.

Vikki was leaning on a car not too far from the side exit and motioned me over.

"Like I said inside, how do you know my name, Greg?"

"The same way you know mine."

She came back with, "Boy, that Cowboy is something else," and we both laughed.

Vikki gestured to her car. "Let's sit inside and talk, 'cause it's too damn hot out here."

She was right about that. My t-shirt was stuck to my body. Inside her car, she turned on the ignition and turned up the AC.

I asked, "Do you smoke weed?"

"Hell yeah!"

I had saved a little of that Cali chronic. I pulled out the small plastic baggie and the stench filled the car. Her eyes widened and I knew she had never smoked true chronic before.

She opened the glove box and pulled out a pack of blunts. "You want me to roll dat for you?"

I passed her the weed and let her do her thing. With well-manicured nails, she split the blunt, emptied the tobacco, and rolled a perfect joint. She put some fire to it and the sweet smell of quality marijuana filled the car.

Vikki took a powerful drag before she passed it to me. She tried her best to hold it in, but started coughing her ass off. I couldn't help but laugh.

When she regained her composure, she said, "I don't see what's so damn funny, Mr. Greg. Wat chu' come all da' way down here from L.A. for anyway?"

"Who said I was from L.A.?"

"E'rbody down here know where you from."

I'd done my homework and Vikki had done hers, too. But before I could say a word, she held up her hand to keep me from telling a lie. "Never mind, I don't even wanna know, boy."

We smoked about half the blunt before I decided it was time to shake Vikki. I couldn't expose my hand until I found out where her head was.

"Are you coming to Black Dot's tomorrow?" I asked.

"Yeah."

"Let's hook up tomorrow, then."

I had put enough on her mind to keep her thinking about me.

My pager went off twice as I stepped from Vikki's car. One was from Jay and the other was from my wife. I slipped back into her car and called Jay.

When he answered, I didn't say anything, so he said, "Tomorrow by twelve noon," and hung up.

I hung up too, and didn't make the other call. My wife would have to wait until tomorrow.

Vikki wrote down her number and handed it to me. "Tomorrow is Friday, so this place is gonna be jumping. I expect to see you here, Greg."

There was something sexy about the way she said my name in that deep country drawl — like it had two syllables instead of one.

I went back inside and got Vince and Cowboy. As we walked to the car I told them, "I've got that deal set up for tomorrow. I want to make sure we're all on the same page."

"We are," Cowboy said, then added, "I'm gonna hang out for a while and fuck with some more hos."

I inched forward so I stood toe-to-toe with him. "Listen playa, don't have your ass out all night. I need you on deck in the morning." I gestured to the club. "Put a bug in a few of those hustler's ears. Let 'em know that you should have something for 'em tomorrow."

"Sho' nuff, Big Homie, I'll hannel dat."

Vince and I headed toward home, but my pager went off, and I had him pull over again. My wife wasn't going to wait until tomorrow, so I called her. "Hey, baby."

"Hey, baby my ass! Why the fuck can't you answer your pager?"

I couldn't focus on my hustle with my wife all in my ear. She had been around me long enough to know my limit. I would shut down to a point where I wouldn't call her at all.

She must have sensed it, because she suddenly changed her tone. "Baby, I was just trying to let you know that Jay dropped your shit off over here and I sent it like I always do. Here's the tracking number."

I repeated the number loud enough for Vince to write down.

She ended the call with, "Baby, please be careful. Make sure you call me as soon as it gets there and I love you."

"I love you, too."

Vince dropped me off and we agreed he would come early the next morning. Even though it was late, my mom wasn't home yet. And neither was Dakari. There was no telling where Dakari was.

It was good to be alone, though, and in the bedroom, I sat on the edge of the bed, thinking about tomorrow.

There was no doubt that I enjoyed living life on the edge, and this was a big risk. But, what else was I supposed to do? Regardless of my intelligence and savviness, I was a felon, had just come off a seven-year stint in prison, and I didn't have a single degree. I had to provide for my family somehow, and to make the kind of money I needed meant that I had to apply my skills to the other side of the law.

And then, just like he always did when I had these dark thoughts, my father came to mind. I didn't think about him often anymore, but when I did, it was heavy. If he had been in my life, would I have made this trip to Natchez to start a hustle that could put me on the outs with my family and land me back in jail? Would I have done all the crazy shit that I had done my whole life? Would I have had a strong moral fiber if he had been around?

Anger filled me, just like it did anytime I thought about my sperm donor.

One specific vision always came to mind. I was twelve years old, out on my bike delivering papers. The rain was pouring so hard that I could barely see.

I was soaking wet and cold as hell. I passed by his house every single day on my route but on that day it stood out. The rain made his bright pink house with the white picket fence look so cozy and warm. Three new cars were lined up in his driveway. A big beautiful light grey Great Dane patrolled the back yard. I couldn't even knock on his door to ask to come out of the cold or get a ride home. His wife didn't like me or my brothers.

Those were questions I couldn't answer, questions I'd never be able to answer.

I went to the boom box on the dresser and turned on the radio. I flipped through the stack of CDs beside the boom box and found Big Syke's first solo album, "Be Yo' Self."

Perfect! This was a CD that always took me back to my neighborhood. Every lyric was profound, every song was a story. He told stories of my life, my past, my present, and my future. The future part is what scared me.

Song four on the disc was "Satellite Niggaz." I turned it up sky high and Big Syke's trademark laugh came through, which made me smile. I got lost in thought as his lyrics told my current story — my worries, my game and my mindset.

Satellite Niggaz all up in your hometown.

Cultivating the game, putting that California grind down.

"Dakari! Dakari!"

Mama was home!

"Dakari, I've told you a hundred times about playing that music so loud." She was still fussing as she burst through the bedroom door.

I stood there, feeling like a kid back in the day. I looked around and said, "Where is that boy, Mama? I just came back here to turn this damn thing down."

Dakari would have to ride this one for me. It was too early for me to be in that type of trouble. "Don't worry, Mama. I'll talk to him about it."

My mother went back to the kitchen and I headed for the shower. As the warm water cascaded over my body, the song's lyrics stayed with me.

How could Big Syke be so accurate about what I was into? Especially the very last line — *it don't take nothin' for me to play a bitch.*

It was too late to let my conscience bother me. Since other people depended on me, I had to focus.

I went back into the kitchen and told my mother about the agreement that I had made with Watani. She seemed relieved that someone would be staying in my aunt's trailer. Now I just had to run it past Uncle Ernest.

My nephew walked through the door and I said, "Dakari, why did you leave that radio on so loud, boy?"

He frowned and I quickly escorted him to the bedroom. "Just go ahead and take your shower, nephew, don't trip."

"Unc, what you done did and blamed on me?"

"Listen little nigga, didn't I just tell you don't trip? Get your ass in the shower so you can help me take my shit up to the trailer."

I'd only been back in the kitchen for about five minutes when Uncle Ernest strolled through the door.

"I've got something to tell you, Ernest." My mother ran the news about my aunt's trailer past him, and he agreed easily.

That didn't make me feel good. *Something's got to go wrong.*

But I didn't focus on that. I'd just have to figure that out later. As soon as we finished eating, my mother gave me the key to Aunt Lena's trailer and Dakari and I headed up there.

I opened the front door to my new spot, then switched on the living room lights. The place felt like a steam room and I located the thermostat and turned on the air conditioning. Next, I went to the master bedroom. I hadn't checked it out last time I was here, but now, I was taken aback; the master bathroom was huge. A skylight was right above the huge sunken tub and a separate shower was off to the left side. Two other bedrooms were on the other side of the living room.

I was ready to crash, but sat on the sofa and turned on the local news.

I picked up the receiver on the phone next to the sofa, and was shocked when I got a dial tone. Perfect! I wanted to put something on Vikki's mind before she went to bed.

She answered, sounding a little cautious.

Without even saying hello, I said, "Who are you thinking about right now?"

"Graeeg, you need to go on somewhere else wit dat mess. Who you think you are, boy? And what you doing callin' me tonight?"

"Baby, I wanted to hear your sexy ass country voice and tell you goodnight before I went to sleep."

Her laugh was low and throaty. "Boy, you sho' nuff is crazy. All right den. Thank you, Graeeg, I'll see you tomorrow, okay?"

"Good night, Vikki."

"Good night, Graeeg."

I hung up. *Yeah, she's all mine. That pillow talk would be coming real soon.*

Chapter 31
Setting Up Shop

I woke up early the next morning. The two hour time difference still had me a little off track, but I went to my mother's house, made a quick breakfast, and hung out with my nephew until Vince arrived.

We rolled on up the road to pick up Cowboy from his grandmother's house, which was about six houses down from where Vince stayed with his grandmother. We smoked a blunt in front of Cowboy's place as we waited for him.

I looked at my watch. Cowboy needed to bring his ass on; he finally came strolling out wearing nothing but a skull cap, jean shorts, and house shoes. He slipped into the back seat.

"Check this out, pretty boy," I said. "I don't know what the fuck you're thinking, but why ain't you ready to roll?"

"Roll where, mane? The package is coming right chere. I wasn't 'bout to take no chance using no bitch on dis first move, pardner."

Vince and I looked at each other for a couple of seconds, then burst out laughing, probably thinking the same thing: *Cowboy was crazy as cat shit.*

I looked back at Cowboy. "Nigga, have you lost your mind?"

Before he could reply, I said, "Vince, start this motherfucking car up. Let's park up under the tree in front of your house until the mail runs."

"I ain't sittin' out here," Cowboy said as he went back into the house.

But Vince and I sat out there, under the tree, in the sweltering heat. About an hour later, the mail truck passed by. My heart was pounding in my chest, but once I saw Cowboy sign for the package, a huge weight lifted from my shoulders. We watched the mailman fly past us on his way out.

Cowboy stood in the middle of the road, waving to get our attention.

"Vince, walk down there and grab the package from that nut. And get his scale, too."

A minute later, Vince and I were ready to take off, but Cowboy flagged us down, grinning like a fool. "Mane, I told you I had dis here shit covered, Big Pimpin'."

"Yeah right, Cowboy. Look, I'm headed to the trailer now. Make some calls to your boys and tell them to hang tight. I'll call you when I'm on my way back."

It didn't take long to get back to the trailer, break open the package and pour the contents onto the table. The marijuana was light green with red hairs all through it. It smelled as good as it looked. This was FIRE!

Seeing the product reminded me that I had to tell Cowboy something. I called him and said, "Hey playa, tell your boys that we only got zips for sale."

"Mane, I done already told a few of dem dat we got *pounds* for sale and —"

I hung up, then glanced at Vince who shook his head. Cowboy had fucked up again. He told them pounds when he didn't wait to hear what we actually had on hand! Even though Vince knew I was angry, I kept it inside; I didn't want him to see me go off.

I was in a better mood once I checked out the product. This was a better quality of marijuana than anticipated. I only paid $325 per pound back in Cali. I could sell the ounces for $100 apiece, which came to $1,600 a pound.

Contrary to Cowboy's plan, I would rather spread that good weed around the whole town, letting as many people as possible get a taste, then word would spread like wildfire.

While Vince and I were working, my pager went off two times: My wife and Misty. I headed into the bedroom, and this time, I called my wife first.

"Hey baby, did you get your mail?" Debbie said with a whole new attitude.

I waited a couple of seconds before I said, "Yeah, baby, thanks."

"Good, now you need to take care of the mailman. You know how this game works."

My wife had already included herself in this new venture. "You know I got you covered, baby. I love you."

Before I could hang up, she said, "Hold on, is this number on the caller I.D. the number to the trailer?"

Damn! I had slipped up. "Yeah, baby, I've got to go now, I'll call you later."

"Don't worry, I'll call *you.*"

So much for peace of mind.

I didn't even think about calling Misty. Really, I wanted to call Jay to give him our status, but like me, he absolutely hated to talk on the phone. My wife would get in touch with him.

I decided to make another call, though, this time to my son. And when he answered the phone, all I could do was smile. It always felt great to hear my son's voice.

"Hey daddy, where are you?"

"In Mississippi,"

And then, Greg, Jr. and I talked for almost half an hour. Before I ended the call, I made sure he had the number.

"Call me anytime," I said. "And I love you, Son."

Just as I hung up, Vince walked in. "Hey, Big Cuz, I done bagged up a whole pound already, but we done ran out of sandwich bags."

"Don't even trip, Li'l Homie. That's all we need to bag up for right now."

But then, my mind went to the next problem: *Where in the fuck am I supposed to keep this shit?*

I was too paranoid to hide it in the trailer. Hustling was one thing, but jeopardizing my family's property was not on the agenda. I walked through the kitchen and out the back door, which led to the woods. I came upon a blue and white ice chest. Perfect!

Returning to the trailer, I told Vince, "There's an ice chest out back. Put the product in there and go down into the woods. Be sure and cross over the fence to the next property and stash it there."

Vince handled the stash, cleaned the kitchen, and put the scale inside one of the cabinets. While he was out back, I put all the marijuana into a semi-clear plastic shopping bag and tossed it onto the kitchen table. Then, I went to the back door to check on Vince. I saw him walking up a small hill a few feet away.

Just as Vince stepped into the trailer, the front door opened and closed. Heavy footsteps shook the trailer.

Damn! I didn't lock the front door.

"Hey Grego! You in here, boy?"

Double Damn! Uncle Ernest! I was a grown ass man and scared as hell.

His deep baritone voice called out my name again.

A frog had caught in my throat, but I moved quickly. I couldn't let him see that bag on the kitchen table.

"Hey, Unc! Whatcha know good?"

I made my way over to the sofa and took a seat. To my relief, so did my uncle. The sounds of the plastic bag crinkling in the kitchen made Uncle's head whip in that direction. "Who dat wit you in here?"

Vince stepped into the living room. "Hey, Ernest. How you doing, Old Timer?"

"Ah! Well, I cain't complain. Get me a glass of cold water from out the fridge while you in der, youngen."

Vince and I briefly locked gazes as he opened the cabinet and tried to hold in his laughter. Uncle Ernest opened his mouth and I knew a story was bound to start. This was so not the right time!

But my uncle talked and talked, until he finally fell asleep, sitting straight up in that chair. Uncle Ernest was snoring so damn loud, people in the next county probably heard him.

And then, the front door to the trailer swung open again. "Hey Unc, how you like yo new spot?"

Dakari's loud ass mouth was right on time. Uncle Ernest woke, gathered himself, and left.

While I talked with Dakari, Vince was in the kitchen rolling us a blunt for the road. All of a sudden, Dakari stopped talking, whipped into the kitchen and took in the bag of weed on the counter.

"I knew you was up to something, Unc."

I grabbed him by the arm, and escorted him to the front. "Like I said before, you ain't seen nothing and you don't know nothing." I pushed him out the door and closed it behind him.

Minutes later, Vince and I jumped into the car, threw Tupac's "All Eyes On Me" in the player, lit the blunt, and drove to Black Dot's.

About five houses down the road, we passed a group of youngsters hanging out under a big tree with their pit bulls. All of them had their pants sagging and they threw up a West Coast W hand sign. They all knew who I was, but I would only know them by their parent's names.

"Vince, back up," I said when we'd driven a little past them. When we pulled up in front of the group, I leaned out of the window. "What's up, li'l homies, what y'all smoking on?"

The biggest one spoke up. "Nuttin'." He leaned my way and said, "Mane, don't you know me? My name is Coron. My mama's name is Van. She said y'all went to school together."

I took a moment to search my memory bank and came up empty. "Naw, not right off hand, but it'll come to me."

I tossed an ounce to the big guy that was the spokesperson and he caught it in midair. Their eyes lit up.

They all talked at once, but I was able to make out: "Mane, dis is dat Cali fire fo' sho', good lookin', Big Homie."

I turned Tupac back up and threw up the W as we pulled off. In the rear view mirror, I saw them standing in the middle of the road returning that W. Their parents were my age; they probably smoked weed, too. The word would spread quickly.

A little down the road, someone was standing in the middle of the lane, waving frantically. As we got closer, I saw it was Cowboy, all dressed up in his Friday gear and fake jewelry.

I told Vince, "Just fly past his ass."

We both threw up the W as we whizzed by. I looked in the rear view mirror and through the cloud of brown dust, Cowboy stood with his hands on his hips. When I could no longer see him, I said, "Go back and get that nut."

When we got back to him, Cowboy looked as if he didn't know whether to laugh or cry.

"Mane, why is y'all playin'?"

I held a poker face for a long minute, then I burst out laughing. "Get in the car, young punk, and start paying attention. This is your last shot, Li'l Homie."

"All right, I got it, Big Pimpin."

We pulled into the parking lot of Black Dot's at three o'clock and finished smoking the blunt as I laid out the plan. Tonight I would have to be more laid back so I could pay more attention to what was really going on.

Both of them would be networking, even though Vince would hang around me most of the time. I also told them that I needed them to find me some heat. "I need a magnum revolver."

Both of them said, "Dat ain't no problem down here, mane."

We walked into the club and all eyes were on me. I scanned the room and saw my cousins at the bar. I sat on a stool next to them and ordered a beer for myself, then watched Vince and Cowboy network.

Cowboy had a few of his boys waiting for him already. Over the next few hours, I watched them go through the side door, then the hustlers would come back with a couple more dudes which meant they purchased some bud, left, smoked some, loved it, told a friend and came back to get some more.

Vince finally sat next to me and ordered his own beer. He waited a few minutes before whispering, "It's all gone."

I waited for my cousins to leave, then went to the car for more weed. Cowboy followed us out and both passed me the money they'd made.

"This shit is going fast," Vince said. "These dudes don't care about price. The same dudes that wanted to buy the pounds are the main ones buying ounces. They're buying three and four at a time."

Not to be outdone, Cowboy told me, "I got a dude on the way to the club with a .44 Magnum, but he don't have no bullets. He wants to trade it for an ounce of weed." Then he nodded toward the packed club. "Vikki and her cousins are on their way over."

I gave Cowboy a hundred dollars to put in his pocket and said, "We're about to make a run to get some more."

Vince and I jumped in the car, but before we headed to the trailer, we stopped at Wal-Mart to get some sandwich bags.

As we rode, I thought about all that had gone down in just four hours. We'd sold all that weed and Cowboy had landed me a gun.

That last part concerned me, though. That meant that damn near everybody had the potential to be packing heat and the small police presence couldn't keep things under control. I would have to carry a gun twenty-four-seven and packing heat all the time troubled me.

Before we got to the store, I decided I had to call Jay to make him aware of what had happened. He didn't like phone conversations, so when he answered, I said, "Hey player, the chicks are out of control down here. I can't handle all of them by myself. There's not enough love to go around, homie, so sign up for school and I hope to see you soon."

I hung up without giving him a chance to say anything. Jay was sharp, he'd figure it out.

Vince and I rode in silence for awhile until he finally said, "Hey, Big Homie, you didn't think it was gonna go like dis, did you? I tried to tell you bout dis when you was back in Cali."

"It's all good, Vince. Believe me. I'm just trying to figure out a way to make a million down here without going to prison for the rest of my life."

Wal-Mart's parking lot was lit up like a huge beacon. We hit the sporting goods section and I slipped Vince a couple hundred dollars. "Get some bullets."

Vince smiled. "You ain't got to be scared 'bout dat down here 'cause dey don't even ask for no I.D."

Damn, forget about the south. Natchez was really the wild, wild west.

After we purchased the bullets, I went to the music section while Vince went to grab the sandwich bags. I picked up Luther Vandross' greatest hits. If Luther couldn't help a brother get some pussy, nobody could.

I wasn't trying to rush having sex because I had always thought with my big head, not my little one. A man who was lusting was out of control — and being in control was one of my greatest assets.

We made it back to the trailer about 10 o'clock and as Vince went to get the stash, my nephew knocked on the front door.

"What do you want now, you fucking pest?"

"Hey Unc, I just walked from up the road and I saw somebody with a flashlight behind the trailer. I was coming to let you know."

I gave him a pat on the shoulder. "Good looking out, nephew, but that's just Vince checking the fence."

"You want me to help him, Unc?"

"Naw, I want you to take your little ass home."

Vince walked in through the back door holding the ice chest in one hand and some shredded plastic in the other.

"Mane, dem fucking raccoons done had demselves a party wit' our shit, Big Homie. It's a good thing we had to come back. Dey only got a chance to fuck wit a small bit of it. Probably 'bout two ounces or so was spread out on the ground."

Dakari cracked up laughing. "See Unc, dat's what happens when you start telling all dem lies."

We all broke up laughing. It was a good thing I had witnessed this with my own eyes. If Cowboy would've used that excuse, I would've fired him on the spot.

We bagged up some more and then Vince suggested that we put the rest in his work truck until morning, rather than stashing it outside again.

I agreed, but before we left, I had one thing I had to do. Inside my bedroom, I pulled back the sheets on the bed and sprinkled a small amount of baby powder on them.

Then I placed the candles that had been in my aunt's bathroom, inside the bedroom.

I told Dakari to run to my mother's house and bring me back his CD player. I wasn't sure if tonight was going to be the night with Vikki — I wanted to take it slow with her, but you never knew. So, I had to be ready.

Dakari was gone and back within five minutes, and I handed him a twenty and told him to go on back home.

But before he left, he just had to get in a few words. "Thanks for the hush money, Unc. You know how we do it."

* * *

The parking lot at Black Dot's was even more packed and I sent Vince inside to get Cowboy. I didn't want to be seen talking to him in front of all of those dudes.

When he ambled over to the car, it was obvious that he'd had a few drinks. He slipped into the back seat.

"So what's the latest, Cowboy?"

"All right, dig dis, Big Pimpin', first of all, check dis here piece out." He slid a beautiful blue steel .44 Magnum with an eight-inch barrel over the seat. "Secondly, yo' tall ass chick is in der. Mane, she done walked way down yonder and back looking for you. Thirdly, you got Black Dot's joint jumping tonight. Da word done already got out 'bout dat Cali fire."

"All right, y'all already know what to do. Cowboy, don't tell Vikki I'm here. I'm just gonna post up inside for a minute and check shit out."

Vince put the gun in the trunk and grabbed a few ounces before they went into the club. About ten minutes later, I slid inside and went straight for the corner on the back wall where I could see everything, but still be in the cut.

Three dudes were sitting at a table with a fifth of Hennessy in the middle. They were smoking on a blunt like it was a cigarette. One of them had a handgun tucked into the small of his back.

I scanned the club and spotted Vikki close to the door with a drink in her hand. She was talking to her cousin and a couple of other chicks. Vikki towered over the other women and her heels gave her even more height. I loved a woman in heels. Though she was deep in conversation, her gaze focused on the door from time to time.

She finally spotted me and we stared at each other for a few seconds. For a brief moment it seemed as though the music stopped and we were the only people in the room.

I mouthed the words, "Will you marry me?"

She rolled her eyes, then gestured for me to come to her. I smiled and walked out of the front door. Moments later, she met me in the parking lot by Vince's car.

"Now what in the hell were you trying to tell me inside?"

I repeated it.

She laughed. "Boy, you sho 'nuff need to go somewhere wit dat mess. Do they teach you how to lie like that in California?"

I looked her in the eyes. "Baby, I was just trying to make you laugh because you were looking so mean."

"Well, it sho 'nuff did work, Graeeg."

"Damn Vikki, I love the way you say my name. I want you to say it just like that when I'm making love to you."

Her eyes widened to the size of saucers. "Boy, I cain't even much believe you juss said dat. You really —"

"I'm just fucking with you, Vikki. Come on, let's go get something to eat."

This was a critical part of the game. I had to be that perfect gentleman. I had to be everything her last boyfriend wasn't.

I gently took her hand and steered her toward her car. I knew that payback on her boyfriend was never far from her mind. And I was going to make sure that she paid back her boyfriend something good!

* * *

Over the next three days, I managed to spread the rumor that I was looking for new talent for a record label while at the same time, Vince and Cowboy got rid of all the weed.   Profits were high. One pound basically covered the cost of the whole five-pound package.

I wired Jay the money and included some to my wife. When Jay got the money, he told me that he finally had his new I.D. and the green light from his people on the twenty pounds.

That was great news. I called Serge. "Get Cheerio ready to go."

I arranged a Greyhound bus ticket for Cheerio and the package. Jay booked a ticket to ride the bus with Cheerio. Cheerio didn't know Jay, so he wouldn't be aware that someone was watching him.

It would be a week before the two of them and the product arrived, so I took that time to relax a bit. Auntie Lena had a white '81 Ford Pinto station wagon that she had brought with her from Cali. I asked her for permission to drive it, which she gave gladly.

Now I had a set of wheels, and I damn sure couldn't be labeled a high roller in that old bucket.

I passed the time by hanging out with Vince. One day, we decided to get in some target practice, and I made sure that Uncle Ernest saw Vince and both of our guns in plain view.

As we walked down the gravel road, Uncle Ernest yelled out, "Grego, ain't too mucha nothin' you can shoot 'round here wit dat cannon, boy."

He was right. Vince had a twelve-gauge hunting shotgun and I looked out of place holding a Smith & Wesson .44 Magnum. But it felt good in my hands, almost euphoric.

Guns had always been my downfall. The blue steel was cool to the touch. The pistol grip was carved from a light-colored wood, which had been smoothed to perfection, and the contrast of the bright red tip on the sight of the eight-inch barrel enhanced its beauty. She was just begging to explode in my hand and I couldn't wait to let her scream.

Vince was my hanging buddy when I went fishing or hunting. He was a fast learner who listened more than he talked.

Target practice was great, but one of the most relaxing times was watching the girls' softball team. They played every Friday and I was actually one of their biggest fans.

The teams were comprised of females from each road. Most of the ones from my road were my cousins and one of my cousins, Neadra, was one of the best players on the team. She might have been petite, but she was tough.

But the best way I passed the time during that week while I waited for Jay was time spent with Vikki. We did the simple things, like going to the movies, or out to dinner. I sent her flowers, too, something my cousin Neadra told me that dudes down here never did. Basically, I did everything that those country boys wouldn't and just waited for nature to take its course.

I never pressured her to have sex, not at all. I just ended our dates with a slow, sensual kiss, making her anticipate our next encounter.

But as it got closer to Jay arriving, I knew that I would have to shift gears soon.

That's what I was thinking about when I was riding around town. It was hot as hell, and all I could think about was having an ice cold beer. I stopped at one of those mom and pop stores and when I stepped inside, the store's air conditioning and the huge fans blowing made it feel like heaven.

I grabbed a twelve pack, but I wasn't in a big rush to jump back into the heat, so I stood in front of one of the fans, closed my eyes, and enjoyed the brief respite.

"You're gonna need more than that fan to cool your big ass off."

I opened my eyes, and standing next to me was a short, thick woman with a light complexion. It didn't take me more than a couple of seconds to figure out that she was at least twelve years my senior. She held a six pack of beer in one hand, Zig Zags and incense in the other.

"Shit, if you got AC in your car, I'm riding with you, lady."

We shared a laugh and walked to the register together. Then, as we walked outside, I asked, "What are you gonna put in those Zags, lady?"

"Some good weed, if I'm lucky."

Exactly what I wanted to hear!

She planted her hands on those curvy hips. "Where you from? I ain't never seent you befo'."

"I'm from Cali, here visiting my family."

She told me that her name was Gina and that she stayed in town. We chatted for a little while longer before I told her, "If you come out to Black Dot's tonight the smoking's on me."

"My kids hang out there, but I'll stop through for a minute and holla at ya."

We exchanged numbers and I jumped back into my hot box, thinking about Gina as I drove away. She was born and raised in Mississippi, but didn't come across as country dumb. She was a little too aggressive, but I needed to connect with an older crowd.

Romancing her was out of the question, though; a little flattery would have to do the trick.

I made it back to the trailer around five o'clock, flopped onto the sofa, opened a cold beer, then looked at my pager. Two messages were from my wife, and five from Vikki.

I dialed my wife first and was blasted with, "You must have lost your motherfucking mind, Greg! I haven't been able to reach your slick ass all week. What the fuck are you doing?"

I laid the phone down, and went to grab another beer. Her voice carried all the way into the kitchen. She hadn't even realized that I wasn't on the other end.

I walked into the bedroom, grabbed some weed, made it back to the sofa, picked up the phone, and she was still going.

Finally, I jumped in. "Baby, you're running up our phone bill for nothing."

"I don't give a fuck about a phone bill!"

Again, I sat the phone down, rolled myself a joint, lit it, and let her blow. She would eventually hang up.

When she did, I called Vikki and she picked up on the first ring. "Graeeg, what you tryin' to do boy, drive me crazy?"

I laughed. "What are you talking about, lady?" Then I turned serious. "Listen Vikki, I just want you to know that I really enjoy your company."

"Well, I really do 'preciate da roses. Thank you, Graeeg."

"You're welcome," I said, thinking about the flowers that I had sent her that day.

"I'll see you later?" I asked.

We agreed to hook up at Black Dot's later that night.

* * *

By ten thirty, Black Dot's was jam packed. Vince and I were in a parking spot that gave me the best view of the whole scene. My .44 Magnum was under the seat and we were sipping from a fifth of Hennessy.

There was a party atmosphere with just as much activity outside as there was inside. Cowboy was hanging outside, though he didn't know that I was watching him. The hustlers approached him one by one. Most were only in his presence for a moment, some stayed for a while.

I pointed things out to Vince so he could learn to read body language. I told him that the ones who stayed for a minute had learned that nothing was happening. The others were potential foot soldiers or wannabes.

I quizzed Vince for information on each person.

Then, I pulled out my phone and called Cowboy. "Slow your roll. You doing way too much talking, homie."

"Mane, where da hell is you at?"

I hung up. Most of the hustlers with him weren't discreet about their business, so I could use that to my advantage.

Vikki and her cousins arrived and all I could say was "Damn!" when I saw her. She wore all red, six-inch heels, and a form fitting linen dress. I couldn't take my eyes off her or her graceful walk. She and her cousins went over to Cowboy and soon passed a blunt around.

Vikki turned and scanned the parking lot. Obviously, Cowboy was talking too much — again. I grabbed the bottle and poured a hefty refill as Vince lit a blunt. Vince passed the blunt and I took a good pull. The combination of weed and alcohol impacted all my senses and sent my mind into a flurry.

I took inventory of the people outside and tried to guess how many of those dudes were packing heat.

A steady stream of nice cars entered the parking lot. The real hustlers — ghetto stars — had arrived and the heavy bass pounded as they passed. They took their time finding parking spaces so the chicks could run up to their cars. I paid close attention, looking for the man who stepped out of his car and adjusted his pants. He would, most likely, be one carrying the heat. I spotted two of five possibilities, which wasn't cool.

Vikki and her crew finally made their way inside the club and I poured myself another drink.

Right after Vikki went inside, Gina showed up wearing tight blue jean shorts, a halter top, and pumps. She had a girlfriend with her and as she made her way toward the door, she spotted Cowboy and moved toward him.

I turned to Vince. "Do you know her?"

"Yeah, e'rbody do. Dat's Ty's momma. She don't fuck wit nuthin' but young niggas. They stay up in town and da whole family sell weed. But she might be bad news 'cause da whole family is scandalous." Vince paused to watch the scene. "I think Cowboy used to fuck wit her daughter, Speedy. Dat was her son, Ty in dat Candy blue Cadillac."

I stepped out of the car and walked toward Cowboy. Wearing all black made maneuvering easy and the two chicks had their backs to me. I was right up on them by the time Cowboy saw me.

I caught the end of his conversation. "Yeah, dat's my cousin. Here he is now!"

I greeted the whole crowd with, "Hey now! What's up country folks?"

Everyone laughed and we kicked it for a few minutes. I gave Gina a sample of the weed, then she invited me to her house to play cards the next day.

After they left for another club, I pulled Cowboy aside and quizzed him about Gina.

He said, "They're cool and they move a lot of weed."

I made the decision to try her out and if it didn't work. . . oh well.

I hung out with Cowboy and his crew for a minute, then waved for Vince to come over. The alcohol had loosened me up. Cowboy passed me a blunt and suddenly everyone went silent, looking past me.

Turning around, I spotted Vikki behind me with her arms folded. And she was not smiling.

"Hey, baby!" I crooned.

"Yo' baby jus' lef', Graeeg."

I was slipping big time! "Baby, that's just business."

"Well, I guess y'all can discuss dat while y'all play cards."

The alcohol had definitely affected my responses, so I tried a different approach.

"Cowboy, grab that bottle out of Vince's car."

I gave everyone — including Vikki and her cousins — drinks, and then we bought some more from the club. It didn't even take an hour; I had succeeded in getting everybody drunk, and I moved our crew of twelve over to Vince's car to stay close to my gun. Vince rolled down his window and turned on a Tupac CD.

I grabbed Vikki's hand and led her to the back of the car where we had a little bit of privacy. Vikki sat on the trunk, placing her heels on the back bumper. She was a little unsteady so I held her small waist and stood between her thick thighs. She threw her hands around my neck and pulled me toward her.

She whispered, "Thanks for the roses, baby."

Vikki leaned in for a passionate kiss. Just as I started to go deeper, the words, "Bitch, come on outside!" interrupted us.

Two chicks tumbled out the door and onto the dirt — fighting. The whole damn club followed them to the parking lot.

Vikki said, "The way they're tearing each other up, it must be over a dude."

The crowd was hyped; I stepped away from the trunk. "It's time to go. Get your car." I nodded to Vince, then hopped in his car and fired it up as Vikki got in her car with her two cousins.

I motioned for Cowboy to lose his crew before he jumped in the car with us. Vikki pulled in front of our car, and then we both peeled out of the parking lot. We only made it about a quarter mile before we heard the gunfire.

Vince pulled ahead of Vikki and I motioned for her to follow us. In just minutes, we were at my trailer. As everyone filed inside, I could hear the faint music from Black Dot's drifting across the bayou.

The six of us sat, talking, listening to music and drinking beer. But after about an hour, I decided that I didn't want Uncle Ernest catching us having a party. So, I told Vince to make sure everyone got home safely.

When Vikki made a move to leave, I told her to stay.

As soon as we were alone, the hustler transformed into the sensitive, caring, romantic, considerate Greg.

For the last week, I had done everything to keep Vikki's mind focused on me. Now it was time to take it to where she had the triple fuck - mind, body, and soul. Only then would I have complete control.

I changed the disc to Luther. His sultry voice flooded the room. I cleared my mind, put on my best dreamy-eyed thug face and slowly turned around.

Vikki wasn't even in the fucking living room! The whirl of the exhaust fan in the master bathroom explained things. So much for presenting a sexy game face.

I grabbed the CD player, hurried to the bedroom, and set the volume. Then I lit the four vanilla candles scattered around the room. The exhaust fan shut off and I had just enough time to kill the lights and lay across the bed.

Vikki stood at the threshold looking like a Black sex goddess. The skylight in the bathroom created a seductive silhouette, outlining her sexy curves.

Her fluid stride was so graceful, those long shapely legs looked like they belonged on a million-dollar fashion model.

Her sweet perfume reached me about three seconds before she did. She stood between my legs and looked down.

The anticipation made my blood race. I started unbuttoning her dress from the bottom and moved up as she spread her feet apart. Her dress flowed open, unwrapping a sneak peek of her red sheer panties and bra.

I reached under the dress and grabbed a firm piece of ass in each hand. The ends of my fingers were close to the prize. She was hot and ready.

Vikki rubbed my head as I kissed her stomach and worked my way up to her full lips. I gave her a deep kiss, then pulled away. She looked at me as though she had been in love with me her whole life.

I slowly laid her down and slipped my shirt off. Power flowed through me as I slipped off my pants, letting my erection do the talking. She kept her eyes on me while she opened her bra. Those dark brown nipples called my name.

She wrapped her arms around my waist and pressed her breasts against me. Her tongue slow danced on my stomach and her slender fingers and sharp nails glided over my ass and down my legs. She looked up at me, then laid back on the bed. I inched her panties down and tossed 'em on the floor.

I toyed with her, playing with her body until she moaned and twisted. I worked on Vikki like a romantic surgeon. With everything I learned and some things I hadn't tried yet, the journey to pure bliss was a wonderful thing.

* * *

Two hours later, we were stretched out on the bed. Sweat glistened on her chocolate skin as those firm breasts rose and fell with each breath. I rolled onto my side, stared into her eyes, and smiled. She looked so peaceful lying there.

I gave her a deep kiss, that oh-so-important after sex kiss.

"Graeeg, I want you to know I ain't tripping off that lady from da club, but you need to be careful wit dat whole family."

I laid back thinking, I'd achieved my goal.

Here comes the pillow talk.

Chapter 32
Trouble Brewing

I'd been in Mississippi for a while, almost three months, on the day that Jay drove down the narrow two lane highway. It was a hot, humid September day, but nothing could spoil my mood. My son, my nephew, and my friend Althea from Sacramento were sitting in the back seat.

Even though I didn't hustle in Sacramento all that much anymore, Althea and I were still close. I loved everything about her. She was a soft-spoken woman, a few years older, with brown eyes that penetrated my soul. But it was the fact that she was down as fuck that kept Althea in my life.

It was Althea who had brought Greg, Jr. on the Greyhound bus all the way from Los Angeles three weeks ago.

I still remembered the way my son jumped into my arms the day they arrived. Whenever we hugged, it spoke volumes — mainly I felt his relief that I was not in prison since I'd promised that I would never go back.

These three weeks with Greg, Jr. had been the greatest time that I had ever shared with my boy. We did all that cool father and son shit. I taught him how to shoot a gun and watched him catch his first fish. I bought a two-seat Go-Cart that gave Dakari and Greg the opportunity to whip through all that open land. We went to the black rodeo every Sunday and practically lived in Super Wal-Mart.

I glanced back, took a quick look at the three of them, and sadness filled me because it was all coming to an end. We were going to spend this last day together at the movies.

Turning back around to the front, I thought about how I really had settled into Natchez. Even Jay had been here about two months and was living in an apartment in town that was our safe house. I was still in the trailer, still driving my aunt's Pinto, and Cowboy still pissed me off. But I could trust him. Vince was still my right-hand-man, and Black Dot's was still my major network source.

Business was good; sometimes I thought, almost too good. Selling weed wasn't the hard part. It was keeping track of all my lies that was becoming impossible.

We were about five minutes away from the movie theater when we passed a liquor store and I spotted Ty's Cadillac. Ty was one of the small time hustlers who'd been working for me for the last two months and he owed me seventy-five dollars. But he'd been ducking me and that was total disrespect. My game required that I get at him in a cool way, though. I didn't want to make enemies in any town.

"Jay, pull into the parking lot," I said, directing him.

Ty was standing next to his car with a few of his homeboys.

I jumped out as the car came to a stop. "What's up, Ty? I been paging you, homie."

He replied, "I caint squeeze blood from a turnip, mane."

The man had nerve to have an attitude. I didn't say another word, just pivoted and walked back to the car. But as I got in, I got a glimpse of Greg Jr. and Dakari. Both of their faces showed deep concern, something I had never witnessed from them before.

Greg Jr. said, "Daddy, you better be careful with that dude."

Dakari chimed in, "Yeah, Unc, you should've seen the way he was looking when you turned your back."

"I ain't worried about him, his little feelings are hurt because his bitch wants to drop him for Jay."

Even though that was funny, it wasn't a joke. It was no secret that Ty's girl wanted Jay real bad. She asked me about Jay every time she saw me, even if Ty was standing right next to her.

Jay laughed. "I don't want that fool's bitch unless she hits the lottery."

We both enjoyed a good laugh before pulling onto the street. But as we drove away, my son and nephew still looked out of the back window.

Greg Jr. and Dakari didn't have a thing to worry about. I had just made up my mind. It was only seventy-five dollars and Ty could keep that change. I needed a reason to quit fucking with him anymore.

Things were going too well for me and Jay; we didn't need anyone like Ty. We had good people working for us, including Jamey, who was Ty's cousin, but one of my best connects.

He'd told me that he had never made much money because he'd always been playing the middle man. I showed him how to make a profit off his hustle and fronted him whenever he came to me. He moved up the ladder real quick and always let me know he appreciated my efforts.

Over a period of time, Jamey and I became cool on the personal tip, too. Whenever he called me for business, I always told him to stop by Krystal Burgers. Jamey loved to eat as much as I did, so it became our ritual.

Even though Ty was his cousin, Jamey and I never discussed the issues I had with him, so we stayed cool. I would just stop fucking with Ty and concentrate on Jamey.

I pushed Ty out of my mind and enjoyed the rest of the day with my son. The time passed too quickly, and the next day, Vince and I drove Greg Jr. and Althea to the Greyhound bus station. When we arrived, I pulled my son aside and we walked to the end of the parking lot.

"I'm really happy you came down here and hung out with me."

"Me, too, dad, but I'm worried about you."

"Why?"

"Because I don't want you to get stuck in the quicksand down in the creek again." Then, he cracked up the way he did the day that happened. He found that incident to be so damn funny.

I reached into my pocket, pulled out two hundred dollars and gave it to him before we walked back toward the bus.

I told him, "I'm proud of the good grades you've been getting, but I think you can do better."

"I promise, I'll do better, daddy."

Back at the bus, I pulled Althea aside, thanked her, and told her I enjoyed her company. I slipped her five hundred dollars, then gave her a passionate kiss and told her to call me when they got home.

On the steps of the bus, Greg Jr. turned back to me. "When are you coming home, daddy?"

"Just as soon as I can, son."

Tears welled in his eyes. "Daddy, please be careful."

I grabbed my son and hugged him for what seemed like forever. I whispered, "I promised you that I would never leave you again. I still mean it."

They disappeared into the bus. I sat on the hood of Vince's car and waved as the bus pulled down the gravel highway. Not even a minute passed and damn...I missed them already.

* * *

When Vince dropped me off at the trailer, I told him, "I'm gonna take the rest of the day off. I'll holla at you later."

I stretched out on the sofa to watch the news, but I couldn't concentrate. For about a month now, I'd been feeling anxious, but having my son around kept me from focusing on that. Now the anxiety came back full force.

I grabbed a pen and tablet and wrote down all the positive and negative shit I was involved in.

I addressed the money issue first. There was plenty of it, and that was one of the main problems. Jay was a meticulous planner and he'd designed a great plan to reach the 60-pound mark. Our profit would be $12,500 each every two weeks and we were just about there; it had only taken two months. The demand exceeded our expectations; we never had enough product.

Unfortunately, we had run out of ways to send the money home. We'd been stuffing 13-inch RCA televisions with $10,500 each and shipping them back. That model was perfect for concealing money, but we had gotten to the point where only three televisions remained and Wal-Mart didn't have any more in stock. And we had already looked out of place when we bought the last five. Consistent activity like that would not go unnoticed.

Getting the marijuana to Natchez was the next crisis. My wife had been stashing fifteen pounds in three-foot-tall stereo speakers, but we could only use a single mail carrier a couple times to do that.

Gossip was the third issue. Jay was tucked away at the safe house apartment, but I was the one who traveled up and down the road under the watchful eye of every neighbor and relative. I had to come up with a legitimate income story real soon.

After making that list, I sat back. Yeah, there were issues, but it seemed like the good outweighed the bad. Life was really good on the business side. And things were well with my personal life, too.

Not only had I just spent three weeks with Althea, but I had a new girl in Natchez — Angela. I had been trying to keep a lower profile and that meant that I couldn't fuck with Vikki too much anymore; she was hot because of her association with me.

So Angela slipped into my life. She was cool and wasn't about attracting attention. She had a dark limo tint on her car, which was great because that meant nobody ever knew when I was rolling with her. I trusted her so much that I even hung out with her at the safe house a few times. Jay would have lost his mind if he knew that.

I had no idea why I was so concerned. Business was good. Life was good. There was nothing to worry about. I tossed the list I had to the side. I didn't have anything to worry about.

But then things went from hustling to hectic and from hectic to crazy in no time flat.

* * *

It was my personal life that first began to unravel and it started with my Aunt Thelma. She became suspicious of me and told my mother that I was probably on the run from the law.

"She's telling everyone to watch America's Most Wanted," one of my cousins told me. "And you know when she speaks, everyone listens."

I hadn't figured out how to handle that headache before another one came into my life.

"Barry is coming to Mississippi," my mother told me. "And he's gonna stay with you in Lena's trailer."

My cousin, Barry the monster? Not that I was scared of him anymore. Not only was I much bigger than him, but he was now the town drunk.

But once he got there, it wasn't so bad, and I found myself actually happy to see him. I didn't feel like I had to hide anything from him since he had taught me everything I knew about hustling. So, I kept on with my business right in front of him.

It was all cool — until Barry took a drink. Once he drank, he became damn near unrecognizable, and I wanted to kick his ass for every second he was drunk.

Maybe Barry being there with me was a warning sign. I don't know, it's just that after he came, all kinds of trouble came my way.

The first problem came when I went against my own judgment. Ty placed an order for a pound and I agreed to sell it to him even though he still owed me money and I had decided to not work with him anymore. Jay thought it was a bad idea, but I don't know why...I agreed to meet Ty on a deserted country road.

I was going strapped, though; I rolled out in the Pinto with a .25 semi-automatic.

When I reached the spot, I saw Ty, rolling five deep when he pulled up behind me. I had the pistol on my lap, but now, I wasn't feeling this deal.

Ty and another guy exited the car and I saw his partner was packing a huge pistol in his waistband. I put the Pinto in drive, pressed the accelerator, and took off. I had a good lead on them, but the four cylinder Pinto was no match for Ty's Cadillac.

My cell phone rang as they closed the distance behind me.

Ty yelled, "Mane, why you take off like dat?"

"Why the fuck is your homeboy jumping out with heat for a fucking pound deal?"

I hung up and floored it toward town, but they rode my ass the whole time. At the first traffic light, I ran right through the red light. They were forced to stop and I got away.

Back at the trailer, I had to evaluate the whole situation. I hadn't considered Ty as a threat. I just assumed that he desperately wanted to buy some good weed.

When I told Jay what happened, he agreed to pay a little more attention to Ty's sneaky ass. Jay started keeping a pistol with him, but I wasn't really concerned about Ty jacking us. I was more concerned about the animosity that had built up toward us behind his bitch. Shit, Ty's girl wasn't the only one. Damn near every bitch in town wanted pretty boy Jay. But he was all about business; he wouldn't give any the time of day.

Our second strike came on the day that Jay and I were to ship a television with money inside back to Cali. I had just shipped one the day before and today was Jay's turn. We always sent our packages a day apart in case something went down.

Natchez only had two post offices, so we were always looking for new ones in other areas, and we'd found one across the river in Louisiana.

I arrived at the safe house and Jay hadn't taken his shower yet. I kicked back under the air conditioning because Jay took hour-long showers! I didn't even bother to tell him that he had to hurry if we wanted to make it to the post office before it closed. That would just be a waste of breath.

When the shower turned off exactly one hour later, Jay didn't trip that we were running late. He had this "Don't Panic" rule that drove me crazy.

"We're not going to make it," I told him.

He still insisted on trying. We threw the box onto the back seat and headed toward the bridge. But then, Jay glanced at his watch and made a quick left off the main highway.

I laughed. "I told you we weren't gonna make it, pretty boy."

He flashed me that million dollar smile. "Yeah, but we still got time to make it to the other one in town."

"We can't use that one. That's the one we used yesterday."

"It'll be okay, because it's a different shift, different people."

I wasn't feeling that and when we walked through the doors, a bad vibe hit me. A quick glance around told me we'd made a mistake. The same faces from yesterday were looking at me today.

But we acted cool and tried to fit in while we stood in line. By the time we made it to the counter, I thought we just might pull the shipment off.

I felt someone's stare. To our left, two female employees were huddled around an older black man who looked like a supervisor. Our glances connected for a brief second and I knew this was trouble.

We finished our business, but as soon as we slipped into the car, I told Jay, "You know that package ain't gonna make it to Cali, homie."

He tried to convince me not to be concerned, but I knew he was worried, too.

His loss would become my loss. We were partners in crime, so I had no choice but to roll with him.

I dropped Jay off at the safe house and headed back to the trailer. Barry was sitting on the steps with a beer in his hand when I pulled up and with the mood I was in, I hoped he didn't say something stupid. When I climbed out of the Pinto, I could smell the liquor.

"Hey, G Man, I've been locked out the house for two hours now. I need a key to my fucking mother's trailer."

I gave him a cold stare, thinking back to all the times when he used to terrorize me and my siblings. "You ain't gonna get nothing but an ass kicking if you don't shut the fuck up, nigga."

He mumbled something as I slammed the door in his face and locked him out.

The telephone rang the moment I sat down and the caller I.D. displayed my wife's number. I ignored the call, turned the ringer off, switched on the television and rolled a blunt.

Visions of that dude at the post office flooded my mind. That package wouldn't make it. Because of Jay's carelessness, we gave away $10,500 dollars.

I pulled the receipt out of my pocket and stared at the tracking number for a moment before I called the 1-800 number. The package was still in Mississippi.

I tossed the receipt onto the table, stretched out on the sofa and fell asleep. Pounding on the door soon woke me up. I could hear Barry talking plenty of shit from outside. He'd had a few more drinks.

I let him in and the moment he set foot inside, he said, "Motherfuckers is gonna have to start showing me some respect around here."

"Check this, Barry, I'm paying the rent in this bitch. You need to take your drunk ass back to Cali."

He mumbled some more stupid shit, went to his room, and slammed the door.

Returning to the sofa, I looked at the receipt once again. We'd sent the package overnight; it should've left the Mississippi office by now. I dreaded making the call, but I did it anyway and used the automated system.

I held my breath and was told the package was still in Mississippi.

Fuck!" I hollered, and threw the cordless phone against the wall.

Barry rushed out from his bedroom. When he saw the shattered phone on the floor, he said, "I hope you ain't tearing up my mother's house, nigga!"

It took everything in me to rein in my anger. But I told him, "Barry, your vacation is over, cousin. Be ready to go back to California in one week."

I walked back to the sofa and finished smoking a blunt when Jay called. He was as chipper as usual.

"What's up, player?"

"Man, that package ain't gonna make it," I told him again.

"Wait until morning before you panic, G Man."

Next, I called my wife and explained what happened. She'd wanted a new car and I had to tell her that would have to be on hold if the money didn't arrive.

Over the next hour I connected with our workers. The last call I made was to Vince who was the only one with a level head all the time. I told him to come hang out with me and bring something strong to drink.

I was sitting in the living room when Barry came out of the bedroom with bloodshot red eyes. He stared at me as he made his way out the door. I was sure he regretted that he couldn't kick my ass like he used to.

That night I tried to stay positive, and I tried to stay that way the next day, too. But after two days, even Jay finally accepted that the package was a lost cause. He shrugged it off, but we had a bigger problem. Our hand had been exposed. The post office had probably alerted the police. We didn't know who would be watching and now we had to find a new way to get the money back home.

Jay considered flying a mule in to carry it back by Greyhound. I thought about switching up the whole game to sell cocaine. It was 80 percent less bulky with a larger profit margin, but it also raised the stakes. The legal penalties were much stiffer and I would become a bigger target for the police and jackers.

I actually wanted to say *fuck all this shit* and find a new town. But unfortunately, I didn't follow my mind.

* * *

Our next shipment from my wife was only thirty pounds, which meant we didn't have enough to hit all of our regulars. We created a priority list. Cowboy and Vince were automatic and after them, Jamey was next in line. The rest of the pounds were spread out accordingly.

At home, Barry and I weren't on speaking terms and he mad-dogged me every time I saw him. I just laughed. What else could I do looking at a drunk?

But I shouldn't have taken Barry so lightly because when Vince showed up at the trailer with an expression on his face that I'd never seen before, I knew there was big trouble.

As he sat on my sofa, he looked like he'd been a witness to a homicide.

Worry was dancing a hole in my stomach. "What's wrong, homie?"

He hesitated a moment. "Mane, we got major problems."

Vince had been up the road and Barry was hanging out there, drunk as fuck, and running his mouth.

"Barry kept telling everyone that he was sick and tired of you selling weed out of his mother's trailer."

Shit!

"Tom Granell, that undercover cop who stays across the road from the bootleg tree heard him, too."

If a freight train ran through the trailer that very moment, it would have been better. I knew exactly the man Vince was talking about. I had hung out up there with him a few times myself and had even told him an elaborate lie about being an ex football player. I also told him that Jay was attending Jackson State University.

"Vince, go get Barry's ass and don't come back without him."

I paced the floor a thousand times as a thousand things went through my mind. I had worked so hard to protect my family's name, especially my mother's. She didn't deserve to be humiliated by me, but this news would be the top story in the country grapevine by morning.

I called Jay and told him, "Get over here right now." Then I called our whole crew and told them to shut down shop immediately.

After all of that, I was finally able to think about Barry and how to deal with him. He'd committed an act of treason that was beyond repair. I thought about taking him deep into the woods to make him dig his own grave. But killing an enemy was too good. Having them suffer for the rest of their lives was a better option. I thought about getting a baseball bat and breaking both of his kneecaps.

But the thing was, he was still my cousin, so I had to settle for simply knocking his ass out cold.

When Vince's car pulled up, I heard Barry's protests; he was angry that he'd been forced to leave his drinking buddies. When they came into the trailer, Barry couldn't even keep his balance. He was so drunk he probably didn't realize what he had done.

How do you beat a man's ass when he doesn't even know why it's happening?

At that point, Barry let loose with a string of, "Bullshit!" and before I could talk myself out of it, I landed a right cross directly on his chin. He crumpled to the floor.

Jay walked through the door seconds later. While my cousin laid there, knocked out, I explained the situation to Jay. He started with that "Don't Panic" shit.

It was too late; I was panicked and I drove Barry's worthless ass to the bus station the next morning.

While I was worried, Jay still wasn't. He told me to stick it out and we would get to the sixty pound mark, then we'd shake this town.

I couldn't think and I definitely couldn't sleep. I felt people closing in on us.

I moved all the paraphernalia from the trailer to the safe house, but that didn't help my paranoia. When I drove up and down the road, it felt like the trees had eyes and were looking at me as I drove butt naked.

There was a basis for my paranoia. I saw Tom Granell's undercover Blazer everywhere. It was like he was following me. I even stopped carrying my gun, though I knew that couldn't be a good thing.

I made a decision — no matter what Jay said, it was time to leave Natchez. I wasn't even going to wait till we hit our mark. I was going to leave now!

Chapter 33
The Shooting

Two days after I made the decision to leave, Jamey called with an order for five pounds. There was no reason for me not to do that deal, so I agreed. He always came down to the trailer in his old work truck, so he really didn't look out of place.

I waited for a couple of hours and Jamey didn't show. That wasn't like him, but I just assumed he got tied up.

The next morning Jamey called and said his truck had broken down, but he still needed those five pounds. He said he'd be there within an hour, but like the day before, he didn't show. He did call this time, though, and said to give him a couple of more hours because he needed to get a few more hundred dollars together.

That was cool with me. Later that afternoon, Jamey called again and said he was running late. But then, the afternoon turned to the evening and the evening became night. Jamey kept calling back, telling me one thing or another and finally he said he had truck problems, but his partner was going to give him a ride.

Jay and I always shut our business down at midnight and it was already after ten. I told Jamey that he'd better hurry.

Usually, I didn't call Jay until after I had the money, but since it was getting so late, I called Jay and told him to bring the weed.

"Okay, I'll come as soon as I take my shower."

I knew what that meant, so I sat down on the sofa and turned on the news.

The lead story was about the shooting death of Tupac, even though it had happened a few weeks ago. I'd done everything to push it out of my mind, but now as I watched the news, I could no longer pretend that it hadn't happened.

I couldn't believe 'Pac was dead. I had only known him for a short time, but the times I spent with him were priceless. I would miss his music, miss his laugh and forever miss that million dollar smile.

That made me want to listen to music. I turned off the television, then the lights except the dim one in the corner and put in the Big Syke CD. I loved Big Syke, but often I didn't listen to my favorite song of his because it made me feel like I was in the middle of a premonition.

"On My Way Out."

The intro was enough to keep something on my mind.

If I die right now there's something I want to say.
Don't plan for the future 'cause the future is today.

I glanced at the table where my Magnum lay. I picked it up, held it for a minute, then opened the cylinder and emptied the shells. The size of the bullets had always impressed me. Having a pistol this huge made me feel like a black superman.

With a rag from the kitchen, I wiped every bullet, cleaning off my fingerprints. Then I reloaded the bullets and wiped the whole gun thoroughly.

I had just finished when the phone rang again. Jamey said, "I'm still coming. You got the five pounds now?"

"Yeah, and you need to hurry up because it's getting close to our cut-off time."

"I'll make it in time."

I looked at my watch. It was already 11:45 and Jay hadn't arrived. After I hung up, I called Jay. "What the fuck are you doing, nigga? Jamey is almost here."

"Calm down, big boy. The next time he calls just tell him to come on down to the trailer."

I hung up. That pretty boy was starting to get on my fucking nerves. We had already lost $10,500; what else would Jay cost us?

I was feeling agitated and uneasy, so I turned off Big Syke and put in Anita Baker. I was upset when the phone rang again, but this time it was my wife. And tonight, I wanted to speak to her. We'd been Bonnie and Clyde for so long and there were times when she read situations better than I did.

After we talked for a couple of minutes, I told her that we were about to sell five pounds.

"Greg, why are you working past midnight? You never do that."

"Baby, I know, but it's only Jamey."

She came back strong. "I don't care who it is! You guys are fucking up down there. All money ain't good money."

When I didn't say anything she continued, "Make sure you take your gun and pager with you."

"I promise. I love you."

Right before I hung up she said, "Baby, please be careful."

"I will, I promise."

Not even a minute passed when Jay pulled up to the trailer. It was twenty minutes past midnight now, but we decided to still do the deal because Jamey was my boy.

Plus, we'd taken that $10,500 hit and we needed this money. More time passed, then I called Jamey.

"How far away are you?" I asked him.

"We're close," he said, sounding a little weird, sounding like he was drunk.

I was frustrated, hungry as fuck, and tired of waiting. "Meet us at the Pine Ridge Market," I told him.

Pine Ridge Market was one of the three stores located along the two-lane paved road leading to and from town. They closed at ten so it would be pitch black out there with the exception of the one light aimed at the front entrance.

I grabbed twelve dollars off the coffee table, and my gun, then Jay and I rolled out. I figured we'd make this deal with Jamey, then get something to eat.

Usually, whenever Jay and I were together, we talked, we laughed, we bullshitted. But it was getting close to one in the morning and I wasn't in the best of moods.

We were almost at the store before I spoke my first words. "Jay, make sure you have your gun where you can get to it. Jamey's acting strange."

Jay pulled over, tossed those five pounds into the trunk, and got back into the car. He reached under the front seat and rested a .380 semi-automatic on his lap. My gun had been on my lap from the moment we left the trailer.

We pulled into the store's empty parking lot; Jamey hadn't arrived. But as soon as Jay put the car into park, a white newer model Mustang passed by. The Mustang traveled several feet, then turned around and pulled in behind us.

Their headlights were off and they were too far away from the store's only light to be able to see. I rolled my window halfway down and called out.

One person got out and I recognized Jamey's voice as he approached alone.

"What's up, fat boy?" I said to him when he got to the car. "Gimme yo' money so we can count that shit and get the fuck on."

He hesitated a moment too long. "My homeboy want to see what it looks like first, mane."

His breath reeked of alcohol and I watched him glance at the pistol in my lap several times.

"Check this, Jamey. We done did this too many times. Go get the money or we're out of here."

Jamey walked back to the car and I hated that I couldn't see what was going on. I kept my eyes on the side view mirror as I grabbed my gun and cocked the hammer back.

I kept thinking, *We need to turn our car around,* but before I could get the words out, a deafening explosion filled the air. The first bullet entered my body behind my right ear. The second one hit me in the right side of my jaw. I lost count after that because I couldn't feel the rest of the bullets.

The explosions were loud and disorientating. It felt like it went on forever, but in reality, it was probably just three seconds. And it was over.

The ringing in my ears didn't stop me from hearing that distinctive sound of a trigger being squeezed on a jammed gun.

I closed my eyes and braced for the next impact of a bullet. It never came, but I kept my eyes closed as I felt somebody lean through the shattered window and go through my pockets, taking my twelve dollars. I cracked my eyes and saw Jamey. I quickly closed them again as he pulled away.

Another dude was on the other side, checking Jay's pockets.

They ran and it wasn't until I heard their car pull off that I opened my eyes again.

*   *   *

"Jay, are you okay?" I croaked in a whisper. But there was no answer. It took me a few more seconds to be able to speak again. "Jay, please don't go, man."

His chin hit his chest and I could see that half of his forehead was gone.

I called out to him again, but he didn't say a word. I kept calling, and then, I got a response!

But it was unlike anything I had ever heard before — the weary sound of a man slipping from life and embracing a not-so-sudden death. He was choking on his own blood and couldn't utter a complete sentence. His chest heaved in an attempt at one last breath and he expired right then. I swear I could feel his spirit move past me.

The car was still running. If I could just get my left hand to work, I could put the car into gear and ram it into the store to set off the alarm. My mind gave my muscles a command to move, but my body didn't respond.

One thought kept going through my mind: I survived the deadly streets of Los Angeles only to get gunned down in Natchez.

The pager signaled a call coming through, but all I could focus on was my heartbeat. The consistent thumps against my chest were so loud. At least it was still beating.

I had never felt so alone in my life and tears pooled in my eyes. But it was too late to cry.

All I wanted to do was think about my life: my mother, my son, my brothers and sister. The times we had spent together and the times we would never be together again.

I lay there and waited for the temperature to change.

My sins, which were too numerous to name, would send me straight to hell, I was sure. I had finally gotten what was coming to me.   I closed my eyes, focused on my heartbeat and prepared to meet my maker.

Just a few minutes passed and a light appeared. Then, a voice. I opened my eyes — slowly, as if that effort alone would be my last move. The temperature was still cool, probably a better sign than any.

I could barely see the face that went with the voice, but I could make out pale skin and deep blue eyes. This was probably that blue-eyed angel my mother told me about as a child. A sense of comfort enveloped my whole being. I had been given a pardon! I was actually going to Heaven.

But then, my angel asked questions and something didn't feel right. I had never died before, but I knew it was not supposed to go this way.

My eyes were too heavy to keep open, but I didn't want the angel to leave me. I could see him more clearly now. A cowboy hat perched on his head. Blue lights from a policeman's cruiser flashed behind him. The crackle of conversation flowed in and out of a two-way radio.

This was an angel? Really? Since when did angels carry a holstered gun? When did they wear a gold badge?

I closed my eyes and thought: Pale skin, blue eyes, and a badge? Maybe he wasn't an angel of mercy.

Maybe he was the angel. . . of death.

"Are you still alive, boy?"

I slowly opened my eyes and looked into the face of the sheriff.

I asked, "How do I look, man?"

He didn't respond.

I told him the name of the guy who shot me, and then recited my mother's phone number.

"Tell my mama I'm sorry and I love her."

I closed my eyes again. This time I was sure that I was really on my way out. The next time I opened my eyes, I would be in Heaven...or hell.

Chapter 34
A Miracle

I heard a flurry of activity. Someone whispered a prayer in a soothing, comforting voice. Someone held my hand, the touch made me feel secure.

I was too afraid to open my eyes; I wasn't ready to find out my final destination. But then, I thought about the prayer and the warm touch. This had to be Heaven.

That was when I let my eyes open and I scanned the area. This wasn't Heaven, this was a hospital. I turned my head just a little and saw my mother's hand holding mine.

Her touch was gentle, but the look on her face was not. There were tears in her eyes and a bunch of worry lines etched in her face.

I wanted to say something, but I tasted blood in my mouth. That was when unconsciousness took me away again. I don't know how long I did that. In and out, in and out. And every time I opened my eyes, my mother was right there, still holding my hand.

Once again I opened my eyes, and this time, my mother wasn't there. I panicked. Had I finally left earth?

"Where is the helicopter?"

That was my mother, that was her voice.

She said, "My son is laying there dying before my eyes! I could've driven him there by now!"

She sounded angry and in control. A few seconds later, she was back at my side. She took my hand again and filled me with comfort.

I wanted to tell her how much I loved her and how sorry I was, but I slipped out of awareness again.

The next time my eyes opened, I summoned the courage to look Mama in her eyes. The pain in them was frightening. She shook her head, but kept her gaze on me.

I heard a whirling overhead. A helicopter? And then, there was all of this activity around me.

Later I would find out that they were helicopter medics, rushing in to get me on a special gurney. They moved me onto it and rushed me outside. I managed to glance back at the bed where I'd left behind a huge puddle of blood.

I didn't have to be totally conscious to realize that I was losing blood as fast as they were replacing it. As they rolled me to the loading zone, I was surprised to see some of my other relatives in the lobby. I made a point to look each one in their eyes knowing this could be the last time I saw them.

The four rednecks had a problem loading me into the helicopter because of my huge frame. One of them even asked if I could move enough to help them fit me in.

One of the medics replied, as they continued struggling, "This is nothing but dead weight, anyway."

* * *

I was floating high above the operating table, looking down at my bullet-riddled body being worked on by a team of surgeons. The doctors worked feverishly, looking like they were doing everything to save my life, but I was at complete peace. Everything around me was white, soothing and serene. Not just white, but a brilliant white — a thousand times whiter than any white I'd ever seen.

There was so much peace around me that I no longer feared death. I even began to think about being reunited with Tupac and Jay.

But my son came to mind, and it all changed. I said a prayer, "God, please don't take me from my son."

I watched the doctor, the one they called Yates, instructing his team to send me back to X-ray. He wanted to know why I was losing so much blood and where I was hemorrhaging.

Time passed, I'm not sure how much, and Dr. Yates picked up the phone in the operating room. He pumped his fist in the air, victory style. "He's stable."

I floated back into a bed and woke in the recovery room...with my mother holding my hand. Her lips were moving, as if she were uttering a prayer. And mine were, too, still asking God not to take me from my son.

* * *

The next few days were traumatic as I found out just how close I came to death. They had told my mother that I only had a ten percent chance of survival. The bullet that hit me behind my ear had traveled downward and severed a main artery in my throat. A second bullet had shattered my jaw. Three other bullets hit me in my right shoulder where all the central nerves were. And my heart had stopped beating on three different occasions.

I was alive, but not in good shape. My mouth had been wired shut; they weren't sure if my jaw would ever heal. I was breathing through a trachea and another hose was inserted into my right lung. My head was swollen to twice its normal size and they'd had to take a vein from my right thigh and placed it in my right bicep. They also took a 10" x 8" piece of skin from the same thigh and grafted it onto my bicep.

The doctors told me that I would have to have extensive physical therapy to learn how to walk all over again, but the worst news was that I was paralyzed from the shoulder down and would never be able to use my right arm again.

That was fine with me...I was happy to be alive.

I was in the hospital in Jackson, Mississippi, but that didn't stop my relatives and friends from coming to see me. First to visit was my wife. While I was still in the ICU, Debbie flew in to be by my side. Though one of our close relatives, Henry, who lived near the hospital opened his home to everyone, Debbie stayed in the hospital with me. She slept on two chairs pushed together, and my mother found a quilt from somewhere that Debbie used as a cover.

She wasn't the only one to fly in from California. Knowing how close Misty was to me, Debbie called her, and that old woman jumped on the first thing smoking from Los Angeles. The day she arrived, I heard that raspy voice all the way in the hallway.

"Where's my son?" she snapped at one of the nurses.

She barged into my room, making a grand entrance like she was the queen of England, wearing a black full-length mink and draped in a couple hundred grand worth of jewelry.

Even though everyone traveled far to be with me, my mother was the one who was there the entire time and she ran the show. She was strict with the visiting rules, making sure that everybody got their fifteen minute visit, but just fifteen minutes, that was all.

While my mother kept visiting rules for my family tight, my wife set the standards for the nursing staff. She made it clear that she wanted the best care for me. I had fresh towels, prompt service, and whatever I needed.

I was amazed by the number of people who came, but there were two overwhelming situations — one that turned out good, the other one, bad.

One of the very best days was receiving a get well card from my son. He printed it up on his computer and my mother delivered it.

Get well, Dad.

Words couldn't describe how special that was.

Right after that it was my father! Debbie told me that my mother was in the hallway talking to my father on the phone.

I had been waiting for this moment my whole life. He did care after all. I couldn't wait to hear his voice.

But when Mama walked into the room, she wasn't holding her cell.

"Mama, weren't you just on the phone with my father?"

Her face filled with dread. "He was calling to see how you were doing. That's all."

I tried to keep my face stiff and my expression neutral, not wanting anyone to know how devastated I was. I wasn't expecting too much from him, just a few encouraging words over the phone. Surely I was worthy of that.

My mind flipped through all the years, all his lies and all his broken promises. This was the last straw. I would hate him for the rest of my natural born life. And from that point, I did my best to put him out of my mind.

Instead, I focused on getting well. I was out of ICU in three days and moved to the third floor to finish my recovery. The first thing I expected was a visit from the police.

The shooting had been front page news the morning after the ambush, and initially it was reported that I was dead. I was considered a miracle, and like I said, I was so glad to be alive. But lying in that hospital bed in University Medical Center Hospital had stripped me of almost everything (though I still had twenty thousand dollars and twenty pounds of marijuana at the safe house.) I felt like I was in a ghetto impeachment.

Now that I had all of these physical issues, I had no idea how I would take care of my family. How would I deal with all the haters who had prayed for my downfall? How far would I have to go to maintain the respect that I'd worked so hard for?

The questions overwhelmed me.

My wife was asleep in her makeshift bed, and I glanced up at the clock, something I did often. It was half past two. My nurse would be coming in the next thirty minutes.

One minute to three, the pain medication had worn off and debilitating spasms hit me with a vengeance.

The nurse walked through the door at three on the dot with a syringe, the solution to my problems. She inserted the syringe into the IV and that liquid heaven flowed into my veins.

I had never experienced a high that wonderful and it was wonderful because the Demerol took my mind away from a single destructive thought that had started to fill my mind.

Suicide.

Visions of suicide kept coming to me as I asked myself all of those questions. It would be a long time before I'd be able to take care of myself. Right now, I couldn't even wipe my own butt. I was totally helpless.

When the nurse left the room, I glanced once again at the clock. Only three hours and forty-seven minutes to go until my next dose.

I couldn't wait.

* * *

It didn't take long before my mind turned away from my injuries and pain. Yes, I was in pretty bad shape, but I didn't have medical insurance and so I had to get back to the business of making money. First up was the safe house.

With a wired-up jaw, I couldn't do much talking, but with a pen and some paper, I instructed Debbie and Serge to go to the safe house and secure the drugs and the money. I then had Debbie call Cowboy and Vince. After they drove to Jackson to see me, I turned my cousins over to Debbie. She ran a tighter ship than I ever did.

With my business rolling a little bit again, I tried to turn my focus back to my healing. But it wasn't easy.

I'd been in the hospital for a few weeks when one day, my wife helped me to the bathroom. She left me alone; I was determined to at least go to the bathroom by myself. But learning how to wipe your ass with your left hand after being right handed all your life was one hell of a task!

On my way back to the bed, I passed the mirror and stopped. My face and head were still swollen. A line of stitches ran along my jawline and a bandage behind my right ear covered another bullet wound. I had a scraggly afro with a matching beard. Intravenous feedings had caused me to lose forty pounds; my massive frame had withered away.

I looked at that stranger whose tears streamed downward. This couldn't be G Man.

I'd forgotten that Debbie was in the room and my wife moved to me and blocked my view of the mirror.

"Don't worry baby, you'll get past this." She gave me a kiss on my scarred cheek. "That scar might be kinda sexy after it heals. You can always change your nickname to Scarface."

I released a much needed laugh and made it back to my bed. But though I laughed, it was still hard to speak with this wired-up jaw.

As the days passed, though, my spirit moved in the wrong direction. I became more and more bitter. I kept going over everything that had happened, asking myself why? In the end, there was no one to blame but me.

But no matter how down I got, my wife wouldn't let me stay there. While I was hospitalized, I saw a completely different side of her. She was patient and kind, loving and strong.

When they wheeled me downstairs for physical therapy, Debbie was with me during every session, helping me, encouraging me.

The workouts were grueling, but soon I was walking again. Just a little at a time, three inches at first, then a few more inches every day.

My wife pushed me hard, expecting the most from me and I did everything I could to live up to her expectations. The day I made it past the nurse's station, the nurses applauded. I was truly a miracle.

I began to feel a little encouraged and I started asking Dr. Yates, during his daily visits, when would I be able to go home.

"As soon as I see you walking."

After he left my room I was forced to think back to those nightmares that I used to have, the ones where I had to choose between losing my arm or leg. I had always chosen my arm, and that was exactly what happened. Then I thought about a comment I made after visiting Auntie Lena one day. I could never imagine being paralyzed — and I wasn't.

It was just a little over a week before Thanksgiving, and I decided to make that my goal. I'd be home for that holiday.

No matter how hard I had to work.

Chapter 35
The Power of Prayer

Even though Thanksgiving wasn't too far away, Debbie had to leave to get back to her job and my stepdaughter. I hated to see her go, but she made me promise that I would see her soon when I was discharged from the hospital.

Once Debbie left, if I thought I would be alone, I was mistaken. My mother stepped in and took over where my wife left off.

Mama stayed with me twenty-four-seven, going through the same ritual as Debbie, sleeping in my room in those two chairs as a makeshift bed.

Having my mother there was amazing, not only because I could feel her love, but because I could also hear her prayers. In the middle of the night I'd wake up and overhear her thanking God for sparing me.

But even with her prayers, I was falling deeper into a depression. Thanksgiving was getting closer and I could only stand on my own for a few moments. If I didn't do something, I wouldn't be going home.

The pressure I'd put on myself made me more depressed, and there were nights when I couldn't sleep. During those times, I'd just stare at my mother, sleeping on those two chairs, and I'd think about how lucky I was to have her.

But my dark thoughts were never far away. I always wondered what was going to happen to me. What in the fuck was I gonna do from here? What in the fuck could I do?

One night I stayed awake for hours, staring at that swollen piece of useless meat that was my right arm. Over and over I commanded my arm to move, but there was nothing. How was I supposed to survive on the streets partially paralyzed?

All I could do was cry, and since my mother was asleep I just let my tears flow. It felt like I'd cried all night, but I must've fallen asleep because I opened my eyes to my mother washing my face with a hot towel.

She rubbed my skin gently and it was so soothing...until one of those spasms hit me.

I let out a deathly scream and grabbed her hand with my left hand. I squeezed her hard, so hard that I was afraid that I'd hurt her.

"I'm sorry," I cried, wishing that they'd just cut my shoulder off!

It took a few minutes for the spasms to pass, and I did feel better after my medication. But after my breakfast (which I was still taking through a straw) my mother went into action.

After she propped me up in bed, she said, "Okay, Grego, let's start walking, son."

I didn't want to. It wasn't like I was going to make my goal, considering the next day was Thanksgiving. But since it was my mother asking, I did it because I would've tried to walk on water if she asked me to.

So, I got up and it didn't take too long for my mother to have my not-quite-as-big ass walking pretty good. My confidence was building by the hour.

On my walk right after dinner, we made it to the end of the hallway. And then, just as we turned around, Dr. Yates stepped off the elevator.

He stopped moving when he saw me. All he could do was shake his head.

"Well, I guess you really want to make that Thanksgiving feast." He smiled. "I'm going to keep my word. I'll let you go home first thing in the morning."

* * *

Thanksgiving morning, only three weeks after I'd been admitted to the hospital, my mother wheeled me out of my room and the whole nurse and doctor team were waiting for me. We said emotional goodbyes and I told them I would never forget them, and I meant it.

It took us a while to get me settled into the car, but finally, I was sitting back. As we rode down the highway, I felt happy at first, as the fresh, crisp air came through the window. My lungs were used to the machine's assistance, so it hurt a little when I breathed too hard.

It didn't take long for the questions to begin to fill my head. What was I going to do now? How would I take care of myself? I couldn't imagine being dependent on someone else for the rest of my life.

About 1:30, when we made that right turn off the highway onto our road, I felt like I was coming home to a hero's welcome.

Familiar faces stared back at me, admiration all in their expressions. I guess they were impressed that I'd survived five gunshot wounds. As we passed, they slowly raised their hands, four fingers up, two twisted—the West coast "W."

What did they think about Jay? He was dead and maybe it was no big deal to them. Youth today were totally desensitized to the most extreme violence. How would I ever be able to tell them that the hustling shit wasn't cool at all? Since they were like me, they probably would never have a positive male role model in their lives.

We finally stopped in front of the trailer, and I had never been so happy to see a doublewide house on wheels in my life. It took about ten minutes for my mother to help me up the steps, before she settled me on the sofa and propped pillows all around me, especially under my right arm.

We hadn't been in the house for ten minutes before a car pulled up, then Angela walked into the house. My undercover cool ass chick came in carrying several bags. She put them down, then came over to embrace me.

"You can go home and relax now," she told my mother.

I knew that my mentally and physically exhausted mother appreciated that.

She left us alone and Angela went to work to help me to feel as normal as possible. She turned on the football game, then said, "I'm going to make you a great Thanksgiving dinner."

She had already cooked the meal: Mashed potatoes, dressing, ham, turkey...all she had to do now was prepare it in the blender.

After a few minutes, Angela brought me a big bowl of a Thanksgiving soup. She held the straw and guided it through the only gap between my wired teeth.

I'm telling you at that moment, this was the greatest meal I had ever had! I understood what it meant to appreciate the simple things.

Afterward, she helped me into the bathroom and gave me a thorough cleaning, before changing my bandages. I hated to look at the raw, pink flesh from the skin graft, but the dressings had to be changed daily. Once that was done, she blended my medication together so that I could swallow it all.

Just when I finished taking my medicine, the phone rang, startling me. Not many people knew that I was home, but Angela picked it up and pressed the receiver to my ear.

It only took me a moment to realize that it was one of my faithful customers calling, taking a chance that someone would answer.

I motioned for Angela to hang up, but the call reminded me of another dilemma. With Debbie gone, I still had fifteen pounds of marijuana to get rid of.

Hustling was in my blood and it didn't take long for a plan to form. I couldn't believe I was about to hustle in my condition, but I needed every dollar I could get.

I was able to get Angela to understand me enough for her to get my stash that Debbie had hidden in my bedroom closet. Next, with wired jaw and all, I gave Angela a crash course on how to use a scale and bag up quarter pounds. For the next hour, we sat in the living room and she did everything that I told her until she had to leave for work. But she didn't plan to leave me alone. She called Vince.

Angela hadn't been gone long before the heavy rumble of thunder roared off in the distance. The sound made me think of Jay, who loved the rain. It had been three weeks now and I still couldn't believe that Jay was gone. The question that had been pressing on my subconscious came to my mind again. *Am I responsible for Jay's death?*

The thunder became louder, and with a couple of the windows open, I could smell the rain. The wind started and became stronger, blowing into the trailer.

The windows needed to be closed, but there was nothing I could do. My only hope was that Vince would arrive soon.

For some reason, the rain, the thunder, the wind all mixed with the memories in my mind. And I heard the sounds of the shooting. I heard the gunshots, I heard Jay gurgling, I heard his last breath.

Panic set in. Sweat flowed from every one of my pores.

Then, "Hey Big Cuz, looks like you done proved dem wrong again!"

That was enough to make my heart slam against my chest. I hadn't heard Vince pull up, let alone come through the front door.

He closed the window and sat on the sofa.

After my breathing returned to normal, we chatted for a minute before I asked, "Vince, do you have any kind of weapon?"

He looked at me like I was crazy. I wasn't sure if the look came from my garbled speech or if it was because he couldn't believe that a person who'd just survived a shooting would ask for a gun.

Finally, he said, "I might have an old .22 revolver."

"Go get it."

He gave me another long stare before he left and returned within fifteen minutes with a rusted gun that had only one side on the handle grip.

"It still works," he told me.

That was all I needed to know. "Reach out to only the most trusted workers and finish dumping the last of the batch."

He scooped up the product, but then he hesitated and slowly sat back down. "I have a few messages for you."

"What?" I frowned.

"A few of your foot soldiers want the green light to hit Ty's whole family."

I'd heard that the word had spread; everyone in town was saying that Ty and Jamey's family had set me up.

"No!" My word could have Ty, Jamey and everyone they knew wiped out, because revenge for the kind of hit they put on me was part of the game. But that was not what I wanted. I didn't want to add murder to the list of all that I'd done; I'd already caused enough damage to my family's name.

I continued, "Tell everyone I said thank you, but that's not the plan."

Not that I was sure of what the plan was. I was in quite a precarious position. It wasn't going to be long before the police came around questioning me, since I was the only eyewitness to a murder. In the hustler's domain, the only witness often turned up dead so that the criminal could walk free. Ty and Jamey had to be thinking that.

I didn't tell Vince that as he left the house. I'd kept that thought to myself.

Right after Vince walked out the door, my eyes felt heavy from the medication cocktail and I finally lay down. I took the gun with me, and used my left hand to grip the handle when I tucked it under my pillow.

After a while, I fell asleep and into a nightmare.

* * *

Suddenly I woke up and felt the presence of someone in the room. I reached for my pea shooter, but before I even pulled it out, I felt her touch and realized that it was my mother.

With her gentle touch, she wiped the sweat from my forehead, then she fed me and gave me my meds before she left.

I was worried about my mother having to take care of me all by herself. But my wife wasn't going to let that happen. I hadn't been home for a week when Debbie came to Mississippi.

We fell into a routine where she took care of me, and helped my mother get me back and forth to the hospital in Jackson. It was hard on Debbie; not my recovery, just living in Mississippi. She was a high-maintenance, big-city girl. I had to do everything I could to get well so that I could return to Los Angeles. That became our focus and Debbie pushed me hard in physical therapy.

My health was number one, but close behind was my business. I kept checking in with Vince and Cowboy, and my cousins were coming through for me. They were moving the product, and soon they were down to the last five pounds

That became my focus, to get better, to move the weed. And both of my goals happened. Just two weeks after I came home, I found out that Cowboy and Vince sold all the marijuana. And just days after that, once Debbie agreed to take responsibility for my care, I got the green light from my doctor to leave Mississippi!

The evening before we were scheduled to leave, the living room was alive with laughter and chatter as my family packed the trailer to celebrate my recovery and to say goodbye. Even though I had been exposed as a hustler, my family acted like nothing had happened. I admired that. This was what a real family was about — people who loved you and who forgave, even if they didn't quite forget.

* * *

317

The next morning, as we pulled away from the house, I scanned every square foot of property, not sure when I would be returning to Natchez. We traveled the same highway that led to and from town and as we approached the store, the place where I'd been shot. I allowed my eyes to do something that I hadn't done since I came home. . . I looked at the scene of the crime.

Right away, I broke out in a cold sweat. I couldn't take in a solid breath. But my gaze was transfixed on the parking lot and the scene played in my mind long after we drove a good distance away.

At the airport, as my wife pushed me in the wheelchair through the terminal, I felt like everyone was looking at me. *Was this how the rest of my life would be?*

It was an ordeal to get on the plane, but once I was on and strapped into my seat, I watched out the window as the plane slowly taxied down the runway. Only when we were in the air did I breathe a sigh of relief. Now I could think about my life. And what were the first words that came to my mind? *What's next?*

Chapter 36
The Casualties of Hustling

Two months after I returned to Los Angeles, not much had changed. My right arm was still paralyzed, and I had to continue to keep it elevated. My mouth was still wired shut and the doctor wasn't sure if my jawbone would grow back.

The nightstand next to the bed, once covered all the time with several thousand dollars, was now only covered with medication.

My frame took up the whole bed, so I slept alone while my wife slept on the floor.

My wife had sacrificed so much for me, including giving up her job so that she could take care of me. That put even more pressure on us financially. We were both worried about where our next dollar would come from, but for Debbie, it was all about me. That was her number one priority, getting me well.

Even though that was her focus, it was always a fight for me. I was filled with constant depression, feeling like I was dying a slow death as the weeks passed and the bills piled high.

We watched our bills (especially medical) grow and grow until they reached a reached a whopping $180,000. Debbie and I then did something that we'd never done. We went to our local county office to get assistance. After being there all day, we left with a promise that we would receive $220 a month in cash and another $180 in food stamps.

All I wanted to do was sleep when we got back home, and I took an extra dose of pain pills to take the edge off. But even though I slept for hours, I awakened in the middle of the night, now unable to sleep.

Debbie had fallen asleep on the living room sofa, and I wanted my wife to rest. It was time for my meds, but I didn't wake her. I had to find a way to take care of myself.

With my good hand, I reached the remote and turned to an army movie, but then the spasms kicked in.

I was determined not to yell out to my wife; I was going to do this myself. I reached for the glass on the nightstand, then dumped the pills. There was no way I could crush them the way Debbie did, so with a shaky hand I poured 7-Up into the glass, ignoring the fact that half spilled on the carpet.

I gathered up enough strength and coordination to drop the pills into the glass one by one, then waited until they dissolved and sipped the meds through my straw.

I'd done it. It was a small accomplishment, but one that was important to me.

I leaned back and watched the army movie, thinking that I would fall asleep soon. But I didn't fall asleep soon enough.

A combat scene filled the screen and the camera zeroed in on two soldiers in a foxhole. A second later, one soldier was shot — in the head. As the soldier lay dying, his partner cradled his head against his chest.

The scene hit me like a freight train going fifty miles an hour. I reached for the remote, but couldn't get to it. I was stuck watching what I didn't want to watch.

Hot tears flowed down my face as I was transported back to Mississippi to that parking lot and the car and the gunfire, to the hole in Jay's forehead and his last breath before his chin dipped toward his chest.

How was I supposed to do this? How was I supposed to live the rest of my life with all of this pain and sadness?

I wanted all of it to just go away.

Reaching toward the nightstand, I put every pill I saw into the glass still halfway filled with 7-Up. As I dropped the pills one by one, I tried not to think about my family; I especially tried not to think about my son.

I knew how many would view this. Some would look at what I'd done and say this was a selfish act, but they hadn't walked in my shoes.

There was no fear inside of me. It wasn't like I'd be alone when I got there. Jay would be waiting for me. I should have been with him anyway. He should have never been the only one to lose his life that night.

My tears were flowing so hard that I couldn't even see the contents in the glass. I picked it up, swirled the liquid around, then looked for the straw.

I couldn't find it; it wasn't on the nightstand. I then spotted it on the floor. I kicked my left leg out of the bed and a spasm shot through my whole right side. The pain was so excruciating! I tried to grab the pillow, but lost my balance and knocked everything off the nightstand, including my farewell cocktail.

"Baby, baby!" my wife shouted from the living room. "Are you all right?" Seconds later, Debbie stood at the door. "What are you trying to do? Why didn't you call me?"

I looked at the cocktail that had seeped into the carpet. Evidently God had other plans for me.

Chapter 37
Surviving the Game

One year later

My ability to walk got better and my jaw healed without the need for more surgery. The only thing was, a year later, there were no changes in my arm.

While my health constantly improved, my relationship steadily deteriorated. With all that had happened, with all that was going on, my wife's patience weakened. It was hard for her; her once powerful, providing husband had been reduced to a struggling citizen. Her frustration eventually turned into verbal abuse, and often her verbal blows hurt more than being shot.

It didn't take long before I tired of her never-ending complaints about money. As much as I hated to do it, I started hustling again.

I called Misty, figuring she would be the best place to start. We'd stayed in touch, though I hadn't reached out to her in months because she was still fucking with her young boyfriend.

When I called Misty, she said, "Hey son, how you holding up over there? Are you ready to make some money yet?"

I wondered if that woman was psychic. I told her about all that was going on, from my healing, to the cost of my medication.

"Tell your wife to bring you up to see your Mama, boy," she said. "I'll have one of my doctor friends help you out with your medication."

I told Debbie, and three hours later, we pulled up in front of her house. The once-beautiful lawn wasn't manicured like it had always been, and the driveway that had always been filled with expensive cars, now held two work vans from her flower shop.

That raised a red flag for me, but the maid was still there; she let me and Debbie in and that distinguishable voice immediately reached my ears. We joined Misty in the den and she greeted us with a hug.

"Have you been taking care of my son?" Debbie nodded and Misty added, "You're right on time, son. The doctor should be here any minute."

We settled in and tried to catch up on what had been going on, but every few minutes, Misty was on the phone. Between what I'd seen when we drove up and her conversations, I got an uneasy feeling.

Her conversations revealed disturbing facts: Her young boyfriend had left and took all of his expensive toys with him, and it seemed she had legal problems pending. What was most frightening, though, was how freely she discussed her illegal business over her phone. Misty's ship was sinking faster than the Titanic!

We'd been there over an hour when she called her doctor friend. Each time she called and he didn't answer, she cussed him out.

After another hour, I looked at Debbie. It was time for us to leave. But before we hit the door, Misty handed me a half-ounce of powder cocaine.

"See if you can make a few dollars off it." She then grabbed a pad. "What're the medications that you're taking?"

I told her and she wrote it all down. "I'll get the doctor to give you three refills of each. Can you come back tomorrow?"

I told her I would. Misty walked us to the car and even once Debbie and I were inside, Misty stayed talking to us. But then suddenly, she stopped in mid sentence, and her eyes fixed on the late model Crown Victoria passing by.

For the first time ever, I saw fear flash in her eyes.

Her voice shook when she said, "Fucking undercover still watching me." She kept her eyes focused on the car. "My phone is probably still bugged, too."

Before I could question her about what was going on, she told me about some white bitch setting her and her doctor up. That was when I knew I had to get the fuck away from there.

On the entire ride back, I went over everything that I saw and everything that I heard. Basically, Misty had officially lost her fucking mind! I would pick up those pills tomorrow, but after that, I would keep my distance.

The next day, Debbie and I drove out to Misty's again, but as we approached the road leading to Misty's place, the hair stood up on the back of my neck. Her house came into view and my shirt became soaked with perspiration. Her driveway was filled with cars and men in dark blue DEA jackets. They were gathered at the open trunk of one car assembling "Evidence" boxes.

Several of the men glanced up as we passed by, but because my windows were tinted, they couldn't see inside.

To get away, we had to turn the truck around since there was only one way in and one way out of her street. As Debbie maneuvered the truck, all I could think about was if Misty had been under surveillance, then they knew about me. My decision to hustle again had just turned into a nightmare.

I braced for the officers to jump in front of my truck with weapons drawn, but nothing happened as we passed.

On our way down the hill, I said, "Keep driving until you see a phone booth." I couldn't get on the freeway until I at least attempted to call.

At a phone booth, Debbie pulled over and dialed the number. When she spoke into the phone, her expression confirmed my worst fear. She didn't have to say a word.

Misty had been a giant in this game. She meant the world to me and I felt like my heart had been ripped out.

The ride home took forever, giving me plenty of time to think about all the *what ifs*. And once I got home, I found out even more. I called Misty's daughter; she told me the doctor had turned informant. He had been wearing a wire for at least a month.

Misty's problems had just become mine. I needed to sell the product she gave me to keep a roof over my head, but with the information they had from the wire, the police could kick my door in at any moment. And the sad part was there wasn't a damn thing I could do. I was too broke to throw the cocaine away and too wounded to run if I had to.

After taking a few days to figure it out, I realized I didn't have a choice; I'd have to take my chances hustling.

It didn't take long for us to find my first customer, a crackhead around the corner. After that, one customer led to another, and finally we were able to pay rent and the other bills. But while money became less of an issue, my wife became a bigger problem.

The arguments with Debbie were getting worse. I couldn't believe someone so close to me could inflict so much pain on my heart. I convinced myself that she was just seeking revenge for all the shit I had done in the past. But hadn't I suffered enough? Wasn't I still suffering every day?

The only things that kept me sane were the visits from my son over the weekends, and then having my son and nephew over the holidays.

But being with Greg and Dakari didn't help with Debbie. There came a point when I began to envision life without my wife. The only thing was, I had to figure out how to make that happen.

Chapter 38
JUNE BUG

Summer, 1999

Three years had passed, but the nightmare of that night remained with me. After all of this time, I still didn't have the use of my right hand; physical therapy wasn't helping me.

But my challenges went way beyond physical.

I was supposed to go back to Mississippi to testify against Jamey and Slick (his accomplice), but they'd taken a plea bargain: twenty-eight and forty-three years, respectively. And to make it worse, I'd been indicted by a grand jury for the marijuana Jay and I had that night.

When my attorney delivered that news, it felt like a death sentence. I couldn't begin to imagine going back to prison. My disabilities would make me completely vulnerable.

But that was a serious possibility because the laws in Mississippi were harsh. I wasn't sure they even acknowledged the Constitution. It was highly probable that I could end up with a sentence just as stiff as the guys who shot me!

Hell, I might as well have killed a motherfucker. The mere thought of being locked up with my assailants was just crazy.

I didn't like the idea of being a fugitive again, but I didn't like the idea of going back to prison, either. That fear consumed my every thought and I needed to find a low-key safe house to lay my head until I could figure out a plan. It only took Debbie days to find a one-bedroom complex, just two blocks West of our apartment. We purchased furniture and all the other comforts of home.

By the time Debbie was done, I had a cozy nest, but all the comforts couldn't get me to relax. I had a king-size bed, but I refused to sleep in it. I slept on the couch with one eye open. I was anxious every minute of every day.

Three weeks after I moved in, Debbie came over one day and the two of us got into one of our heated fights. To this day, I don't remember what it was about, definitely something stupid. But we were loud enough for the neighbors to call the police.

Before I even knew what happened, the police showed up at my door. I was trembling, not only because I was on the run, but Debbie and I had just brought four ounces of cocaine into the house.

The female officer who came to the door was cool, until she asked my name. I had to say something, so I gave her a fake name. She accepted it and I felt like I'd gotten away with this. She then wrote down the license plate number of my wife's car...which was registered in my *real* name.

Even though the officer left (it was the end of her work day) I knew I'd be seeing her again real soon.

That night I couldn't even sleep, and when daylight came I was just as paranoid. I sat by my front door, checking out everything. Nothing seemed too unusual, except all of these cars with tinted windows that kept passing by.

At first, I was not too alarmed. But then, when I stood to make a run to the kitchen, I watched a tall black guy stroll past my front door. He kept moving, but I checked out his expensive New Balance tennis shoes, his Levi jeans, and the way his shirt was tucked in nice and neat. But it was the Ray Ban sunglasses and USC hat that were a dead giveaway. The icing on the cake was the tight ass jeans he wore. He couldn't squeeze a quarter into his back pockets! I didn't know of any street dudes or college kids that wore jeans that tight. I kept my eyes on him until he turned right at the end of my block two houses away.

I wasn't one hundred percent sure that he was a cop, but I wasn't going to take any chances. I somehow had to get the drugs and my handgun out of my apartment.

I grabbed the phone and called my wife, telling her what I'd just observed.

"I'll be right over," she said, with the same alarm in her voice that I felt.

I hung up, then walked out the front door and headed down the driveway. But before I could make it to my truck, the words, "Freeze motherfucker! Lay flat down on your stomach!" rang in my ears.

Ol' boy who'd just passed my house was right on top of me. He had brought ten other cops with him.

"Is your name Greg Marshall?"

No sense in telling a lie. "Yeah, that's me, man."

He handcuffed me, then lifted me to my feet. They took me back into the apartment and dumped me onto the couch as they searched the apartment. The four ounces of dope were under the couch in a cigar box and my pistol was under the cushion where I sat. Once they discovered the drugs and the gun, I was going back into the pen for good.

I sat there just waiting, waiting for them to come over to me. And then I heard Debbie.

"My husband is in there," she said.

But the cops outside wouldn't let her inside.

Still I sat, waiting for this to be over, then one of the detectives grabbed me off the couch. "We've finished our search," he said as he led me toward the door.

What? They hadn't found my gun or the weed!

I guess that didn't matter too much, they'd gotten what they'd come for. They'd captured a fugitive.

The moment I stepped outside, I locked eyes with my wife.

As I walked past her, she asked, "What did he do? Why are you taking him away?"

She was still asking hundreds of questions as they stuffed me into the back of one of those cars that I'd seen earlier. Before they closed the door, one of the officers answered Debbie when she asked where they were taking me.

"He'll be housed in the Los Angeles County Jail until he's extradited back to Mississippi."

Mississippi! It was all over now for me.

* * *

Thirty minutes later, I was escorted through the doors of The Twin Towers, a new state of the art facility that was the men's central jail. The stench from the other inmates was the first thing that hit me.

We were herded into one of the holding tanks that was designed for twenty inmates, but were packed with at least fifty bodies.

I thought I would never see this kind of place again. And this time I had more to worry about. Human vultures laid in the cut for that weak or wounded prey.

But I was still an old-school-convict. I would have to adapt. My life literally depended on it. However, I found out that a little luck was on my side. My disability earned me the privilege of being placed in the medical ward.

Getting processed into the county jail was pure torture, taking hours and hours to finish. I was finally taken to my bed. Well, it wasn't really a bed. The jail was so overcrowded that I had to sleep on a two-inch thick mattress on the cement floor.

By the time I had that primitive bed prepared, it was close to three o'clock in the morning. Even though I was exhausted, I couldn't get to sleep. All I could think about was my situation. What was going to happen to me now? I had to make it, especially tomorrow. The first day in any jail was the most important.

Just before I closed my eyes, I took one last look around. True convicts always slept with one eye open and I needed to spot those men. They would surely be looking at me, too.

* * *

I had about two hours of sleep before blinding lights snapped on and the voice of a redneck sheriff boomed through the loud speakers. I lay on my mattress and scanned the whole room once again, evaluating any potential threats. No immediate red flags popped up, so I rolled up my mattress and headed to the sink to brush my teeth.

I ate breakfast, then settled into the dayroom to watch television. There were four pay phones in the middle of the unit and getting on the phone was the only thing on my mind.

I waited at one of the stainless steel tables until it was my turn, and I called Debbie first. She was bred for a crisis like this and she assured me that she would take care of the lawyer situation.

Just like Debbie promised, the lawyer was there early the next morning. I let him do all the initial talking so that I could evaluate him.

My first impression was that he seemed knowledgeable about my case considering the short amount of time it had been on his plate. He was also straightforward.

He told me my options: I could fight extradition to Mississippi or I could go and face the music. He gave me a day to think about it since Mississippi had ten working days to come and get me.

Just before he stood to leave I asked, "How much money did my wife pay to retain you?"

"Two grand."

I was a little ticked that we had given this man that much money to tell me what I already knew.

My next visitor was my wife. Debbie came the next morning and we talked through my options and the possibilities. At the end, I told her to call my cousin, Watani. I was thinking that maybe with his connections, he would be able to help. He was really the only hope I had.

Over the next days, all I did was count down: Seven, six, five, four, three, two, and finally one.

When it got to just a few hours left, I began to think that maybe those Mississippi officers weren't coming for me. Maybe they realized that hell, I was the victim!

At the end of the day, I laid on my bunk to relax and read. But then the sheriff made that dreaded announcement over the PA system, "Greg Marshall, booking #732-45563. Roll your shit up! Mississippi is here to get your ass."

I wrote my wife's phone number down and instructed my cellmate to call her as soon as possible.

Two hours later, I was in a holding tank dressed in civilian clothes with about a half dozen other prisoners who were being extradited to different cities. Two U.S. Marshalls came and shackled us.

We were escorted to a heavily secured transport van to begin our cross-country journey. I looked out of the window as we pulled away from the county jail, wondering if I would ever see Los Angeles again. I had no clue what was ahead since down South, Red Neck Justice prevailed.

Two guards drove the transport van. One was a twenty-seven- year-old beet red, 5'8", 350 pound white dude. The other one was a much taller slim, dark-skinned black guy in his late 40's. Five seconds of listening to him and I knew he was an Uncle Tom Negro.

It seemed like we stopped at every jail along the I-10 Interstate and it took us two days to get to Texas. Three days later, we crossed the Mississippi River Bridge. The lights on the River Boat Casino glowed, and I took in all the other familiar landmarks. I never imagined that I would see it all through the window of a prisoner transport van.

The van pulled up in front of the tiny town jail, which looked more like a large two-story brick house.

I was the only prisoner getting off and several officers were on the front steps to greet me. Two of them grabbed me, one for each arm, and escorted me through the front door.

All eyes were on me as I entered the lobby. I wasn't surprised. I was the big news. In this small town, my case was the equivalent to the OJ Simpson case.

They stripped me of my personal clothing and handed me a black-and-white two-piece jailhouse uniform. The two-sizes-too-small uniform with its huge stripes reminded me of the chain gang movies.

I made it to a cellblock close to five in the morning. As I walked through, I couldn't see the faces in the pitch-black darkness, but I could feel the stares. The jailer ushered me into my new home and locked the gate behind him.

I didn't even get a chance to sit down on my bunk before the silence was broken.

"What's happen' wit you, mane?" The voice paused for a moment. "Dis here is Sonny from the Cut Throat apartments, mane. Wheez been waiting on you. Mane, I cain't even much believe dat dem bastards done brought you way down here."

Sonny was one of Cowboy's right-hand men, a proven foot soldier. I acknowledged him and then more voices greeted me once Sonny stopped talking. Obviously he was the shot caller in that cellblock.

The next voice belonged to a man we named Brrrr Rabbit because he spoke so slowly. "Mane, we done gave Jamey an' dem boys the blues e'r'time we see dem."

The chatter was loud and excited and as they talked, I listened, evaluating it all.

The bottom line was that Jamey and Slick had created what would have to be a future prison war. Eventually, I would have to deal with them, and when I did, I would need some real foot soldiers.

I thanked them for taking care of business and fell silent.

The jailer showed up about thirty minutes later pushing a cart with breakfast. He disappeared and came back with another cart loaded with brown paper lunch sacks. I thought this was an extra treat, but learned that the bags held our second — and final — meal of the day. Hard times were definitely ahead.

Before I even started my breakfast, though, the jailer came to my cell and told me to get my things together.

He escorted me down two flights of stairs to a part of the jail that had nothing but silence and empty cells.

"What's going on?" I asked him.

"You're being isolated for your own protection."

This was the last thing I needed! Now I'd have to explain to my crew that I was not part of a protective custody case. That title ranked right up there with a snitch jacket.

Once he locked me in, I sat down on my bunk and looked around. The silence felt like I was a million miles from the whole world. There was a payphone on the wall. I grabbed it, but there was no dial tone, so I was truly completely alone.

I tried to sleep, but all I did was lie there. I felt a bulge beneath the mattress, and at first I didn't move. But after a while I stood, lifted the mattress, and found a Bible.

I grabbed it, then stared at it for a few moments, thinking about how important that book had been in my life as a child. I wondered where my life would have been if I had just listened to my mother.

I opened it and went straight to Proverbs, read a few pages, then placed the book on the bed. It had just been a few pages, but I didn't want to read anymore. Too much truth in the Good Book.

Plus, I knew that God had given me every chance. How many times had he spared me from certain death? But I ignored all the warnings.

After a few minutes, I picked up the Bible again. I read and read, taking in all the words that told me I still had a chance to change my life. After reading for about two hours, I got down on my knees praying like my mother had taught me. I had to pray; I needed His help in the worst way and I knew He could save me.

I got off my knees and started reading again. I read until I fell asleep.

I was startled awake by the jailer opening my cell. This wasn't the same jailer, this white dude was huge and had to be at least 6'3" and 375 pounds, though he was very polite. He left my cell door open and gave me permission to use the pay phone.

"Just give me a couple of minutes to turn it on from upstairs." He paused at the door for a few seconds before he closed it. "Looky here, Mr. Marshall, dere's a Sheriff been askin' bout you. He da one dat saved yo' life. His name is Julius Cotton. He wants to know if you're up ta seein' him after he gets off work dis evening."

"Of course I don't mind."

After he locked the door, that's all I could think about. I was about to meet the man who had saved my life. I remembered him being a redneck, but couldn't care less about that now. I had never had to thank anyone for saving my life. How would I put my gratitude into words?

I waited a few more minutes, then checked the payphone to find it was on. The first call I made was to Debbie. My wife brought me up to speed. Watani had found a local lawyer, but his fee was $3,500 just to get started. We had no choice but to pay him.

After I hung up, I called my mom. She already knew I was back in Mississippi; Debbie had called her the moment the police had arrested me.

"We're working on some things," I told her. "Don't worry."

Of course, I knew telling her that wasn't going to stop her from worrying, but at least I could try.

I went back into my cell, picked up my Bible and went back to reading where I had left off last night. I read and read until the jailer came and told me to follow him.

We navigated upstairs into the inmate visiting area and he told me to have a seat. The door closed behind him and while I waited, all kinds of emotions flooded me.

Then, I felt his presence before I even turned around.

The first things I saw were his eyes. My mind flashed black to that tragic night and I remembered when I saw his eyes, I'd thought he would be the last living person that I'd ever see.

Even as I stood, I kept my eyes on his eyes. There were tears in his and tears in mine and we hugged for the longest time.

We sat down and talked like old friends. Sometimes when he looked at me, he shook his head.

"It was by the grace of God that you survived, you know that, right?"

I learned that he was a religious family man. "God has given you a second chance," he told me and then quoted scriptures to go along with that.

Hours passed and we just kept going until he had to leave.

"Good luck, Greg," he said before he shook my hand and left.

For the rest of the day and night, I felt so good. Not a bad way to spend my first day in jail. And then, that good feeling continued into the next day when I called Debbie and she told me about the judge I'd have to face.

The regular judge was an old white guy who was known for giving out serious time. But right now, he was on vacation. I would be going in front of a black female judge.

And not only that, the judge was in a legal battle and who was *her* attorney? My attorney!

God could not have set it all up better for me. I was ready to face the judge, and no matter what happened, I knew I was being given the best chance possible.

Chapter 39
Judgment Day

I'd only been in jail two days, and now I was standing in front of the judge.

With everything Debbie had told me, I had a great feeling, but then the judge walked in, and I wasn't sure anymore. I knew all the things that were working in my favor, but when the judge sat down to preside over the court, she didn't look all that friendly. In fact, she was serious and stern, totally professional, and the confidence I had began to wane.

Plus, the way she looked at me, I could tell that it didn't matter to her that I was black.

"Mr. Marshall," she said, looking down from the bench, "you do know that you're facing a sentence of thirty-three years in prison?"

I swallowed hard. "Yes." Maybe I had gotten happy for nothing. Maybe she was going to give me the same sentence that the white judge would have given me.

After giving me a lecture about the dangers of drugs, she handed down my punishment. "Mr. Marshall, you will reimburse the court one thousand, eight hundred dollars, which is the cost of transporting you from California to Mississippi, and then one thousand dollars for court costs."

She slammed the gavel down.

I paused for a moment...was it over? Was that it?

I shook my attorney's hand, and for once I couldn't wait to get back to my cell. I had to call my wife.

Debbie was excited. She got right on it and said she would wire the fine to my lawyer. After that, I called my mother and told her the good news. Then, I went back to my cell to wait for all the paperwork to get squared away.

As I waited, I sat on my bunk and counted my blessings. This was unbelievable. Right next to me was that Bible and I picked it up. As I held it, I had so many questions. What role did God play in all of this? And was this another warning for me to get my shit together?

As I meditated on that, I was full with all kinds of thoughts. Truly, I wanted to change my life this time. I wanted to be the man my mother raised me to be, not the hustler that I had become.

I knew that a lot of what I'd been through came from the scars I'd carried, and many of those emotional scars came from my father. But at some point I was going to have to stop using my father as an excuse. I needed to find and focus on the positive aspects of my life.

Just hours later, I was dressed in my own clothes and two days after I'd stumbled into the jail in shackles, I walked out the front door a free man — in more ways than one.

After my lawyer greeted me, he said, "Today was your lucky day. The presiding judge is due back tomorrow. Don't waste any time getting out of Mississippi."

I shook my attorney's hand and told him he didn't have to worry. I was going to get the hell out of Mississippi.

* * *

My mother pulled up just as my attorney turned to leave. I had never been happier to see her, but then, my smile fell away when my cousin Roy, the police officer, pulled up in his Natchez Police Department patrol car. He didn't get out of his car; he just glared at me from the front seat.

I couldn't blame him. I'd been down here selling drugs right under his nose and he'd probably caught some flack for that.

But after a couple of seconds, he managed to flash me a smile. "Boy, youza lucky son of a gun!" he shouted out. "I hope thangs work out fo' you back in California, cousin."

I smiled and nodded, letting him know I got his message. Just like my attorney, my cousin was letting me know that I needed to get my ass on the first thing smoking.

Well, neither my attorney nor Roy needed to worry about that. I was only going to spend one more night in Natchez; Debbie had booked a flight for me for early the next morning.

But before I got on that plane, I was going to spend the day with my mother. I jumped into her car and hugged her before we took off.

We were chatting until we came close to the scene of the shooting. My mother was silent, I was silent; and I wasn't even going to try to handle it. As we passed the parking lot, I closed my eyes, doing my best to control the emotions inside of me.

Once we got to my mother's house, though, I was back to feeling free. And I enjoyed the time with her, just talking. I apologized to her for what I'd done, and I made a promise that I was out of that life.

I wasn't sure if my mother believed me, but that was fine. I could show her a whole lot better than I could tell her.

The next morning, I was on that first flight to Los Angeles, so happy and so determined to get my life together. I had a new chance and a new outlook. I was ready to begin a new life.

But when I arrived in California, I had a new crisis. I was broke again. This case had cost all of our savings. I was back to the place where I was before. How was I supposed to keep food on the table? Was I strong enough to make something happen without letting the hustler inside of me come out?

I just wasn't sure. I just didn't know.

Chapter 40
The Ultimate Lie

Now that the criminal case in Natchez had been resolved, I gave up my safe house apartment and we sold all the furniture. But of course, that wasn't enough to hold us down. Our financial struggles were back.

I was doing my best to keep a good attitude, but depression was like a cloud and constantly loomed over me.

Hustling seemed like the only way, but I just didn't want to do that anymore, not only because of what happened while I was in jail in Mississippi, but also because having been a victim, now I trusted no one — except God.

Reading that Bible while I was in jail had put a lot of things on my mind. Faith in God is what really stood out to me. Faith and redemption.

I had to have faith in all the promises of God and all the things that I believed He wanted for me. I had to believe that I'd eventually regain use of my arm. I had to believe that everything would be all right. I had to believe that God would take care of me.

I had to believe.

But as the months moved on, our situation became worse. Financially, we were drowning and I wondered why the decision I'd made to stop hustling hadn't opened some doors that would have made my life easier. We had to have a roof over our heads, we had to have food, we had to have just the basics to live. Surely God knew that!

But we dropped so far to the bottom that even the ground was a step up.

It got to the point where I had no choice. All of those spiritual life changes that I wanted to make? All of that would have to wait. I got back in the game.

Selling dope in the streets at my level wasn't complicated. There was a universal formula: Have the best product and one customer will lead to two, two will lead to three, and word of mouth will do the rest.

But it didn't take long for hustling to bore me. I found ways to keep myself out of the streets totally. I found a new hobby, customizing my '86 Toyota pickup truck. *Mini Trucking Magazine* became my new Bible.

What gave me the greatest joy was the time I spent with my children. But that joy was also the source of a great pain, a pain that inside I knew would one day come.

* * *

Even though I still had doubt about Julius being my son, I had decided to stop pressing it. Maybe it was because I'd been in his life since his birth and I was glad to be taking care of him. Maybe it was because I was the only father he knew, so I didn't want to take anything away from him. Whatever it was, I treated Julius as if he were my son.

That meant I had weekend visits with him, and every time he came over I was thrilled to have him with me. Julius really was a special little boy, very handsome with a smile that lit up a room.

Whenever he came to visit, I made sure that he felt like a king for the entire weekend. It was all about watching movies from Blockbuster Video and doing anything else he wanted. We'd end every weekend visit with a feast at Sizzler's All-You-Can-Eat buffet.

I loved the way Debbie interacted with both of my sons. During one visit I found myself sitting back, watching and enjoying the way Debbie got down on the floor and played with Julius.

As I watched him, I wondered why I had any doubts about him being my son. The way he tilted his head, or the way he held his hand under his chin. . . he had so many of my mannerisms, there were so many things that he did that reminded me of myself. I often found myself saying, "That's my boy!"

Sometimes Julius would catch me off guard and ask in his little innocent voice, "Am I your boy, daddy?"

Whenever he asked me that, it warmed my heart.

"We're going to work on numbers now," Debbie said to Julius. "We're going to count all the way to one hundred, okay?"

My son beamed. "Okay!"

Debbie asked, "When's your birthday?"

Julius didn't hesitate. He told her a date that was thirty days later than I thought.

My heart dropped to my toes. My wife looked me straight in my eyes for a brief moment and without speaking, I knew what she was thinking. She, like so many others, had always doubted Julius's paternity. And for Debbie, this was proof because she knew what I knew — every parent taught their child the exact date of that special day.

My wife, the warden, smelled blood. She stood up. "Do you want some ice cream?"

"Yes!" my son cheered, forgetting all about learning to count to one hundred.

She fixed him a large bowl, using an interrogation technique that police often utilized to relax a suspect.

Then, Debbie asked him again. The same question. And he gave her the same answer.

I couldn't even look at my wife, even though she was trying to make eye contact with me. Surely my boy must be mistaken, but she kept asking him over and over. And over and over, he gave the same answer.

I was crushed, because all I had to do was the calculation. Julius was a prison baby, allegedly conceived during one of our conjugal visits. I was locked away; there was no way I could confirm the exact date. I had to rely on my son. And if the date that Julius was telling us was true, then he wasn't my son.

And then, innocently, Julius confirmed the lie in another way: "Yeah, my mama said I got two daddies."

This time when Debbie looked over at me, she smiled.

I was devastated. I thought back to Precious's pregnancy. She had disappeared during the last four months, but Precious was like that. When Julius was born, I just accepted it, never requesting a copy of his birth certificate.

I don't know why I was so willing to accept Precious's word. Maybe it was because she'd touched my heart by naming the boy after my mother. She positioned Julius to carry the name of a great woman into the next generation.

But now I knew. . . that crazy bitch had been lying for six years!

Actually, this was more than a lie. This was the *ultimate* lie. This was a moral crime, an assault on my heart and soul.

I felt the heat of Debbie's gaze on me, but I still wouldn't look at her. I didn't want her to see my hurt, or to see the rage boiling inside.

As Debbie offered Julius another serving of ice cream, I grabbed a joint and stormed out of the living room just as my wife asked him, "So when was the last time you saw your other daddy, Julius?"

I closed the door behind me before I could hear his answer.

* * *

Thirty minutes later, Julius, Debbie and I were rolling down the freeway, the car filled with nothing but silence as we drove toward Precious' apartment. Smoking that joint had been a mistake; my high had me overthinking and remembering everything.   There had been a rumor for years that this dude, Kenny Ray, was Julius's father, but I'd ignored that. Now, I had a feeling that was true.

As we got closer to Precious' place, my thoughts turned to violence...violence against Precious.

Fifteen minutes later, we parked in front of Precious' apartment building on 85th and Broadway. Crack cocaine had devastated this area and the streets were crawling with dope dealers and junkies.

I called Precious and told her to come downstairs, then I jumped out of the car and stomped to the building. Julius and I were waiting in the lobby when Precious stepped off the elevator and practically skipped toward us.

She glanced down at the shopping bags holding the new clothes I'd bought him over the weekend and a huge smile spread across her lips.

That infuriated me even more. She finally made eye contact with me and her smile disappeared faster than all the money I'd given her for the last six years.

I made sure to hold her gaze as the words blared from my mouth as if I were a fire-breathing dragon. "How's Kenny Ray doing?" I asked.

I could see the blood draining beneath her brown skin and her body stiffened.

"Precious, I need to see an *authentic* birth certificate *tomorrow*." I gave her a false smile and stomped toward the door. I was just about to jump into the car when I heard that sweet, innocent voice behind me.

"Bye, Daddy. Am I still your boy?"

I turned around and my heart constricted, but I managed to say, "Of course you are, son."

I made my way back to him and gave him a hug, then kissed him on one of those soft, chubby cheeks.

The ride back home was as silent as the ride over. I was so numb I couldn't form a word. I also didn't feel like hearing the warden brag about how she was right once again.

All of that faith I'd built up, and now this situation made me question my faith in God. Not that God was responsible for what Precious had done, but how could He allow my heart to hurt so badly?

When we reached the valley, I asked my wife to stop at the liquor store and I jumped out and grabbed a fifth of Hennessy. Back at our place, I went straight to the loft, opened the bottle, and took a swig. The heat of the liquor made its way through my throat, into to my stomach.

I had mastered the art of using my weed roller with one hand and I took another hefty gulp before I lit that joint. I couldn't get high fast enough.

I turned on some mellow music and waited for that great escape to begin. It didn't take long before I was drunk and singing along with every song. The music was probably too loud, but I didn't give a fuck. I wished somebody, anybody would complain so that I could fight.

The DJ broke out with Al Green's, "How Can You Mend a Broken Heart."

My tears flowed before I could blink. All I could do was cry. When the song ended, I summoned enough strength to reach for the remote and turn the music off.

I needed to talk to somebody, but not Debbie. Maybe my mother, but it was really too late to call her. I had no one.

And then, I realized that I did.

I fell to my knees. I knew what I wanted to pray, but didn't know how. I managed to pull a few words together, asking God to help take away this pain. That's all I kept saying over and over and then ended with a confident, "Amen."

Sitting up, my thoughts turned back to Precious. But now, my heart had softened. I thought back to the things Precious had told me, disturbing stories of her abusive past that included both sexual and emotional abuse.

Telling that lie about Julius, a lie of that magnitude had to be a cry for help. I really was in no position to pass judgment on her, especially since God had forgiven me of my sins. Shouldn't I do the same for Precious?

Even though my pain had waned, I couldn't help but think about Julius. I was the only father he had ever known and I loved him so much.

Visions of my fatherless life flashed through my mind and I wouldn't wish that pain on any child. Right then, I made the decision to continue being Julius' father, no matter what.

But dealing with Precious was another issue. I picked up the phone and called her.

"Precious, I still need to see that birth certificate by noon tomorrow."

I then fell into a restless sleep.

By five minutes to twelve the next day, I had became a clock watcher. I stared at the clock as the deadline came and then passed. At 12:01, I accepted the fact that Julius really wasn't my child. At 12:02, I made the decision to turn this negative event into a positive one. I still had my other son. Precious couldn't take *that* one away from me.

Chapter 41
The Transition

The year 2000 came faster than I thought. My right arm was slowly starting to show some positive signs of healing, but my heart hadn't. I tried my best to put Precious and her bullshit behind me, but it wasn't easy. Not a single day went by when I didn't think about Julius, and how he wasn't my son.

I had reached out to Precious a couple times since that day almost a year ago and begged her to come clean. But she still insisted on holding to the lie. And in order to do that, she never produced that birth certificate.

I eventually gave up hope and kept myself going through those bad times by working on my truck. I started reading *Mini Trucking* magazines regularly and got enough information to eventually start customizing my truck. I became that young electronically inclined kid again; The Brainiac was back!

That filled my days, and at night I hung out in my old neighborhood, Inglewood. That once all-white city had become so bad that it was now known as Inglewatts. But I couldn't stay away.

I spent my time at this little hole in the wall club called Tag's located on the infamous Crenshaw

Boulevard and Imperial Highway. Tag's reminded me of the juke joints down in Mississippi with its one pool table and a jukebox. The place was much too small and always packed.

Tommy, a Korean guy, had owned the club since forever. He was like family in our hood and very well protected. Tag's was famous for potent alcoholic drinks. Tommy purchased his liquor off the streets for pennies on the dollar and could afford to be generous.

But what Tag's was really known for was that it was a one-stop shop for anything criminal and was the neighborhood gang stronghold.

Hanging out there gave me the opportunity to explore several illegal business opportunities. After I checked them all out, I decided to join the highjacking crew. Their specialty was taking diesel trucks loaded with electronic goods at gunpoint. Since I still only had the use of one arm, I was only responsible for locating the goods and mapping out the plans.

We had a couple of lucrative runs before I backed off. I only wanted to earn enough to pay bills and pour into my new hobby.

But even though I backed off the illegal activity, I still hung out at Tag's. On one Friday night, I noticed that the gang presence was unusually thick and when I scanned the people, there were too many niggas packing heat. Something was up.

After asking a few questions, I found out that the word around the hood was that Pookie just got out from doing eleven years in the Feds.

Pookie was a serious gang member and shot caller. As kids, everyone in the hood feared him, even me. He was ruthless, a killer.

I'd first met Pookie back in '72; he was one of the dudes that tried to rob me at knifepoint on my first day in our new neighborhood. I'd avoided him until I became a respected thug in my own right, but I always knew I could never do business with him. If something went wrong, I would have to kill him before he killed me.

When I heard this news, I fell into the shadows. I needed to be able to read Pookie's body language before he read mine. About an hour later, Pookie strolled across the parking lot like he owned the place. He looked as dangerous as ever. I watched his loyal soldiers embrace him, though I was sure that it was mostly from fear.

Pookie eventually made his way to me. We shook hands, embraced, and he seemed sincerely happy to see me.

"I heard about you getting shot," he said.

We chopped it up for a few more minutes, basically, just a bunch of bullshit small talk. He had to respect me as an O.G. just as I had to respect him. I respected him, I still didn't trust him.

We exchanged numbers and promised to keep in touch. Then, I hit the highway about two in the morning and turned the music down to think about how I was leaving the safety of the valley to hang out in the hood, placing myself in harm's way, even though I'd made promises to God, my son, and myself to change my ways.

But I still had to pay the bills and hustling was all that I knew. I had no choice but to do what I did.

That meant that I still went down to the hood every Friday. I couldn't help it.

Pookie made his appearances at Tag's around the same times that I did. And every time I saw him, I kept close tabs on him, watching every move he made. He had mellowed out, and eventually I let my guard down enough to have some decent conversations with him. He was selling cocaine, just like I was, but he told me of his plans to go legal and open a custom car shop. I told him to give me a call if he ever needed anything.

Four months later, he made that call to me. I was lying on my couch, nursing a bad cold when my phone rang.

"Hey, G Man," Pookie said. "I need four ounces and can't find any anywhere. Can you help me?"

I knew he was telling the truth. The city of South Los Angeles was experiencing a money-controlled drought on cocaine.

I explained to Pookie that my usual supplier had me on hold, too. "But, I'll make a couple of calls and get back to you."

When I hung up, though, all I did was drink a hot cup of Theraflu and then passed out on the living room sofa.

Two hours later, the ringing phone woke me up. Pookie sounded desperate this time, so reluctantly I made a call to Rick, my alternate connection.

I hadn't known Rick that long. I met him through an acquaintance, another street thug who vouched for him.

I talked to Rick, then called Pookie back and confirmed that the deal was made. He and I agreed to hook up at Tag's later that night.

When I hung up the phone, Debbie stood in front of me with her hands on her hips. "Have you lost your fucking mind, nigga? You ain't got no business getting involved with somebody else's shit. Besides that, your ass is too sick to go outside anyway."

I was too sick to hear her talking shit to me, so I waved her off, and pulled the cover over my head for a few hours. But then I got up and went down to Tag's. I was still sick as I sat there in that parking lot waiting for Pookie.

I went over the deal in my head. This would be simple, and it would be quick since only twenty-five hundred dollars was at stake.

When Pookie pulled up, I made eye contact with him and gestured for him to follow me. We made the drive to the city of Pomona where Rick stayed. I hated doing drug deals on another man's home turf. The advantage always went to the home team.

We pulled off the freeway and made our way to the Jack-in-the-Box where Rick told me to meet him. He wasn't there when we arrived and I called him.

"Man, I'm sick as a dog," I told him when he answered. "I need to get this shit over so I can get back to bed."

"Okay, I'll be right there."

Pookie and I sat in the lobby of the restaurant and made small talk until he arrived.

Rick was about 5-feet-8-inches with shoulder length dreadlocks tied back in a ponytail. He walked into the place flashing a big smile and signature gold teeth, which always annoyed me. He was originally from Alabama, and there was something about him that reminded me of the dudes that shot me.

I made the introductions and he explained to us that he needed to count the money first. He didn't have the product on him, but his homeboy was on the way and should be pulling up any minute.

No red flags went off. The move was typical for a drug deal.

Pookie handed over the money, but just a couple of seconds later, Rick said, "Man, I've been drinking beer all day." He stood and grabbed his crotch like his bladder was about to burst.

He walked to the restaurant's counter, and asked for the key to the restroom. The bathroom was on the other side of the lobby and out of sight.

Pookie and I sat there talking, but then the minutes passed and my stomach began to sink. It didn't take that long to piss.

I got up and walked around to the bathroom with Pookie on my heels. The men's restroom door was wide open, the key still in the lock.

Panic set in.

I ran out the side door into the parking lot, but knew his car wouldn't be there. Pookie and I just stood there and I locked eyes with him.

His eyes were bloodshot red, his shoulders tense and his hard glare spoke volumes.

"I didn't have anything to do with this," I said. "But I'll get your money back."

"Where he stay at?" he asked.

"I don't know, but I'll get on it first thing in the morning."

Still, the two of us stood there in that parking lot for another hour, looking stupid. As if Rick would come back.

This scenario was a potential death dance, but Pookie and I finally left. I thought long and hard about this crisis during my silent ride home. Once this was over, it was definitely time for me to find another profession.

Debbie was sitting in the living room when I walked in at midnight. One look at my face was all it took. She was already shaking her head before I even sat down and told her what happened.

All I wanted to do was lie down and rest. I took some more medication, thinking that I would handle this thing with Rick in the morning. It didn't take long for me to fall asleep.

It seemed like only minutes had passed when my wife shook me awake. I was groggy, but aware enough to hear the panic in her voice as she called my name.

She couldn't even speak as she handed the cordless phone to me.

My heart slammed against my chest, even before I said, "Hello, hello."

All I heard were voices and commotion.

Then I heard a familiar voice. My brother!

"Greg, please help me!" Serge cried out. "Pookie and another dude kidnapped me. He wants me to bring him to your house. Please bro! Just give him his money back!"

My heart stopped beating and everything around me went silent. My little brother's voice was all I could hear as my grip tightened around the cordless phone.

The line went dead.

That sick motherfucker thought that I was in on beating him out of a measly twenty-five hundred dollars? So, he had kidnapped my brother?

This is deadly. . . and personal!

My thoughts were interrupted by the phone ringing again. My wife answered, listened and hung up.

"Greg, Pookie says that they're fifteen minutes away and have his money when he gets here or give him your truck."

Now my fear turned to rage. That motherfucker had fucked up. He had violated a major rule of the game: Never involve innocent folks.

I didn't have that kind of money and I wasn't giving him my truck. It was time for a showdown.

My whole body flamed with such rage that I felt like I had a fever of 125 degrees.

I grabbed the cordless and headed downstairs to the front of my apartment building; Debbie was right behind me. Pookie had told her that they were fifteen minutes away, but they could be closer. The thing was, my wife and daughter were home and I couldn't let them make it to my front door.

I ran back into the apartment, pulled out that Magnum, then stood in front of my apartment with my wife; the gun was tucked in my waist.

My heart was so heavy as I thought about my baby brother. I loved Serge so much and couldn't believe this was happening to him.

Standing there, just waiting, I visualized how this would end. I thought about how Pookie was going to look with his brains hanging out. I had never wanted to kill a man as much as I did that very minute.

I glanced at my watch. According to the call, there were seven minutes left. My hand slid down under my shirt, searching for the gun handle. I needed to feel it.

That movement caught my wife's attention. She glanced downward, then looked me straight in my eyes. "Greg, what the fuck is wrong with you! You can't do this!"

She gripped my wrist. I tried to pull away from her, but as I did that, all the "what if's" played in my mind: What if I couldn't handle the weapon with my left hand? What if I missed Pookie and shot my brother? What if I missed Pookie and he still killed my brother? What if they found out where I stayed and just let my brother go?

But the biggest question wasn't a what if. It was what would I tell Mama if I got my brother killed?

That's when I had that moment — the one that would change my life forever.

I looked at my wife and told her to do something that I had never done in my entire life.

"Dial 911."

Relief was all over her face as she ran into the house. Still, I waited outside, just in case. But only a minute or two passed before I heard the police helicopter above us.

A minute after that, police cars raced down the street toward us. I tossed my gun into some nearby bushes, slumped against the chain link fence, and waited for the rest of the scenario to play out.

I didn't care what happened to me from that point on. All I felt was relief that my family would be safe.

* * *

I listened to the sounds coming from the police radio. Pookie and his thug helper were in custody and my brother was safe.

The police on the scene questioned me and my wife at length for at least two hours, but the whole time, I worried about my little brother. I could only imagine how traumatized he must have been.

I waited for the rest of the night for a call that never came.

The next morning I found out that Serge had packed his possessions, jumped in his car, and headed to Atlanta. He never even called me.

I was consumed with guilt and grief. I accepted the things that I had done to myself, but now I was truly responsible for hurting a close family member.

I'd made this promise many times, but I had to get out of the game — for real. No excuses, no justifying, no falling back on my word.

I fell to my knees and once again, I called on God, and this time when I talked to Him, I meant all the promises I made. This time I would keep this promise to God and myself.

And in the process, I'd have to find a way to make up all of this to my little brother.

Chapter 42
Back to the Future

November 22, 2008
LAX Airport, Gate A-19

My flight didn't leave for another hour. I put my bags down and walked to the large windows that looked onto the runways. Huge passenger jets formed a line, waiting their turn to take off.

Twelve years had passed since the shooting and seven years since Serge's kidnapping. And now here I was today, heading back to Natchez, Mississippi.

This was going to be the Thanksgiving to remember. It had been twenty-five years since all my siblings had been together on such a joyous occasion.

So many thoughts flooded my mind. The last time I'd flown to Mississippi, I was up to no good. This time I was totally legit with the law and with God.

I took a moment to rewind the tape to my crazy life and a song popped into my head.

This may only be a dream

Tomorrow may never come....

The lyrics from the Will Downing song played in my mind. It was like the world stopped spinning every time I heard that song. It forced me to think about the shooting and how I'd been left on this earth for a reason — to make a difference.

Now, I appreciated life and the simple things that others often took for granted. Simple things like buttoning a shirt or tying shoes could cause a crying marathon for me, though I had learned to keep those crying stints to a minimum.

The human mind was amazing when it came to survival. In this world of physically disabled misfits, there were only two kinds of people: quitters and fighters.

I became a fighter. I accepted every challenge and now I knew there wasn't any goal out of my reach, including writing an autobiography and pecking out the story with one finger.

With God all things are possible.

The announcement over the loud speaker called out the numbers for my flight, but before I stood up, I glanced up at the television. It was tuned to CNN and a news story was on about Barack Obama.

I couldn't hear what was being said because of all the noise, but whatever they were saying, it didn't matter. Admiration filled me every time I saw Barack Obama's face. He had been an unknown just six months ago.

I'd read an article outlining his journey to the Presidency. He started his quest at about the same time I decided to write the story of my life.

He had his reasons for running for office and I had my reasons for writing this book. My hope was that maybe someone, somewhere could learn something from what I had experienced. Maybe someone could know that God could make anyone whole again. Maybe someone could understand that it all began and ended with God — every thought, every action, every reaction, every consequence, and every reward.

The Bible says, *"Lo, I will be with you until the ends of the earth."*

I might not have reached the end of the earth, but at times I had made it to the end of my rope. And even then, God threw one lifeline after another.

For a few moments longer, I focused on the image of Barack Obama on the screen. As an African American, most people thought he didn't stand a chance. But he did the impossible, didn't he?

Well, most people didn't believe that I could write a book, but here we are at the end of my story.

Or should I say. . . the beginning?

Check out an excerpt from the next book in the G Man series. . .

Dead Man Walking

By Gregory Marshall

A raw and gritty look at G Man's seven years on California's death row.

Coming Fall 2015
From

BROWN GIRLS BOOKS

They have a saying here in the county jail: *Pressure Bursts Pipes!*

I didn't know what that meant when I first heard it, but I know what that means now.

Sitting on my bunk, I was in deep thought; I'd never had so much on my shoulders. My current crisis was crazier than any movie I'd ever seen.

And not just for me, for Lala, too.

The air conditioner felt like it was ten degrees colder than last night, but I wasn't thinking about that right now. There was too much on my mind. First, there was Lala. I hadn't spoken to her in three days and regrets flooded my mind. Turning Lala out at such an early age was a huge mistake. Agreeing to let her dance at the strip club was the beginning of the end. I'd taken a naïve eighteen year old, groomed her into a pure hustler, and created a monster. And now, there was no way that I could manage my fiancée's activities in the free world from where I sat.

But, there was no time for the moral police. My life was on the line and getting shorter by the minute. I had to find a way to get that shipment of black tar heroin into the right hands. The last note that had been delivered to my cell was a hidden threat disguised as a friendly reminder.

Just seventy-two hours ago I was living the privileged life of a powerful convict. Now I was scrambling and regrouping just to survive another day. I couldn't let day number four catch up with me without any good news for the Syndicate.

I caught Deputy Gray's nosey ass walking the tier, and I stopped him, knowing that even he was beginning to panic.

"I need you to let me out for an emergency phone call," I told him.

He didn't respond, but I knew it was only a matter of time before he came back. He'd gotten used to that weekly thousand-dollar pay off from us.

Just like I expected, thirty minutes later, my cell door slowly opened. The P.A. system cracked with his voice, "You got fifteen minutes, Marshall."

I almost ran to the pay phone and called my best friend, Eric, but he didn't answer. I called him several more times as if somehow that would change things and he'd pick up.

But after the fifth time, my forehead began to sweat and desperation set in. I couldn't panic now, so I settled down and thought back. Recently, Eric had given me a phone number to his cousin, Debbie. He told me to call her if I ever needed to make a call and couldn't reach him. I ran back to my cell, grabbed her number off my desk, then went back and dialed Debbie's number.

"Hello?"

Silently, I thanked God that she answered. When I told her who I was, she said, "Well, well, well. Heard a lot about you Mr. Greg." Her voice was sultry, it reeked with confidence.

Turning on my hustler charm, I made a little small talk with her before I got right to business. I asked

Debbie to make a few calls for me on the three-way so that nothing would be traced back.

As she dialed my first number, I thought about how Eric and I had already gone into phase two: get enough money to replace that shipment by any means necessary.

Nobody answered the first number, and so I called my girl, Wendy next.

When she answered, I had to think fast. I created a story about getting bailed out, but was short five hundred dollars. A little more lying and smooth talking was all it took.

"I'll get the money to Eric tonight," she told me. Then, there was an awkward silence as I waited for Wendy to hang up.

I wondered what she was waiting for, and then, I remembered those three important words, "I love you, Baby."

She lovingly replied, "I love you, too."

Not taking any chances of a slip up on the three-way, I hung up and called Debbie back. I gave her another number to dial. This time I called Jackee.

Jackee was a little more street savvy than Wendy; it took a lot more conversation to convince her. But eventually she bought it. "All right, Greg, I'm gonna give the money to Eric, but I expect to see your black ass as soon as you hit these streets."

Trying my best to hide my excitement, I agreed with any and everything she aid.

Another awkward silence followed at the end of the conversation. I was slipping big-time. "I love you, Jackee."

Once again I hung up and called Debbie back. My fifteen minutes was almost up, but I wanted to thank her for making the calls. This time, she sounded a little irritated.

"You need to be ashamed of yourself, boy. I can't believe they went for that bullshit. Who do you think you are?"

I slid into hustler mode and spit a little game at her. But Debbie was no pushover. As a matter of fact, she was downright aggressive. She represented the ultimate challenge. It was pretty obvious that she and I both loved a worthy opponent.

Just before I get off the phone, she told me that she was gonna come visit me in the morning. With all the confidence in the world I replied, "If you come once, you'll come again."

"Yeah, we'll see," she said with confidence, then hung up.

I dialed Lala's number one more time, still no answer. I slammed the phone down and muttered under my breath, "Shit!" This was so out of character for my fiancée; where was she?

Deputy Gray was standing three feet away from me. Only the steel bars separated us. In his business-as-usual voice he said, "Times up, lock it down, Mr. Marshall."

Knowing that everyone was observing us, I openly thanked him for the emergency phone call, then gave him a reassuring wink before I turned and headed back to my cell. I sat at my desk and evaluated the day's events.

I was in too deep this time around. There was no turning back. I should've been content with Deputy Gray bringing me the weed and small gifts from the street. Having a crooked Sheriff on my team provided me a position of power, but I had wanted more.

So now, I was involved with the most powerful prison gangs in the state of California: The Aryan Nation, Black Gorilla Family, Crips, Bloods and the most notorious of them all, The Mexican Syndicate.

This venture started out as a cool hustle, but now it was a major operation. And with thousands of dollars at stake, killing me was always a realistic option for any of the gangs. At this point I could care less about the power I had, I just wanted to get these dudes their shit.

I stretched out on my bunk, clasped my hands behind my head, stared at the ceiling, and thought about Lala. Again I wondered, where was she? She had never disappeared like this. She knew the position that I was in.

But then, my thoughts drifted to Eric's cousin, Debbie. He'd told me a many stories about her. Told me she drove men crazy. They both were raised on the Eastside of Los Angeles and the Eastside was known for breeding true street hustlers. I was from the Westside and considered as just another pretty boy from the streets.

That was okay with me, I just let my game speak for itself. I closed my eyes and thought about what Debbie might look like. I couldn't wait to meet her. She was about to meet a real Westside hustler tomorrow.

* * *

Sleep didn't come easy that evening. I tossed and turned all night. I wasn't surprised when I heard Deputy

Gray's voice early the next morning. He normally worked evenings, but I figured he was working a double shift.

I was sure that Deputy Gray would be the one to escort me to my visit. I wondered what time Debbie would get there; visiting hours began at ten.

It was ten-thirty when I heard my name called over the P.A. system.

"Marshall, you have a visitor; you have ten minutes to get ready."

A smile came to my face. Even though I really wanted to meet Debbie I would rather see Lala sitting at that window. Twenty minutes later, Deputy Gray was standing in front of my cell waiting to escort me. I was the only one called for the early visit so that allowed me a little one-on-one time with Deputy Gray.

I explained the whole situation to him and reassured him that everything would be back to normal soon. We both laughed and talked like we always did, but the concern on both our faces was obvious.

I was all settled into my visiting cage and waiting on that moment when I would see Debbie for the first time. I still had a few minutes to spare, so I turned my back to the window and continued my conversation with Deputy Gray.

Two minutes later, he looked past me with a puzzled expression. I turned around immediately and saw Wendy sitting there grinning like a Cheshire cat. I did my best to hide the disappointment. The phones finally came on and I sat there, pretending that I was glad to see Wendy. But we had just gotten started when I saw her walk up behind Wendy.

I knew it was Debbie as soon as I saw her. She was absolutely stunning. The way she walked was the very first thing that captured my attention. Every move she made was graceful.

She wore a bright red leather miniskirt, matching waistline jacket, black silk blouse, six inch red pumps, and a red and black leather brim to top it off. Her hair was pulled back into a very neat ponytail that went down her back.

Her hazel eyes grabbed and held me, but her legs were her greatest assets.   I forgot all about poor Wendy. Defeat was written all over her face as soon as she turned to look at Debbie. I didn't give her permission to bring her ass down here anyway. I didn't care how much money she'd given me. I was gonna just have to reschedule. It was Debbie's time right now.

A first impression is a lasting impression. I had to show Debbie that I was in control of things.

I spoke to Wendy for about five more seconds before I asked her to leave.   The fireworks started as soon as Debbie spoke, "I told you not to have a bitch down here when I came."

She was bold and ready. That broke the ice. We talked like old friends from that point on and I checked out every square inch of her as we talked. Her make-up was applied perfectly. Sexy lips and subtle cheekbones. Debbie definitely had class.

Our conversation turned to business ten minutes into our twenty-minute visit. She got right to the point. "Eric tells me there's trouble in paradise."

That statement caught me off guard. That meant that she was well-informed about Lala and the crisis. It also meant that my game wasn't as tight as I led her to believe.

She ran the show from that point on. Debbie told me that she'd talked to Eric before she came. He told her that everything was coming together and for me not to worry. Debbie saw the deep concern on my face as we talked and she offered to help.

"No, but thank you for asking," I said. Even though I was lusting, I still was engaged to Lala. I already had my team in place. Debbie would just have to remain as eye candy for now.

Then without any warning, the phones were shut off. Our visit had come to an end. Since I still had a few minutes to sit there while I waited for my escort to take me back upstairs, I gestured for Debbie to stand up and turn around for me. I couldn't take my eyes off her. Neither could the other inmates or Deputy Gray.

Then, I heard his voice behind me. "Damn, that's all woman, Marshall. You might as well let me have that one."

I replied, "She'll chew your lame ass up and spit you out, dude."

Debbie stood there until he put the handcuffs on me. She made a gesture with her hand for me to call her and then, she turned to leave. Debbie had left a lasting impression on me. She was the ultimate trophy. My mind was made up, I had to add her to my collection.

But Deputy Gray seemed more excited about Debbie than I was. She was all he talked about on our way back to my cell. She definitely had made my day, but I still had pending matters to deal with.

"Can you give me five minutes to use the phone before you lock me down?" I asked Gray.

He agreed and I grabbed the phone. I had to try Lala one more time. This time, her phone didn't just ring -- someone answered.

"Lala?" I said, knowing that wasn't her voice on the other end. Then, what I noticed besides the fact that this wasn't my fiancée's voice was all the commotion in the background. Unmistakable anguished screams and gut wrenching crying filled my ears.

The hair stood up on the back of my neck.

"Who is this?"

"This is Greg, who's this?"

"This is Lala's mother." I heard nothing but pain in her voice as she cried.

"What's going on? Where's Lala?"

She struggled to release her next words and then, she spit the words at me like fire, "Lala is dead, Greg!"

I said, "What do you mean she's dead?"

This time she screamed it at the top of her lungs as if directing it solely at me. "I said she's dead!" She slammed the phone to the receiver before I could get another word out.

Deputy Gray and I locked eyes for a brief moment. Total disbelief was written all over his face.

I didn't say a word. All I wanted to do was get to the safety of my cell. I was in cell number twelve. It seemed like a mile away as we walked toward it.

The first five cells were within earshot of my conversation and one of them held a Mexican Syndicate member. It was only a matter of time before the rest would know. Lala's death had just sealed my own fate.

I was already facing the death penalty for murder. The state of California wanted to legally kill me. Now, I'd have four prison gangs that wanted to do the same.

I was trapped in this City Within a City. There was nowhere to hide.

I was just a dead man walking!

55245409R00211